Lecture Notes in Artificial Intelligence   8982

Subseries of Lecture Notes in Computer Science

More information about this series at http://www.springer.com/series/1244

Patrick Lambrix · Eero Hyvönen
Eva Blomqvist · Valentina Presutti
Guilin Qi · Uli Sattler
Ying Ding · Chiara Ghidini (Eds.)

Knowledge Engineering
and Knowledge Management

EKAW 2014 Satellite Events,
VISUAL, EKM1, and ARCOE-Logic
Linköping, Sweden, November 24–28, 2014
Revised Selected Papers

 Springer

Editors
Patrick Lambrix
Linköping University
Linköping
Sweden

Eero Hyvönen
Aalto University
Espoo
Finland

Eva Blomqvist
Linköping University
Linköping
Sweden

Valentina Presutti
STLab ISTC-CNR
Rome
Italy

Guilin Qi
Southeast University
Nanjing
China

Uli Sattler
University of Manchester
Manchester
UK

Ying Ding
Indiana University Bloomington
Bloomington
USA

Chiara Ghidini
Fondazione Bruno Kessler
Trento
Italy

ISSN 0302-9743   ISSN 1611-3349   (electronic)
Lecture Notes in Artificial Intelligence
ISBN 978-3-319-17965-0   ISBN 978-3-319-17966-7   (eBook)
DOI 10.1007/978-3-319-17966-7

Library of Congress Control Number: 2015936681

LNCS Sublibrary: SL7 – Artificial Intelligence

Printed on acid-free paper

Springer International Publishing AG Switzerland is part of Springer Science+Business Media
(www.springer.com)

Preface

This volume contains the Satellite Events proceedings of the 19th International Conference on Knowledge Engineering and Knowledge Management (EKAW 2014), held in Linköping, Sweden, during November 24–28, 2014. This was the first EKAW conference in a Nordic country. It was concerned with all aspects of eliciting, acquiring, modeling, and managing knowledge, the construction of knowledge-intensive systems and services for the Semantic Web, knowledge management, e-business, natural language processing, intelligent information integration, personal digital assistance systems, and a variety of other related topics. The special focus of EKAW 2014 was Diversity.

For the main conference we invited submissions for research papers that presented novel methods, techniques, or analysis with appropriate empirical or other types of evaluation, as well as in-use papers describing applications of knowledge management and engineering in real environments. We also invited submissions of position papers describing novel and innovative ideas that were still at an early stage. In addition to the regular conference submission, we established a combined conference/journal submission track. Papers accepted for the combined track were published as regular research papers in the EKAW 2014 Springer conference proceedings (LNAI 8876) and authors were also invited to submit an extended version of their manuscript for a fast-track in the Semantic Web Journal (SWJ) published by IOS Press.

In these proceedings we have gathered papers related to the other events at EKAW 2014.

EKAW 2014 hosted three satellite workshops: VISUAL 2014 - International Workshop on Visualizations and User Interfaces for Knowledge Engineering and Linked Data Analytics, EKM1 - the First International Workshop on Educational Knowledge Management, and ARCOE-Logic 2014 - the 6th International Workshop on Acquisition, Representation and Reasoning about Context with Logic. The organizers of the workshops have provided summaries and selected best papers of their workshops of which the revised versions are included in these proceedings. Further, there were two tutorials: K4D: Managing and Sharing Knowledge in Rural Parts of the World, and Language Resources and Linked Data. The workshop and tutorial programs were chaired by Eva Blomqvist from Linköping University, Sweden, as well as Valentina Presutti from STLab ISTC-CNR, Italy.

This volume also contains the accepted contributions for the EKAW 2014 demo and poster session. We encouraged contributions that were likely to stimulate critical or controversial discussions about any of the areas of the EKAW conference series. We also invited developers to showcase their systems and the benefit they can bring to a particular application. The demo and poster programs of EKAW 2014 were chaired by Guilin Qi from the Southeast University, China, and Uli Sattler from the University of Manchester, UK.

Further, the EKAW 2014 program included a Doctoral Consortium that provided PhD students an opportunity to present their research ideas and results in a stimulating environment, to get feedback from mentors who are experienced research scientists in the community, to explore issues related to academic and research careers, and to build relationships with other PhD students from around the world. The Doctoral Consortium was intended for students at each stage of their PhD. All accepted papers are included in this volume. The presenters had an opportunity to present their work to an international audience, to be paired with a mentor, and to discuss their work with experienced scientists from the research community. The Doctoral Consortium was organized by Ying Ding from the Indiana University Bloomington, USA, and Chiara Ghidini from The Fondazione Bruno Kessler in Italy.

The conference organization also included the Program Chairs Krzysztof Janowicz from the University of California, USA, and Stefan Schlobach from Vrije Universiteit Amsterdam, The Netherlands. Axel-Cyrille Ngonga Ngomo from the Universität Leipzig, Germany, was the Sponsorship Chair. Henrik Eriksson and Patrick Lambrix both from Linköping University, Sweden, took care of local arrangements, while Zlatan Dragisic and Valentina Ivanova from Linköping University, Sweden, acted as Web Presence Chairs. Eero Hyvönen from Aalto University, Finland, and Patrick Lambrix from Linköping University, Sweden, were the General Chairs of EKAW 2014.

We want to thank Karin Hendry from Linköping University and Tina Malmström from Grand Travel Group Sweden AB for their excellent help with local arrangements as well as EasyChair and Springer for excellent cooperation regarding conference organization and publication of the proceedings. Thanks to everybody, including attendees at the conference, for making EKAW 2014 a successful event.

February 2015   Patrick Lambrix
                                                    Eero Hyvönen
                                                    Eva Blomqvist
                                                 Valentina Presutti
                                                       Guilin Qi
                                                      Uli Sattler
                                                      Ying Ding
                                                    Chiara Ghidini

Organization

Program Committees

Posters and Demos

Alessandro Adamou	ISTC CNR, Italy
Pierre-Antoine Champin	Université Claude Bernard Lyon 1, France
Liang Chang	Guilin University of Electronic Technology, China
Stefan Dietze	Leibniz University Hanover, Germany
Miriam Fernandez	Open University, UK
Tudor Groza	University of Queensland, Australia
Matthew Horridge	Stanford University, USA
Yue Ma	Université Paris Sud, France
Nicolas Matentzoglu	University of Manchester, UK
Pascal Molli	Nantes University, France
Guilin Qi (Chair)	Southeast University, China
Bernhard Schandl	Universität Wien, Austria
Hala Skaf-Molli	Nantes University, France
Uli Sattler (Chair)	University of Manchester, UK
Christopher Thomas	Wright State University, USA
Boris Villazon-Terrazas	Intelligent Software Components S.A., Spain
Haofen Wang	East China University of Science and Technology, China
Stuart Wrigley	University of Sheffield, UK

Doctoral Consortium

Sören Auer	University of Bonn and Fraunhofer IAIS, Germany
Eva Blomqvist	Linköping University, Sweden
Stefano Borgo	ISTC CNR, Italy
Elena Cabrio	INRIA Sophia-Antipolis, France
Michelle Cheatham	Wright State University, USA
Paolo Ciancarini	University of Bologna, USA
Oscar Corcho	Universidad Politécnica de Madrid, Spain
Mathieu d'Aquin	Open University, UK
Ying Ding (Chair)	Indiana University Bloomington, USA
Mauro Dragoni	Fondazione Bruno Kessler, Italy
Aldo Gangemi	ISTC CNR, Italy
Chiara Ghidini (Chair)	Fondazione Bruno Kessler, Italy
Giancarlo Guizzardi	Federal University of Espírito Santo, Brazil

Martin Homola	Comenius University, Slovakia
Maria Keet	University of Cape Town, South Africa
Juanzi Li	Tsinghua University, China
Diana Maynard	University of Sheffield, UK
Matteo Palmonari	University of Milan Bicocca, Italy
Anna Perini	Fondazione Bruno Kessler, Italy
Marco Rospocher	Fondazione Bruno Kessler, Italy
Satya Sahoo	Case Western Reserve University, USA
Guus Schreiber	Vrije Universiteit Amsterdam, The Netherlands
Vojtech Svatek	University of Economics Prague, Czech Republic
Valentina Tamma	University of Liverpool, UK
Jun Zhao	Lancaster University, UK

Contents

Demos

Tutorials

Language Resources and Linked Data: A Practical Perspective

Jorge Gracia[1](✉), Daniel Vila-Suero[1], John P. McCrae[2],
Tiziano Flati[3], Ciro Baron[4], and Milan Dojchinovski[5]

[1] Ontology Engineering Group, Universidad Politécnica de Madrid, Madrid, Spain
{jgracia,dvila}@upm.es
[2] CITEC, University of Bielefeld, Bielefeld, Germany
jmccrae@cit-ec.uni-bielefeld.de
[3] LCL, Sapienza Università di Roma, Roma, Italy
flati@di.uniroma1.it
[4] AKSW, University of Leipzig, Leipzig, Germany
cbaron@informatik.uni-leipzig.de
[5] Czech Technical University in Prague, Praha, Czech Republic
milan.dojchinovski@fit.cvut.cz

Abstract. Recently, experts and practitioners in language resources have started recognizing the benefits of the linked data (LD) paradigm for the representation and exploitation of linguistic data on the Web. The adoption of the LD principles is leading to an emerging ecosystem of multilingual open resources that conform to the Linguistic Linked Open Data Cloud, in which datasets of linguistic data are interconnected and represented following common vocabularies, which facilitates linguistic information discovery, integration and access. In order to contribute to this initiative, this paper summarizes several key aspects of the representation of linguistic information as linked data from a practical perspective. The main goal of this document is to provide the basic ideas and tools for migrating language resources (lexicons, corpora, etc.) as LD on the Web and to develop some useful NLP tasks with them (e.g., word sense disambiguation). Such material was the basis of a tutorial imparted at the EKAW'14 conference, which is also reported in the paper.

Keywords: Linked data · Language resources · Multilingual web of data

1 Introduction

Linked data (LD) is a set of best practices for exposing, sharing, and connecting data on the Web [2]. Recently, researchers working on linguistic resources have shown increasing interest in publishing their data as LD [4]. Nowadays, there are many good examples involving important organizations and initiatives that stress the opportunities offered by LD and foster the aggregation of multilingual open resources into the Linked Open Data (LOD) cloud. By interlinking multilingual

© Springer International Publishing Switzerland 2015
P. Lambrix et al. (Eds.): EKAW 2014 Satellite Events, LNAI 8982, pp. 3–17, 2015.
DOI: 10.1007/978-3-319-17966-7_1

and open language resources, the Linguistic Linked Open Data (LLOD) cloud is emerging[1], that is, a new linguistic ecosystem based on the LD principles that will allow the open exploitation of such data at global scale. In particular, these are some key benefits of linguistic LD:

– Provide enhanced and more sophisticated navigation through multilingual data sets and linguistic data
– Support easier integration of linguistic information into research documents and other digital objects
– Support easier integration of linguistic information with LOD datasets, enhancing the natural language description of those datasets
– Facilitate re-use across linguistic datasets, thus enriching the description of data elements with information coming from outside the organization's local domain of expertise
– Describe language resources in RDF [10] and make them indexable by semantic search engines
– Avoid tying developers and vendors to domain-specific data formats and dedicated APIs.

With the aim of contributing to the development of the LLOD cloud, we organised a tutorial at the EKAW'14 conference[2] on the topic "Language Resources and Linked Data". The tutorial tackled the following questions:

1. How to represent rich multilingual lexical information (beyond `rdfs:label`) and associate it to ontologies and LD?
2. How to generate multilingual LD from data silos?
3. How to represent multilingual texts, annotations and corpora as LD?
4. How to perform word sense disambiguation and entity linking of LD?

The tutorial aimed at answering the above questions in a practical way, by means of examples and hands-on exercises. In this paper, we summarise different theoretical and practical aspects concerning the representation and publication of LLOD on the Web, and give a summary of the mentioned tutorial including pointers to the educational material and practical exercises used on it.

The remainder of the paper is organised as follows. In Section 2, the patterns based on the *lemon* model for representing ontology lexica are introduced. Section 3 summarises a methodology for generating and publishing multilingual linguistic LD. In Section 4, we show how to integrate NLP with LD and RDF based on the NIF format. In Section 5, disambiguation and entity linking methods based on BabelNet are explained. Section 6 summarises the outline and outcomes of the EKAW'14 tutorial on "Language Resources and Linked Data" and, finally, conclusions can be found in Section 7.

---

[1] A picture of the current LLOD cloud can be found at http://linghub.lider-project. eu/llod-cloud. The picture was jointly developed by the Open Knowledge Foundation's Working Group on Open Data in Linguistics (http://linguistics.okfn.org) and the LIDER project (http://www.lider-project.eu/).
[2] http://www.ida.liu.se/conferences/EKAW14/home.html

2 Modelling Lexical Resources on the Web of Data: The *lemon* Model

In this section we will see how to represent rich lexical information associated to ontologies and LD, and how to use a set of design patterns to facilitate such representation in a practical way.

2.1 Modelling Ontology-Lexica

Lexical resources such as WordNet [14] are one of the most important types of data sources for linguistic research. Such resources are complementary to another type of Web resources that contain a large amount of taxonomic data described in RDF such as DBpedia [3]. Bridging the gap between these two types of resources means that rich linguistic information found in lexical resources (e.g., lexicons) can be used to describe information on the Web, enabling novel applications such as question answering over LD [18]. This leads to a new type of resources that is termed *ontology-lexicon*, which consist of an ontology describing the semantic and taxonomic nature of the domain and a lexicon describing the behaviour of the words in a language.

Building on the existing work of models such as LexInfo [5] and LIR [15], *lemon* (Lexicon Model for Ontologies) [11] was proposed to provide a "de facto" standard which is used by a cloud of lexical LD resources such as WordNet [13], BabelNet [7], and UBY [6] among many others. The *lemon* model's core consists of the following elements depicted in Figure 1:

Lexical Entry. A lexical entry, which may be a word, multiword expression or even affix, is assumed to represent a single lexical unit with common properties, especially part-of-speech, across all its forms and meanings.

Lexical Form. A form represents a particular version of a lexical entry, for example a plural or some other inflected form. A form may have a number of representations in different orthographies (e.g., spelling variants) or media (e.g., phonetic representations).

Lexical Sense. The sense refers to the usage of a word with a specific meaning and can also be considered as a reification of the pair of a lexical entry used with reference to a given ontology. The sense is also used as a node for the annotation of many pragmatic features such as register.

Reference. The reference is an entity in the ontology that the entry can be interpreted as, or alternatively that can be represented by using the lexical entry.

In addition to the core, *lemon* provides a number of models to enable representation and application of the model to a wide variety of domains. Firstly the **linguistic description** module enables annotations to be added to entries, forms or senses. Secondly, the **phrase structure** module allows description of how the words within a multiword entry relate. Next, the **syntax and mapping** module is used to represent how a syntactic frame corresponds to one or more

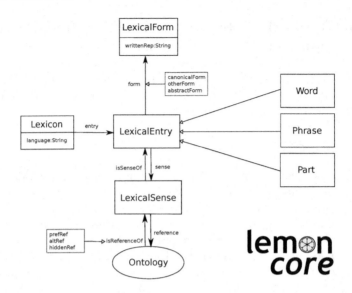

Fig. 1. The *lemon* core model, indicating the classes, the properties used to connect them and their subclasses.

semantic predicates in the ontology. The **variation** module captures the representation of variants between terms. Finally, the **morphology** module allows for regular expression representation of morphological variants avoiding the need to represent many forms for a single lexical entry.

Additional extensions have been also developed, such as the **translation** module [8], which allows for representing explicit translations between lexical senses documented in different natural languages, or the **lemon-BabelNet** extension required for the LD representation of BabelNet (see Section 5).

2.2   The *Lemon* Design Pattern Language

When creating a lexicon from scratch, common patterns quickly emerge for the creation of lexical entries and associated ontology axioms. These patterns have been assembled into the *lemon* Design Pattern Language[3], which provides a compiler to generate a standard RDF/XML representation of the data.

These patterns describe the ontological type and the part-of-speech of the entry, such as for example the 'class noun' pattern which describes a noun referring to a class in the ontology. In addition, to the triples stating these two facts the entry is also associated with a noun predicate frame ('X is a N'). The 'object property noun' pattern is similar but takes as parameters not only the lemma but also a property (p) and an individual (v) and generates an anonymous class (C) with the axiom $C \equiv \exists p.v$ which is associated with the noun like in the 'class

---

[3] http://github.com/jmccrae/lemon.patterns

noun' pattern. Examples of these patterns are given below, which indicates that "cat" refers to a class dbr:Cat the noun "German" refers to all elements whose dbp:nationality has a value of dbr:Germany:

```
@prefix dbr: <http://dbpedia.org/resource/> .
@prefix dbp: <http://dbpedia.org/property/> .

Lexicon(<http://www.example.com/lexicon>,"en",
  ClassNoun("cat", dbr:Cat),
  ObjectPropertyNoun("German", dbp:nationality, dbr:Germany))
```

Verbs are divided into state verbs which express a general ontological fact and consequence verbs where the ontological fact is a consequence of the event described by the verb[4]. In addition there are patterns to model verbs with more than two arguments to multiple ontology predicates. For adjectives, there are also patterns describing adjectives as classes ('intersective adjectives'), comparable properties ('scalar adjectives') and relative adjectives, which is described more completely in McCrae et al. [12].

3 Methodology for Multilingual Linguistic Linked Data Generation

The previous section presented a way of representing lexical data in RDF. However, representing linguistic data is only a part of the whole process required to expose language resources as LD. In this section we will give an overview of such process and some methodological guidelines.

In fact, several guidelines [20] have been proposed to produce and publish LD on the Web. These guidelines are meant to provide a set of tasks and best practices to generate and make available high quality LD. More recently, Vila et al. [19] proposed general guidelines for generating *multilingual* LD. In addition, the W3C Best Practices for Multilingual Linked Open Data community group[5] has recently published specific guidelines for generating and publishing LD out of several types of language resources (e.g., bilingual dictionaries, WordNets, terminologies in TBX, etc). The core activities identified in such guidelines are[6]: (i) selection of vocabularies, (ii) RDF generation, and (iii) publication.

Selection of vocabularies. In this activity the goal is to select standard vocabularies to represent linguistic data. The diverse options depend on the type of data. For example the *lemon* model, described in Section 2, is an appropriate vocabulary for representing lexica, and NIF, described in Section 4, to represent annotations in text. For other (non linguistic) information associated to the language resource, other extendedly used vocabularies can be used such as Dublin Core[7] for provenance and authoring or DCAT[8] for metadata of the RDF dataset.

---

[4] Generally, state verbs express the triple in the present tense, e.g., 'X knows Y', and consequence verbs express the triple in the past tense, e.g., 'X married Y'

[5] http://www.w3.org/community/bpmlod/

[6] See for instance http://bpmlod.github.io/report/bilingual-dictionaries

[7] http://purl.org/dc/elements/1.1/

[8] http://www.w3.org/ns/dcat#

Furthermore, if we need to model more specific features, a growing number of vocabularies is available on the Web and they can be found in catalogs such as the Linked Open Vocabularies catalog (LOV)[9].

RDF generation. After selecting the vocabularies that will be used to model the linguistic data sources, the main steps to be performed are: (a) modelling the data sources, (b) design the identifiers (URIs) for the RDF resources that will be generated, and (c) transform the data sources into RDF by mapping them to the selected vocabularies and following the identifier patterns previously designed.

Publication. The last activity can be organized in two tasks: (a) dataset publication, and (b) metadata publication. As for dataset publication, there are several architectures available such as having a triple or quad-store to persist and query the data and setting up what is known as LD front-ends, which are basically an access layer on top of a triple-store.

As an example of the above steps, let us imagine that we want to transform a set of spreadsheets containing a set of terms in one language and their correspondent translations into another language. The first step would be to select an appropriate vocabulary and in this case *lemon* and its translation module[10] are a good choice. The next step would be to decide how to model the data contained in the spreadsheets. For instance, we could decide to create a separate lexicon for each language, each row in the spreadsheet corresponding to a different `lemon:LexicalEntry`, and interlink them through translation relations. The following step would be to define the identifier scheme, that is, how URIs are created. There exist several guidelines to design URIs such as the one published by Interoperability Solutions for European Public Administrations [1]. For instance, if the files contain unique identifiers for each lexical entry we could use those identifiers to create the URIs of the lemon lexical entries and append them to a namespace that we own and where we will publish the data. Finally, the last step would be to map and transform the sources into RDF. There are various open source tools to generate RDF depending on the type and format of data[11]. In our case, LODrefine[12] provides an easy way to transform many kinds of tabular and hierarchical data into RDF and its interface is similar to commercial tools to work with spreadsheets. The result of this transformation is the set of RDF files that have to be published on the Web. Finally, regarding publication, LODrefine provides an automatic way to upload the data into Virtuoso, which is a triple store available as open source[13], or we could manually load the data into light-weight alternatives such as Fuseki[14].

---

[9] http://lov.okfn.org

[10] http://purl.org/net/translation

[11] See for example http://www.w3.org/2001/sw/wiki/Tools

[12] http://sourceforge.net/projects/lodrefine/

[13] https://github.com/openlink/virtuoso-opensource

[14] http://jena.apache.org/documentation/serving_data/

4   Integrating NLP with Linked Data: The NIF format

In the above sections we have explored how to represent lexical information in *lemon* and how to generate and publish it as LD on Web. However, in addition to lexica, the representation and publishing as LD of multilingual texts, annotations and corpora is also important. In this section we will explore the use of the *NLP Interchange Format* (NIF) to that end.

NIF [9] is an RDF/OWL based format which provides all required means for the development of interoperable NLP services, LD enabled language resources and annotations. Other than more centralized solutions such as UIMA[15] and GATE[16], NIF enables the creation of heterogeneous, distributed and loosely coupled NLP applications. The NIF format is based on a URI scheme for minting URIs for arbitrary strings and content in Web documents. It is supported by the NIF Core Ontology[17] which formally defines classes and properties for describing substrings, texts, documents and the relations among them.

The following code presents an example of a simple NIF document with an annotated substring. We will further use this example to explain the NIF basics.

```
1   @base <http://example.com/exampledoc.html#> .
2   <char=0,> a nif:Context , nif:RFC5147String ;
3   <char=86,90>
4          a    nif:RFC5147String , nif:String , nif:Word ;
5          nif:beginIndex        "86"^^xsd:nonNegativeInteger ;
6          nif:endIndex          "90"^^xsd:nonNegativeInteger ;
7          nif:isString          "July" ;
8          nif:referenceContext  <char=0,> ;
9          itsrdf:taIdentRef     dbpedia:July .
10         nif:oliaLink penn:NN .
11         nif:oliaCategory olia:Noun .
```

NIF Basics. Every document in NIF is represented using the `nif:Context` concept and identified using a unique URI identifier (line 2). Further, each annotated substring is represented using the `nif:String` concept, or more specifically, as `nif:Word` (line 4) or `nif:Phrase` concepts. The substrings are also uniquely identified with URI identifiers (line 3). The surface forms of the substrings and document's content are referenced as literals using the `nif:isString` property (line 7). Each substring, using the `nif:referenceContext` property is linked with the corresponding document where it occurs (line 8); an instance of the `nif:Context` class. The begin and end indices are also attached to each substring and document using `nif:beginIndex` and `nif:endIndex` (lines 5–6).

NIF is also aligned with well–established linguistic ontologies and standards such as the Ontologies of Linguistic Annotation (OLiA) and Internationalization Tag Set 2.0 (ITS). OLiA provides NLP tag sets for morpho-syntactical annotations. In NIF it can be used, for example, to assign grammatical category to a `nif:Word` (lines 10–11). ITS 2.0 standardizes attributes for annotating XML and HTML documents with processing information, however, it

---

[15] https://uima.apache.org/

[16] https://gate.ac.uk/

[17] http://persistence.uni-leipzig.org/nlp2rdf/ontologies/nif-core/nif-core.html

also provides an ontology, which can be reused in NIF. For example, using the `itsrdf:taIdentRef` property we can link particular substring representing a named entity mention with its corresponding DBpedia resource (line 9).

Annotating Strings with NIF. Strings can be easily annotated with NIF using Command Line Interface (NIF–CLI) or using Web service (NIF–WS) implementations. Both methods share a similar set of parameters. This includes, for example, parameters for specifying the input and output format, the base prefix URI for the newly minted URIs and the input text submitted for processing. In the following example we show the annotation of a string using NIF–CLI implementation for the Snowball Stemmer[18]. The result for the submitted text will be a single `nif:Context` document, all the `nif:Word`(s) present in the text and the stem for each word (line 9).

```
java -jar snowball.jar -f text -i 'My favorite actress is Natalie Portman.'
1   @base <http://example.com/exampledoc.html#> .
2   <char=0,> a nif:Context , nif:RFC5147String ;
3   <char=3,11>
4           a      nif:RFC5147String , nif:Word ;
5           nif:isString           "favorite" ;
6           nif:beginIndex         "3"^^xsd:nonNegativeInteger ;
7           nif:endIndex           "11"^^xsd:nonNegativeInteger ;
8           nif:referenceContext   <char=0,> ;
9           nif:stem               "favorit" ;
```

Using NIF-WS we can expose a particular NLP functionality of a tool (e.g. tokenization, POS tagging or Named Entity Recognition (NER)) on the Web. Hence, it is not necessary to download, setup and run the NIF software making possible the creation of a small NIF corpus using an available NIF-WS service. Some of the implementations which are already exposed as Web services includes Stanford NLP[19], DBpedia Spotlight, Entityclassifier.eu[20], Snowball Stemmer and OpenNLP[21]. The following URL exemplifies the annotation of the string "I'm connected." using the Snowball Stemmer NIF-WS implementation.

```
http://snowball.nlp2rdf.aksw.org/snowball?f=text&i=I'm+connected.&t=direct
```

The parameters used for NIF-WS are similar to NIF-CLI implementations and are summarized at the API specification website[22]. For instance, *informat* (f) specifies the input format, *input* (i) holds the actual string that will be annotated, and *intype* (t) defines how the input is accessed (directly from stdin, from an URL or file).

Querying NIF Annotations. Existing NIF corpora or created RDF documents with NIF annotated strings can be further queried, for example, using a SPARQL interface. Twinkle[23] is a simple tool for loading RDF corpora and querying it using standard SPARQL. Upon starting the Twinkle tool (`java -jar`

---

[18] http://snowball.tartarus.org/
[19] http://nlp.stanford.edu/software/
[20] http://entityclassifier.eu/
[21] https://opennlp.apache.org/
[22] http://persistence.uni-leipzig.org/nlp2rdf/specification/api.html
[23] http://www.ldodds.com/projects/twinkle/

twinkle.jar), we can load the corpora such as the Brown corpus (**File** button), write a SPARQL query (e.g. list all words in a document) and execute it (**Run** button).

```
1   prefix nif: <http://persistence.uni-leipzig.org/nlp2rdf/ontologies/nif-core#>
2   prefix rdfs: <http://www.w3.org/2000/01/rdf-schema#>
3   prefix olia: <http://purl.org/olia/brown.owl#>
4
5   SELECT  ?uri, ?word WHERE {
6              ?uri a nif:Word.
7              ?uri nif:anchorOf ?word
8   }
```

The query in the example above will return all the words along with their URI identifiers.

```
1   <char=4405,4407> "he"^^<http://www.w3.org/2001/XMLSchema#string>
2   <char=7596,7599> "had"^^<http://www.w3.org/2001/XMLSchema#string>
3   <char=2031,2034> "set"^^<http://www.w3.org/2001/XMLSchema#string>
4   <char=9916,9922> "reform"^^<http://www.w3.org/2001/XMLSchema#string>
5   ...
```

When querying a document that contains POS tags it is possible to create elaborated queries, for example selecting nouns, verbs and OLiA links using the OLiA mapping.

Available NIF Corpora. A number of NIF corpora from different domains and sizes have been published in the NIF format. For instance, the *N3 collection*[24] of datasets, which can be used for training and evaluation of NER systems. *Wikilinks*[25] is a very large scale coreference resolution corpus with over 40 million mentions of over 3 million entities. It is available in the NIF format and published following the LD Principles. The Brown corpus[26] is another showcase corpus of POS tags in NIF. The NIF dashboard[27] contains a list of these corpora as well as their access address and size. Adding a new corpus to the list is possible by uploading a description file using the DataID[28] ontology.

NIF Resources and Software. The *NIF dashboard* exposes the current status of NIF Web services, as well as access URL, demos, converted corpora, wikis and documentation. The NLP2RDF website[29] contains the last NIF related news and resources of previous publications.

NIF Combinator is a Web application which allows to combine output from multiple NIF-WS in a single RDF model. It is possible, for example, to annotate a string using Stanford NLP and then perform NER using the DBpedia Spotlight Web service, this way creating an enriched corpora. When a corpus is created it is recommended to validate it. For this task another useful application is the *NIF validator* which uses the framework RDFUnit and grants the validation of NIF annotated documents.

---

[24] http://aksw.org/Projects/N3NERNEDNIF.html
[25] http://wiki-link.nlp2rdf.org/
[26] http://brown.nlp2rdf.org/
[27] http://dashboard.nlp2rdf.aksw.org
[28] http://wiki.dbpedia.org/coop/DataIDUnit
[29] http://nlp2rdf.org/

The source code of the NIF related software is available at *NLP2RDF GitHub web page*[30]. The NIF core engine is developed in Java and the RDF models are manipulated using Apache Jena[31]. The NIF reference code is flexible and implementations for new NLP tools might be done extending NIF classes. The NIF packages also provide helpers for tokenization and creation NIF-CLI and NIF-WS interfaces. In addition, the GitHub repository is used to maintain the core NIF ontology.

5   Multilingual WSD and Entity Linking on the Web

In the previous sections we have focused on how to represent, publish and make linguistic data interoperable on the Web. In the following paragraphs we will review some useful NLP-related tasks that can be done with such data. In fact, the recent upsurge in the amount of information published on the Web requires search engines and machines to analyze and understand text at sense level and in any language. News aggregators and user recommendation systems, for instance, often have the problem to suggest new information to the user such as places or celebrities. For example, in the following sentence it would be useful to understand the senses intended for `Mario` and `strikers`.

`Thomas and Mario are strikers playing in Munich.`

This task, however, is affected by the lexical ambiguity of language, an issue addressed by two key tasks: Multilingual Word Sense Disambiguation (WSD), aimed at assigning meanings to word occurrences within text, and Entity Linking (EL), a recent task focused on finding mentions of entities within text and linking them to a knowledge base. The goal shared by the two task is to have multilingual information disambiguated/linked so as to perform better text understanding.

On the one hand EL systems have always been concerned with identifying and disambiguating mentions of named entities only (e.g., `Thomas`, `Mario` and `Munich` are three valid mentions), while WSD algorithms are supposed to disambiguate open class words such as nouns, verbs, adjectives and adverbs (e.g., `strikers` and `playing` are two target words needing disambiguation). The main difference between WSD and EL is thus in the inventory used: the former draws word senses from dictionaries, which usually encode only open and close class words, the latter are instead supposed to link mentions of named entities to concepts to be found in encyclopaedias, such as Wikipedia, DBpedia, etc.

Babelfy [16] is a state-of-the-art WSD/EL system which for the first time solves the two problems jointly, by using BabelNet [17] as the common sense inventory, both for WSD and EL.

5.1   BabelNet

BabelNet is a huge multilingual semantic network at the core of which is the integration of the encyclopaedic information coming from Wikipedia and the

---

[30] https://github.com/NLP2RDF/
[31] https://jena.apache.org/

lexicographic information of WordNet. By the seamless integration of these resources, BabelNet merges the two sense inventories used by WSD and EL systems separately. With new versions being released (the latest version 3.0 is available at http://babelnet.org) BabelNet now contains more than 13 millions of concepts and named entities lexicalized in 271 languages and has integrated also other several resources such as OmegaWiki, Open Multilingual WordNet, Wiktionary and Wikidata. In order to foster interoperability across linguistic datasets and resources and to further support NLP applications based on the LLD cloud, BabelNet has also been converted into LD [7] by using *lemon* as the reference model (see Section 2) and is also accessible through a SPARQL endpoint.[32] Lemon-BabelNet features almost 2 billion triples and is interlinked with several other datasets including DBpedia as nucleus of the LOD cloud.

By means of the SPARQL endpoint it is possible, for instance, to query the service for all the senses of a given lemma (e.g., *home*) in any language:

```
SELECT DISTINCT ?sense ?synset WHERE {
    ?entries a lemon:LexicalEntry .
    ?entries lemon:sense ?sense .
    ?sense lemon:reference ?synset .
    ?entries rdfs:label ?term .
    FILTER (str(?term)="home")
} LIMIT 10
```

or to retrieve definitions for a given concept (e.g., the first sense of *home* in English) in any language:

```
SELECT DISTINCT ?language ?gloss WHERE {
    <http://babelnet.org/rdf/s00000356n> a skos:Concept .
    OPTIONAL {
        <http://babelnet.org/rdf/s00000356n> bn-lemon:definition ?definition .
        ?definition lemon:language ?language .
        ?definition bn-lemon:gloss ?gloss .
    }
}
```

5.2   Babelfy

Babelfy[33] is a unified, multilingual, graph-based approach to EL and WSD which relies on BabelNet as the background knowledge base from which to draw concepts and lexicalizations to perform the identification of candidate meanings.

From the task point of view, EL on the one hand involves first recognizing mentions contained in text (fragments of text representing named entities) and then linking the mentions to some predefined knowledge base, on the other hand WSD has mentions already identified and consists in selecting the right sense for the word of interest. By generalizing the idea of mention, instead, be it either a named entity or a concept, Babelfy unifies the two sides of the coin by tackling two problems in one. The joint disambiguation and entity linking is performed in three steps:

---

[32] http://babelnet.org/sparql/
[33] http://babelfy.org/

– Each vertex of the BabelNet semantic network, i.e., either concept or named entity, is associated with a semantic signature, that is, a set of related vertices. This is a preliminary step which needs to be performed only once, independently of the input text.
– Given an input text, all the linkable fragments are extracted from this text and, for each of them, the possible meanings are listed, according to the semantic network.
– The candidate meanings of the extracted fragments are interlinked using the previously-computed semantic signatures, so as to obtain a graph-based semantic interpretation of the whole text. As a result of the application of a novel densest subgraph heuristic high-coherence semantic interpretations for each fragment are finally selected.

A possible application of Babelfy is to easily disambiguate and produce multilingual LD starting from free text written in any language, such as snippets returned by search engines or recommendation websites. The free text is initially enriched with semantic links thanks to Babelfy and then transformed into LD by using the NIF model (cf. Section 4). This feature is of particular interest to the LD community since it provides a means for true interoperability across sense-tagged datasets, one of the concepts at the foundations of the NIF format. In order to produce LD from free text with Babelfy, the following steps are needed:[34]

1. Open the configuration file *babelfy2nif.properties* under the *babelfy/config/* directory;
2. Set up the appropriate parameters so as to account for the language of interest, as well as for the output format (turtle, n-triples or rdf/xml) and type of stream (file vs. standard output). It is also possible to customize the conversion by choosing the algorithm for handling overlapping annotations (either `LONGEST-ANNOTATION-GREEDY-ALGORITHM` or `FIRST-COME-FIRST--SERVED ALGORITHM`). Since Babelfy by default enriches the text with all the possible semantic annotations (including annotations of short, long and even overlapping fragments) these algorithms allow to discriminate annotations whose fragments overlap: the former selects the annotations from the longest to the shortest one, the latter accepts non-overlapping annotations in order of appearance, from the left to the right;
3. Execute the following command 'sh `run_babelfy2nif-demo.sh`' (on Linux) or '`./run_babelfy2nif-demo.bat`' (on Windows).

For example, given the sentence "The Semantic Web is a collaborative movement led by the international standards body World Wide Web Consortium (W3C)", an excerpt of the enriched and converted file in NIF is:

---

[34] All the material referred here (configuration files, executables, etc.) was distributed at the EKAW tutorial and it is now available online (see section 6 for more details).

```
<http://lcl.uniroma1.it/babelfy2nif#char=0,16>
        a                       nif:Word , nif:RFC5147String ;
        nif:anchorOf            "The Semantic Web" ;
        nif:beginIndex          "0" ;
        nif:endIndex            "16" ;
        nif:nextWord            <http://lcl.uniroma1.it/babelfy2nif#char=17,19> ;
        nif:oliaCategory        olia:Noun , olia:CommonNoun ;
        nif:oliaLink            <http://purl.org/olia/penn.owl#NN> ;
        nif:referenceContext    <http://lcl.uniroma1.it/babelfy2nif#char=0,128> ;
        itsrdf:taIdentRef       <http://babelnet.org/rdf/s02276858n> .
```

where the fragment "The Semantic Web" has correctly been linked to the Babel-Net synset <http://babelnet.org/rdf/s02276858n>.

6   Tutorial on Language Resources and Linked Data

As referred in Section 1, a hands-on tutorial about the above topics was orga-nized on 25th November 2014 in Linköping, Sweden, collocated with the 19th International Conference on Knowledge Engineering and Knowledge Manage-ment (EKAW'14) and with the title "Language Resources and Linked Data". The aim of the tutorial was to guide participants in the process of LD generation of language resources in a practical way. This tutorial was the last of a series of related tutorials that were imparted at the International Conference on Lan-guage Resources and Evaluation (LREC'14)[35] and at the International Semantic Web Conference (ISWC'14)[36] respectively. The first one was about "Linked Data for Language Technologies"[37] and took place in Reykjavik, Iceland on 26th May. The second took place in Riva del Garda, Italy, on 20th October with the title "Building the Multilingual Web of Data: a Hands-on Tutorial"[38].

The tutorial at the EKAW'14 conference was a full day tutorial divided in five sections: one introductory section and the other four sections covering each of the topics treated previously in this paper (Sections 2 to 5). Each section was divided into a theoretical introduction and a practical session. The practical work consisted of completing some short guided examples proposed by the speakers in order to immediately apply and understand the theoretical concepts. All the instructional material and presentations used in the tutorial were available online in the tutorial's webpage[39] beforehand. Further, a USB pendrive containing all the data and software required to follow the sessions was distributed to every participant. Such material is now available in the tutorial's webpage.

There were no major prerequisites for the attendants to follow the session. Only a certain familiarity with the basic notions of RDF and OWL. Neither pre-vious experience on LD publication nor prior knowledge on NLP techniques or computational linguistics were required. The audience profile ranged from PhD

---

[35] http://www.lrec-conf.org/lrec2014
[36] http://iswc2014.semanticweb.org/
[37] http://lrec2014.lrec-conf.org/media/filer_public/2013/12/23/t10-tutorialoutline.doc
[38] http://www.lider-project.eu/iswc14_MLWDTutorial
[39] http://www.lider-project.eu/ekaw14_LRLDTutorial

students to research group leaders. Most of them worked in the intersection of Semantic Web and NLP and were interested in exploring the potentiality of linguistic LD in their own research lines. The tutorial was actively followed by 18 attendants (including speakers)[40]. In general, according to feedback received in the discussion session that followed the tutorial, the audience found the experience satisfactory and recognized the interest of an event that covered most of the relevant aspects in the conversion of language resources into LD.

7   Conclusions

In this paper we have summarised different theoretical and practical aspects concerning the representation and publication of LLOD on the Web. In particular we have reviewed: (i) how to represent ontology lexica based on the lemon model, (ii) how to follow a methodology for generating and publishing multilingual linguistic LD, (iii) how to integrate NLP with LD and RDF based on the NIF format and, (iv) how to perform word sense disambiguation and entity linking based on BabelNet. The key notions of such topics have been presented along with pointers to further materials and relevant information.

The paper reports also on the EKAW'14 tutorial on "Language Resources and Linked Data" that treated all the above concepts in a practical way. Pointers to the tutorial's instructional material and required software are also given, with the aim at helping developers and interested readers to acquire the basic mechanisms to contribute to the LLOD cloud with their own resources.

Acknowledgments. This work is supported by the FP7 European project LIDER (610782) and by the Spanish Ministry of Economy and Competitiveness (project TIN2013-46238-C4-2-R).

References

1. Archer, P., Goedertier, S., Loutas, N.: Study on persistent URIs. Technical report, December 2012
2. Bizer, C., Heath, T., Berners-Lee, T.: Linked data - the story so far. International Journal on Semantic Web and Information Systems (IJSWIS) **5**(3), 1–22 (2009)
3. Bizer, C., Lehmann, J., Kobilarov, G., Auer, S., Becker, C., Cyganiak, R., Hellmann, S.: DBpedia - a crystallization point for the web of data. Web Semantics: Science, Services and Agents on the World Wide Web **7**(3), 154–165 (2009)
4. Chiarcos, C., Nordhoff, S., Hellmann, S. (eds.) Linked Data in Linguistics - Representing and Connecting Language Data and Language Metadata. Springer (2012)
5. Cimiano, P., Buitelaar, P., McCrae, J.P., Sintek, M.: LexInfo: A declarative model for the lexicon-ontology interface. Web Semantics: Science, Services and Agents on the World Wide Web **9**(1), 29–51 (2011)

---

[40] Compare to the 40 and 31 participants that followed the related tutorials at LREC and ISWC respectively. Notice, however, the smaller size of the hosting conference in the case of EKAW.

6. Eckle-Kohler, J., McCrae, J.P., Chiarcos, C.: LemonUby-A large, interlinked, syntactically-rich lexical resource for ontologies. Semantic Web Journal-Special issue on Multilingual Linked Open Data (2015)
7. Ehrmann, M., Cecconi, F., Vannella, D., McCrae, J.P., Cimiano, P., Navigli, R.: Representing Multilingual Data as Linked Data: the Case of BabelNet 2.0. In Proceedings of the 9th Language Resource and Evaluation Conference, pp. 401–408 (2014)
8. Gracia, J., Montiel-Ponsoda, E., Vila-Suero, D., Aguado-de Cea, G.: Enabling language resources to expose translations as linked data on the web. In Proc. of 9th Language Resources and Evaluation Conference (LREC 2014), Reykjavik (Iceland), pp. 409–413. European Language Resources Association (ELRA), May 2014
9. Hellmann, S., Lehmann, J., Auer, S., Brümmer, M.: Integrating NLP using linked data. In: Alani, H., Kagal, L., Fokoue, A., Groth, P., Biemann, C., Parreira, J.X., Aroyo, L., Noy, N., Welty, C., Janowicz, K. (eds.) ISWC 2013, Part II. LNCS, vol. 8219, pp. 98–113. Springer, Heidelberg (2013)
10. Manola, F., Miller, E.: RDF primer. Technical report, W3C Recommendation (February 2004)
11. McCrae, J.P., Aguado-de Cea, G., Buitelaar, P., Cimiano, P., Declerck, T., Gómez-Pérez, A., Gracia, J., Hollink, L., Montiel-Ponsoda, E., Spohr, D., et al.: Interchanging lexical resources on the semantic web. Language Resources and Evaluation **46**(4), 701–719 (2012)
12. McCrae, J.P., Unger, C., Quattri, F., Cimiano, P.: Modelling the semantics of adjectives in the ontology-lexicon interface. In: Proceedings of 4th Workshop on Cognitive Aspects of the Lexicon (2014)
13. McCrae, J.P., Fellbaum, C., Cimiano, P.: Publishing and linking wordnet Dusing lemon and RDF. In: Proceedings of the 3rd Workshop on Linked Data in Linguistics (2014)
14. Miller, G.: WordNet: A Lexical Database for English. Communications of the ACM 38(11), November 1995
15. Montiel-Ponsoda, E., Aguado de Cea, G., Gómez-Pérez, A., Peters, W.: Modelling multilinguality in ontologies. In: Proceedings of the 22nd International Conference on Computational Linguistics, pp. 67–70 (2008)
16. Moro, A., Raganato, A., Navigli, R.: Entity Linking meets Word Sense Disambiguation: a Unified Approach. Transactions of the Association for Computational Linguistics (TACL) **2**, 231–244 (2014)
17. Navigli, R., Ponzetto, S.P.: BabelNet: The automatic construction, evaluation and application of a wide-coverage multilingual semantic network. Artificial Intelligence **193**, 217–250 (2012)
18. Unger, C., Bühmann, L., Lehmann, J., Ngonga Ngomo, A.-C., Gerber, D., Cimiano, P.: Template-based question answering over RDF data. In: Proceedings of the 21st International Conference on World Wide Web, pp. 639–648 (2012)
19. Vila-Suero, D., Gómez-Pérez, A., Montiel-Ponsoda, E., Gracia, J., Aguado-de Cea, G.: Publishing linked data: the multilingual dimension. In: Cimiano, P., Buitelaar, P. (eds.) Towards the Multilingual Semantic Web, pp. 101–118. Springer (2014)
20. Villazón-Terrazas, B., Vilches, L., Corcho, O., Gómez-Pérez, A.: Methodological guidelines for publishing government linked data. In: Wood, D. (ed.) Linking Government Data, ch. 2. Springer (2011)

From Knowledge Engineering for Development to Development Informatics

Stefan Schlobach[1], Victor de Boer[1][✉], Christophe Guéret[2], Stéphane Boyera[3], and Philippe Cudré-Mauroux[4]

[1] VU University Amsterdam, Amsterdam, The Netherlands
{k.s.schlobach,v.de.boer}@vu.nl
[2] Data Archiving and Networking Services, Amsterdam, The Netherlands
christophe.gueret@dans.knaw.nl
[3] SBC4D Consultancy, Toulouse, France
stephane@sbc4d.com
[4] eXascale Infolab, University of Fribourg, Fribourg, Switzerland
phil@exascale.info

Abstract. Knowledge Sharing is a key enabler of development of the rural poor. ICTs can play a critical role, providing for instance market data or weather information to sustenance farmers, or education to children in remote areas. While advanced knowledge technology has proven its use in many applications in the so-called developed world most of the tools cannot be easily applied in developing countries, because of restricted infrastructure, unsuitable modes of communication or ignorance of the local context. In the K4D tutorial at EKAW 2014 we argued that a new of kind of research in Knowledge Engineering is needed in order to make knowledge technology useful outside privileged developed countries. This research will have to include existing social and economic structures as fundamental requirements in order to be successful. Finally, we claim that this holds for a broader spectrum of subdisciplines of Computer Science, and not just for Knowledge Engineering, which lets us advocate Development Informatics: a joint forum for CS researchers who try to make their research relevant for the developing world as well.

1 Introduction

The tutorial "K4D - Managing and sharing knowledge in the developing part of the world"[1] took place on November 24, 2014 as part of the workshop and tutorial program of the EKAW 2014 conference. It was targeted at the broader audience of Computer Science researchers interested in knowledge engineering and management and attracted an audience that was as mixed in provenance as in its professional interests.

Throughout this paper we will use the term *knowledge sharing* for the exchange of complex information (often contextual and not necessarily formalised). The most common forms of knowledge sharing do not rely on technology and are mostly

---

[1] http://worldwidesemanticweb.org/events/k4d-2014/

© Springer International Publishing Switzerland 2015
P. Lambrix et al. (Eds.): EKAW 2014 Satellite Events, LNAI 8982, pp. 18–29, 2015.
DOI: 10.1007/978-3-319-17966-7_2

oral or textual in natural language. *Knowledge Technology* on the other hand deals with the tools to use technology (e.g. computers, mobiles, radios, etc) to support knowledge sharing.

The tutorial was organized as a series of lectures, divided into four sessions:

1. Knowledge sharing in the development context
2. Knowledge technology in development practice
3. Knowledge technology as an enabler for development?
4. Development Informatics

The goal of the tutorial was to shed light on the specific conditions that Billion of people in developing countries face daily and that are too often unknown to the research community working on the design of knowledge information systems. This fell directly under the "diversity" topic of the conference in 2014 and more generally under the knowledge management theme of EKAW. The tutorial argued that the design of information systems for developing countries calls for specific tools, practices and patterns.

The goal was to equip the participants with an analytic toolkit to identify, in their own work, opportunities to broaden their research to be relevant to the people on the other side of the *digital divide*, as well as interesting research challenges that are specific to a development context.

There is a need for Computer Science to open up to development challenges. In this paper we argue for the emergence of a coherent CS sub-discipline, encompassing specific knowledge representation, information retrieval and software engineering research topics.

2   Knowledge Sharing in the Development Context

Knowledge sharing can play an important role in overcoming poverty in the developing world. One of the most impressive, and famous, examples of the power of knowledge and knowledge sharing in the developing world is the work of Yacouba Sawadogo, a farmer from Burkina Faso, who extended existing knowledge in sustainable land management, which had an astonishing effect on efforts to re-green the Sahel zone. The power of his approach was the local context in which this knowledge was created and embedded as well as the spread of the knowledge by means of the almost missionary power of the knowledge sharing capabilities of Yacouba and others involved.[2]

By making knowledge sharing more effective and scalable, Knowledge Technology can become a key enabler of development for the rural poor. Before analysing the specific requirements to Knowledge Technology in a developing context we report on previous research into knowledge sharing case studies in rural, developing regions. For a number of cases, we have already developed and deployed ICTs using a living-labs method [1]. Other cases are currently under development.

---

[2] There is an documentary made about Yacouba Sawadogo work: http://www.1080films.co.uk/project-mwsd.htm.

Market Information Sharing. This use case was developed in a living-labs collaboration between Malian sustenance farmers, radio hosts, a local NGO and CS4D researchers [1]. Local farmers expressed the need to share information about prices and availability of local produce such as honey or cereals. A Market Information System (MIS) called RadioMarché was developed in collaboration with the stakeholders. RadioMarché allows for information creation and access using simple mobile phones through voice interfaces in local languages. The market information is locally relevant for the farmers and their clients, but also monitored on an aggregate level by the local NGO.

Radio Information Platform. A second case and system was developed in the same area. The Furoba Blon system allows radio hosts to collect information from remote villages using citizen journalists who call in with their news items. This is a more generic platform in the sense that the type of information is less restricted. Local radio hosts manage and access the information using a web-interface or a voice-interface using their mobile phones in a local language [1].

Weather Prediction Using Pluviometric Data. Weather prediction is important for planning, securing and assessing farming and its products. Global weather prediction systems exist, but due to climate change and local conditions, it is important to use local observation data to analyse data on local levels. In rural Burkina Faso and Mali, we are developing a system for gathering, sharing and aggregating pluviometric data. Local farmers expressed the need for effective and efficient creation, curation and sharing of rainfall and weather data. This data is locally shared and can be combined with (Open) satellite data into a larger observation system. Based on aggregate knowledge, one can understand large scale hydrologic processes, such as flooding, irrigation and vaporization.

Land Rights. More complex knowledge is being created and shared in this case in rural Burkina Faso which centers around land rights. Local farmers are often unaware of the complex issues around land ownership and usage rights. This is sometimes exploited by others to illegally use land for mining or building purposes. Local NGOs have mapped these land rights and seek solutions to share this knowledge amongst farmers in an effective and timely manner.

Innovative Farming Techniques. In collaboration with local NGOs, innovative farmers in rural West-Africa are developing innovative farming techniques to deal with soil degradation and desertification. Examples of these techniques are the use of stone walls or the timely digging of holes (so called *zaï*) to recover and retain water on farmland. This complex and locally created knowledge is currently being aggregated by the NGOs to be shared between farmers using folders, videos and extension workers. Here, knowledge representation and knowledge sharing techniques can assist in increasing the reach of these techniques.

Education Statistics. Among the different approaches for improving education in deprived part of the world, the foundation One Laptop Per Child (OLPC) decided to go for giving one laptop to every child and let them progress on their own under the guidance of a teacher. Monitoring this learning process is needed as educators and state institutions need to know how all the young learners are performing. Several solutions have been proposed to gather and aggregate this data[2], turning private nominative data into anonymous public statistics.

These case studies each bring their own specific challenges to using ICT and knowledge technologies. However, we can make a number of generalizations about the specific challenges and approaches to knowledge technologies for development.

3 Technology for Knowledge Sharing in Development

Common to all these examples is that there is a clearly identified need for knowledge sharing, and that there is some basic infrastructure to apply Knowledge Technology. On the other hand, in none of the examples can state-of-the-art Knowledge Technology directly be applied. In the following sections we will describe some initial attempts to close this gap, and explain why this is non-trivial, both from a technological, methodological and socioeconomic perspective.

3.1 Requirements and Challenges

First of all, any knowledge technologies need to be embedded in existing infrastructure and social context to ensure local uptake and sustainability of solutions. This calls for "downscaling" of knowledge technologies solutions to existing infrastructures [3]. These include mobile telephony as main intercommunication device. Where in rural developing areas personal computers and tablets are hardly used, mobile devices have been recognized as having the greatest potential for development[4]. In Africa, mobile telephony has become the primary mode of telecommunication [5]. More specifically, most mobile phones in use in these areas are simple (2G) compared to current generation smartphones or feature phones. To ensure the maximum reach of knowledge technologies, we therefore should consider making them available through voice or text messaging.

Another information sharing platform that is currently used in large parts of the developing world is that of radio. Radio is for example still the most popular mass-medium in Africa and currently used to distribute a wide variety of information amongst listeners. Examples include services for farmers (market prices or weather reports) or health services. Incorporating radio as a platform for Knowledge Technologies can drastically improve its reach [6].

It is also paramount that ICT solutions -including knowledge technologies, operate within existing socioeconomic and business processes. To ensure that developed technologies are sustainable, they need to be owned by local stakeholders. At the same time, the socioeconomic context needs to be understood to a degree where the Knowledge Technology is able to be used by the users it is designed for. For example, if local power structures prohibit users to enter information in a system, such a system will lose effectiveness.

3.2   Example for Paradigm Shifts

There are many challenges and opportunities for new approaches to knowledge technologies for development. This requires an open mind and in some cases a radical shift in paradigms. For example, where most knowledge technologies assume broadband networks to transfer information, in low-connected environments this does not hold. In these cases, information can be distributed using the mobile network or through radio. Sneakernets[3] employ physical transportation of data-carrying devices, which in some cases can result in high bandwith throughput (albeit with a high latency). For existing knowledge technologies we can consider to what extent they can use these alternative networks and as computer scientists, we can adapt them where necessary. We present two examples of current work on using Linked Data technologies in these new paradigms.

- **Linked Data and Voice Technologies.** In [7], the authors present work on using Voice access for simple mobile phones to Linked Data for to rural communities in the Sahel region. This work builds on RadioMarché, a market information system (MIS) which can be accessed using first-generation mobile phones. Linking the locally produced market data to other data sources will increase its value for use by local NGOs but also for subsistence farmers themselves. The RadioMarché data was made available as Linked Open Data. At the same time, the authors present an ontology for describing RDF resources as voice recordings in multiple languages. These voice fragments can then be used in a voice interface that can be accessed by simple mobile phones. The authors present a prototype demonstrator that provides voice-based access to this linked market data. As such, these are first steps towards opening Linked Data to local users that do not have appropriate hardware to produce and consume Linked Data.
- **Entity Registry System** Semantic Web solutions typically assume the availability of Web architectures: including access to global network access. However, in rural environment, these assumptions do not hold. In many cases where internet connectivity is available, these are not stable. The Entity Registry System (ERS) [8] is software that provides Linked Data solutions for local "not-always-online" networks. ERS is a decentralised registry which is designed to be read/write, track the provenance of the contributions and be usable offline and online. This registry creates a global data space where every user is able to say something about any entity. Just like Wikis allows for the collaborative of a web site, ERS will enable the collaborative editing of a registry on a de-centralised basis. The data associated to an entity is its description, recorded as RDF data. An implementation of ERS was developed that allows for effective information exchange for the Sugar Learning Platform[4] originally developed for the XO laptop of the One Laptop Per Child initiative (OLPC)[5].

---

[3] http://en.wikipedia.org/wiki/Sneakernet
[4] http://sugarlabs.org/
[5] http://one.laptop.org/

– **Localising Open Data** The "Open" movement also has caught on in International Development and a number of development researchers and practitioners recognize the benefits of building openness into policies and technologies for development. As is noted by Davies and Edwards [9]: "*Governments, companies and non-governmental organisations (NGOs) across the world are increasingly exploring how the publication and use of open and linked data can have impacts on governance, economic growth and the delivery of services*". However, it remains a challenge to bridge the digital divide and have open development data have significant impact for the rural poor themselves since these people often lack access to data portals on the Web or lack the literacy to interpret the data. The World Bank has recently experimented with bringing Open Data about development contracting to rural villages in Indonesia and Kenya[6]. They developed print material that was shared with local community members in intensive interactive sessions. This is an example of sharing knowledge using alternative modalities. Other examples are the usasge of icon-based communication or development of video or animation material to share knowledge.

4 Knowledge Technology as an Enabler for Development?

In the previous sections we have provided examples of potentially useful and promising applications of Knowledge Technology in development. An important basis for these approaches was the local embedding and the careful adjustment to the social context of each individual application of Knowledge Technology.

In this section we want to expand on this theme, by discussing Knowledge Technology in development in a broader socioeconomic perspective. First, in Section 4.1 we will briefly revisit existing arguments with respect to ICT4D in general, before identifying some specific challenges to Knowledge Technology in Section 4.2.

4.1 Knowledge Technology in ICT4D

The application of information and communication technologies (ICT) in development might be considered at first thought to be an uncontroversial tool for development, but there have been heavy discussions about their role and impact from sociological, political and economic perspectives. In this section we will briefly summarise some of these arguments to clarify the challenges and responsibility researchers in Knowledge Technology face when working in development case studies.

What is Development? Originating in the ideas of the Enlightenment, development is about economic, social and political progress, and technology seen as one of the driving vehicle for this kind of progress. This is a disputed, and

---

[6] http://www.open-contracting.org/bringing_open_contracting_data_offline

highly European, notion, where progress is often considered an essential part of the functioning of our societies. It should, however, be noted that this a very biased notion, which is meaningless, and non-desirable, in many societies. This undermines the very foundations of many approaches to ICT4D, which aims at transforming societies to resemble what we consider to be successful role-models. This colonial view is very often at the core of misunderstanding in ICT4D.

Another argument questions the role of ICT for benefitting society: competition about technological leadership can lead to innovation, but mostly for the those already in a leading position, which increases, rather than decreases, global disparity. In words of Tim Unwin, an outspoken critics of traditional ICT4D approaches, *"technology has all too often been used mainly to enable the rich and privileged to retain their positions of economic, social and political power"* [10].

Neo-liberal approaches have mostly focussed on trade rather than aid, free markets and privatisation of state-owned companies. As a consequence 70% of Ghana Telecom is, e.g., now owned by Vodafone. Although some of this kind of involvements potentially increases the availability of advanced technology critics identify the risks that this technology is not used in the interest of the people, but mostly to increase the gain of usually Western companies.

What is the Role of Information and Communication Technologies for Development? In this paper we adopt a broad view ICT, meaning all kinds of electronic means of capturing, processing, storing and communicating information, such as computers, phones, Internet, radio or tv. Access to information has been identified as one of the core human rights, and Universal Declaration on Human Rights by the United Nations in 1948 states in Article 19: *"Everyone has the right [...] to seek, impart information and ideas through any media and regardless of frontiers."* In this respect there is nowadays a central role for ICTs, as they are one of the central carriers of information in modern times. Considering this role of ICTs for information and knowledge sharing, access to and usability of such technology is of crucial importance.

The potential benefits of ICTs in development are therefore enormous: at the most abstract level Knowledge Technology can play an important role in knowledge and information sharing, with potential contributions to empowerment, education, advances of democratic process and emancipation. Given the previous discussion about ICT4D, though, this optimistic look has to be relativized, as those positive benefits are not guaranteed, and require a careful analysis of the application scenario at hand. Some of the risks have been identified in the ongoing debate about ICT4D.

The Big Debate About ICT4D The debate about ICT4D has been ongoing for decades. From an economic perspective the importance of science and technology for economic growth has been emphasised often referring to positive examples from Asia, where a combination of skilled labour forces and excellent infrastructure turned ICTs into main vehicles for impressive economic growth. ICTs in these cases helped accessing information and facilitate trade, which ensured those countries a strong position on growing marked. Many questions remain though in how far those effects can be reproduced more globally. On the African continent, *e.g.*, there is hardly any production of hardware or software, not is there a sufficiently educated labour-force to deliver ICT services even to the own people. This means that the supply chains of ICT remain between US, Europe, India, China, Taiwan, South Korea, Japan, Russia *etc.*, with Africa paying for services without further profiting economically.

Many critics have pointed to the environmental impact of current approaches to ICT4D where hardware, sometimes old leftover hardware from developed countries, is delivered to the developing countries. Combine this with a lack of expertise to apply this hardware in local contexts, development aid of ICTs often simple results in uncontrolled dumping of old, and often highly toxic, technology.

From a social-cultural and socioeconomic viewpoint new, Western, ICT approaches are often radically deviating from traditional communication models, with two possible unwanted outcomes: either the technology is simply not used and the development effort wasted at best, or the technology destroys existing and successful communication structures, replacing them with often unsuitable and untested new paradigms.

4.2   ICT4D Specific Challenges to KT

The case studies described in Section 2 have shown us that users in poor rural areas are as we speak creating knowledge in the field, in schools, *etc.* The stakeholders express the need for more effective and efficient creation, curation and sharing of this knowledge. Currently, they are hindered in doing so using ICTs mainly because of the lack of infrastructure (Internet access, lack of electrical power, *etc.*); incompatible interfaces (which do not take into account local languages or literacy levels) and the lack of generic platforms for creating bottom-up knowledge sharing solutions. This calls for new designs of knowledge sharing architectures that take into account these issues. Our ongoing efforts helped shape three distinct aspects to focus research agendas on:

Interfaces Such architectures should allow knowledge creation, curation and sharing through relevant interfaces that take into account local languages and levels of literacy. Voice-based[1] or icon-based interfaces have shown great promise here, especially when combined in multi-modal interfaces.

Infrastructure Similarly, the systems should be designed to work with non-standard infrastructures. On the one hand, there is often a lack of persistent power grid, internet connectivity and ownership of computing devices. On the other hand, mobile networks and simple first- or second-generation mobile phones are widespread in many developing areas. Effective knowledge sharing platforms should make use of these assets. At the same time, small hardware solutions are affordable both in price and cost of ownership (low power consumption). They are robust solutions to serve as data sharing nodes[3].

Contextualisation of knowledge A characteristic of these cases is that often, the information that is created is primarily locally used. However, a secondary usages lies in the aggregation to higher levels (regionally, country-level, global). The other way around, this more generic data is also relevant locally when combined with the local information. Knowledge sharing platforms should take this issue into account. For example, when global (internet) connectivity is temporarily unavailable, knowledge can still be shared locally using local networks. In Table 1, we list the use cases and some characteristics of the knowledge being shared. This includes where it is created, uses of the knowledge (primary and secondary) and whether Peer-to-Peer exchanges are needed. In some use cases, the knowledge being exchanged is fairly simple. In other cases, the knowledge is much more complex. The innovative farming techniques are made up of relatively complex sequences of farming actions depending on weather, soil structure etc. Table 1 shows the diversity in the complexity of the knowledge across the use cases. The complexity will have its consequences for the interface design as well as how knowledge is shared and aggregated. A generic platform should be able to deal with the creation, sharing and curation of knowledge of different levels of complexity.

Table 1. Overview of the different aspects of the knowledge in the use cases. *Knowledge creation and usage* : the importance of locally created knowledge (*e.g.* produced by the end users) versus its global counter part (*e.g.* governmental or country level). *P2P exchanges* : amount of local communication among peers from a different level of communications. *Complexity* : appreciation of the number of entities and level of communications that can be observed, leading to simple to more complex systems.

Use case	Knowledge creation	usage	P2P exchanges	Complexity
Market Information	local	local+global	important	simple
Radio Platform	local	local	not needed	simple
Pluviometry	local+global	local	not needed	simple
Land rights	local+global	local	useful	complex
Farming techniques	local+global	local	useful	complex
Education statistics	local	global	not needed	simple

Our experience so far through different projects[7] taught us that it is important not only to consider all these specific topics together in one holistic view but also to ensure the target population and ICT experts are always part of the discussions. We consider this as part of the bottom-up living-labs approach, working from local needs and focus on markets and using locally sustainable ICTs.

---

[7] See the papers cited in this paper but also the community landing pages http://worldwidesemanticweb.org/ and http://w4ra.org/ for an overview.

5   From KT4D to Development Informatics

There is a duality in Computer Science as it can be considered either as a discipline or as a tool. As a tool computer science is key to processing large amount of data whereas the development of the novel algorithm needed for such computation would appeal more to the discipline facet of Computer Science. The consequence of doing ICT4D without Computer Scientists is that standard and simple ICT solutions are applied (and often fail) following a "one size fits all" idea. The expertise needed to adapt existing technical solutions and develop new solutions when those existing can not fit is missing. Multi-disciplinary approaches combining the expertise of ICT4D practitioners and that of Computer Scientists hold the promises of better optimised computational systems.

The reasons this is only rarely happening now have not be sought in the lack of interest for Computer Scientists to help improve the life of underprivileged world citizens, nor in the lack of motivation for ICT4D experts to collaborate with Computer Scientists. There are fundamental thresholds Computer Scientists have to overcome:

- There is an intrinsic difficulty to work in multi-disciplinary contexts. As we have argued, successful development and deployment of Knowledge Technologies for development will have to be done in collaboration with experts able to investigate the socioeconomic context. Other collaborations will include language technology specialists or hardware designers.
- There is a very high threshold to work in ICT4D:
  - The knowledge gap is huge (on both sides). On the one hand, Computer Scientists do not know about development issues, and on the other hand, ICT4D practitioners and development experts are unaware of the benefits that CS research can bring.
  - Intrinsic uncertainty and carefulness of researchers to work in new research fields.
  - Scientific recognition (still) rather limited. To be able to draw consistent and sustained support contributions from Computer Scientists, this recognition will have to grow larger.
- The scientific challenges of Computer Science in a development context are not well understood
- In most cases there is a physical distance between the researchers and the target population. This causes development challenges to remain unknown to researchers and makes working efficiently difficult.
- There is also a cultural distance between researchers and target population, which, together with language barriers cause for difficulties in communication.
- It can finally be noted that, in an ever going globalisation of the World economy where competition among (groups of) countries is tough levering funding from on part of the World to help another can prove to be challenging.

Besides the necessary discussions among all those are concerned[8], we believe the definition of a coherent research discipline is a first step into solving them.

---

[8] Face-to-face as during this tutorial and other events we organise but also on-line in discussion community groups.

We therefore propose establishing *Development Informatics* as a sub-discipline of Computer Science. Development Informatics research integrates development specific problems into computer science research efforts. These can be in Distributed Systems, Computational Linguistics, Human-Computer Interaction, or, in the case of K4D: Knowledge Engineering. Those Computer Science experts will face common development-related challenges: technologically, as well as legally, ethically, sociologically and politically.

In this Development Informatics, some not so common research questions can emerge related to the specific challenges listed above. For example, looking at the specific topics of knowledge representation, information retrieval and software engineering :

- Knowledge representation
  - How to relate textual and vocal data representations to enable voice interfaces to data ?
  - What level of common semantics can be reached among several communities speaking all a different dialect among them ?
  - What are the impact of the digitization of content and data collection on the life of people living in developing economies ?
- Information retrieval
  - Can visualisation and voice be leveraged to bridge the literacy gap in computer-human interfaces ?
  - What is the role of information sharing in development[9] ?
  - Can insights from development experts be used to better understand the dynamics of informal economies and drive the design of optimised computational systems ?
- Software engineering
  - What are the sensible assumptions to make when designing a computational system for a developing economy ?
  - What are the Technological Challenges for system change ?
  - Can data intensive computational systems be made to fit contexts with limited resources (hardware, connectivity, ...) ?

6   Conclusion

Supporting knowledge sharing through state-of-the-art knowledge technology in the developing world can not be achieved by simply deploying well-established ICT solutions in a top-down manner. The Knowledge Engineering community has to take on the problem of development by increasing the applicability of its technologies in developing countries. For this, the global discussion of ICT4D has to be understood, with its implications on global and local political, socioeconomic, and socio-cultural processes but, most and foremost, the local context of the applications has to be understood, which often implies a radical paradigm

---

[9] Eventually focusing on development related datasets such as health-care data, aid money spending, votes, contracts, or education indicators.

shift. In previous work we identified 3 main dimensions in which the knowledge engineering community has to broaden its approach: study alternative (often weaker) infrastructures, novel interface paradigms, and contextualisation. In this paper, we claim that these findings call for an even larger effort, the creation of a new subdiscipline of Computer Science, which we call Development Informatics.

References

1. Gyan, N.B., de Boer, V., Bon, A., van Aart, C., Akkermans, H., Boyera, S., Froumentin, M., Grewal, A., Allen, M.: Voice-based web access in rural africa. In: WebSci, pp. 122–131. ACM (2013)
2. Verma, S.: The quest for data (2014). http://www.olpcsf.org/node/204
3. Guéret, C., de Boer, V., Schlobach, S.: Let's downscale linked data. IEEE Internet Computing 18, 70–73 (2014)
4. Boyera, S.: Mobile web for social development (MW4D). Technical report, W3C (2008). http://www.w3.org/2008/MW4D/ (accessed March 19, 2010)
5. UNCTAD Secretariat: Science and technology for development: the new paradigm of ict. In United Nations Conference on Trade and Development, ed.: Information Economy Report 2007–2008, United Nations Publication (2007). http://unctad.org/en/Docs/sdteecb20071_en.pdf (accessed August 8, 2011)
6. Bon, A., Boer, V.D., Leenheer, P.D., Aart, C.V., Baah, N., Froumentin, M., Boyera, S., Allen, M., Akkermans, H.: The web of radios- introducing african community radio as an interface to the web of data. In: Proceedings of the 1st International Workshop on Downscaling the Semantic Web - Downscale 2012 (2012). http://ceur-ws.org/vol-844
7. de Boer, V., Gyan, N.B., Bon, A., Tuyp, W., van Aart, C., Akkermans, H.: A dialogue with linked data: Voice-based access to market data in the sahel. Semantic Web (2013)
8. Guéret, C., Cudré-Mauroux, P.: The entity registry system: Publishing and consuming linked data in poorly connected environments. ERCIM News 2014 (2014)
9. Davies, T., Edwards, D.: Emerging implications of open and linked data for knowledge sharing in development. IDS Bulletin 43(5), 117–127 (2012)
10. Unwin, T.: ICT4D. Cambridge University Press (2010)

Workshop Summaries and Best Papers

Acquisition, Representation and Reasoning About Context with Logic (ARCOE-Logic 2014)

Alessandra Mileo[1]([✉]), Martin Homola[2], and Michael Fink[3]

[1] INSIGHT Centre for Data Analytics, National University of Ireland, Galway,
Republic of Ireland
alessandra.mileo@deri.org
[2] Faculty of Mathematics, Physics and Informatics, Comenius University,
Bratislava, Slovakia
homola@fmph.uniba.sk
[3] Institut für Informationssysteme Technische Universität Wien, Vienna, Austria
fink@kr.tuwien.ac.at

Abstract. In recent years, research in contextual knowledge representation and reasoning became more relevant in the areas of Semantic Web, Linked Open Data, and Ambient Intelligence, where knowledge is not considered a monolithic and static asset, but it is distributed in a network of interconnected heterogeneous and evolving knowledge resources. The challenge to deal with the contextual nature of this knowledge is brought to an unprecedented scale. The ARCOE-Logic workshop aims to provide a dedicated forum for researchers to discuss recent developments, important open issues and future directions in the area of contextual knowledge representation and knowledge management.

Preface

Contextual nature of knowledge is one of the most important problems studied within the fields of data and knowledge management and engineering. Knowledge is often crafted and stored under some assumed context, such as spatial and temporal coordinates under which the piece of knowledge holds, relevant associated topic, purpose of the particular knowledge set. However, knowledge is also often published, redistributed and reused beyond the originally intended application, and that is when the relation between the originally assumed context and the new application context needs to be dealt with and accommodated.

With the emergence of the Semantic Web, and especially the Linked Data initiatives, enormous amounts of data have become available, and knowledge is not considered a monolithic and static asset, but it is distributed in a network of interconnected heterogeneous and evolving knowledge resources. Furthermore, data is handled and processed not only in form of datasets published on the Web, but more and more in form of sensor data streams. The challenge to deal with the contextual nature of this huge and dynamic data is therefore brought

© Springer International Publishing Switzerland 2015
P. Lambrix et al. (Eds.): EKAW 2014 Satellite Events, LNAI 8982, pp. 33–34, 2015.
DOI: 10.1007/978-3-319-17966-7_3

to an unprecedented scale; however, also increasing opportunities arise to build novel applications combining and reusing semantic data across domains, depending on the ability to deal with the problems associated with context and data contextuality.

ARCOE-Logic 2014, the 6th International Workshop on Acquisition, Representation and Reasoning about Context with Logic, was held in Linköping, Sweden, on 25 November 2014, in collocation with EKAW 2014. The workshop aims to provide a dedicated forum for researchers to discuss recent developments, important open issues and future directions in the area of contextual knowledge representation and management. It follows from five previous edition of ARCOE (Int'l Workshop on Automated Reasoning about Context and Ontology Evolution) and two previous edition of Logic (Int'l Workshop on Logic-based Interpretation of Context).

The current edition of the workshop received nine submissions which were all peer-reviewed by at least three members of the program committee and of which six were accepted. One submission was later withdrawn. The papers were selected based on their quality, relevance to the workshop topics, and potential to bring forward interesting ideas to be discussed during the workshop. Authors of two selected papers accepted to submit a revised and extended version and they passed a second round of reviews. The two resulting revised papers are included in this volume.

We would like to thank to the authors for their valuable contributions and program committee members for providing high quality feedback, and we look forward to the next edition.

February 2015   Alessandra Mileo
                                                                       Martin Homola
                                                                         Michael Fink
                                                                    ARCOE-Logic 2014

Knowledge Propagation in Contextualized Knowledge Repositories: An Experimental Evaluation
(Extended Paper)

Loris Bozzato[✉] and Luciano Serafini

Fondazione Bruno Kessler, Via Sommarive 18, 38123 Trento, Italy
{bozzato,serafini}@fbk.eu

Abstract. As the interest in the representation of context dependent knowledge in the Semantic Web has been recognized, a number of logic based solutions have been proposed in this regard. In our recent works, in response to this need, we presented the description logic-based Contextualized Knowledge Repository (CKR) framework. CKR is not only a theoretical framework, but it has been effectively implemented over state-of-the-art tools for the management of Semantic Web data: inference inside and across contexts has been realized in the form of forward SPARQL-based rules over different RDF named graphs. In this paper we present the first evaluation results for such CKR implementation. In particular, in our first experiment we study its *scalability* with respect to different reasoning regimes. In a second experiment we analyze the effects of *knowledge propagation* on the reasoning process. In the last experiment we study the effects of *modularization* of global knowledge with respect to local reasoning.

1 Introduction

Recently, the representation of context dependent knowledge in the Semantic Web has been recognized as a relevant issue. This lead to the introduction of a growing number of logic based proposals, e.g. [6,7,10–13]. In this line of research, in our previous works we introduced the Contextualized Knowledge Repository (CKR) framework [1,4,5,10]. CKR is a description logics-based framework defined as a two-layered structure: intuitively, a lower layer contains a set of contextualized knowledge bases, while the upper layer contains context independent knowledge and meta-data defining the structure of contextual knowledge bases.

The CKR framework has not only been presented as a theoretical framework, but we also proposed effective implementations based on its definitions [2,5]. In particular, in [5] we presented an implementation for the CKR framework over state-of-the-art tools for storage and inference over RDF data. Intuitively, the CKR architecture can be implemented by representing the global context and the local object contexts as distinct RDF named graphs. Inference inside (and

© Springer International Publishing Switzerland 2015
P. Lambrix et al. (Eds.): EKAW 2014 Satellite Events, LNAI 8982, pp. 35–51, 2015.
DOI: 10.1007/978-3-319-17966-7_4

across) named graphs is implemented as SPARQL based forward rules. We use an extension of the Sesame framework that we developed, called *SPRINGLES*, which provides methods to demand an inference materialization over multiple graphs: rules are encoded as SPARQL queries and it is possible to customize their evaluation strategy. The rule set encodes the rules of the formal materialization calculus we proposed for the CKR framework [5] and the evaluation strategy follows the calculus translation process.

In this paper we present the results of an initial experimental evaluation of such implementation of CKR framework over RDF. In particular, the experiments we present are aimed at answering three different research questions:

- **RQ1 (scalability):** *what is the effect on the amount of time requested for inference closure computation with respect to the number and size of contexts of a CKR?*
- **RQ2 (propagation):** *what is the effect on the amount of time requested for inference closure computation with respect to the number of connections across contexts?* (considering a fixed number of contexts and a fixed amount of knowledge exchanged).
- **RQ3 (modularization):** *what is the effect on the amount of time requested for inference closure computation with respect to the distribution of knowledge across global and local modules?*

As we will detail in the following sections, by means of our experiments we answered the questions with these findings:

- **F1 (scalability):** reasoning regime at the global and local level strongly impacts on the scalability of reasoning and its behaviour. Considering only global level reasoning, results suggest that the management of contexts does not add overhead to the reasoning in global context; by considering also reasoning inside contexts, inference time appears to be influenced by the expressivity and number of contexts.
- **F2 (propagation):** knowledge propagation cost linearly depends on the number of connections. Moreover, the representation of references to local interpretation of symbols using context connections is always more compact w.r.t. replicating symbols for each local interpretation: the first solution in general requires more computational time, but outperforms the second solution in case of a larger number of connections.
- **F3 (modularization):** the representation of global knowledge as a module shared by all contexts is always more compact w.r.t. replication of knowledge for each local interpretation. For an adequate dimension of the module and number of contexts, reasoning with modularization outperforms the overhead of context management.

The remainder of the paper is organized as follows: in Section 2 we summarize the basic formal definitions for CKR and its associated calculus; in Section 3 we summarize how the presented definitions have been implemented over RDF named graphs; in Section 4 we present the test setup and experimental evaluations; finally, in Section 5 we suggest some possible extensions to the current evaluation and implementation work.

2   Contextualized Knowledge Repositories

In the following we provide an informal summary of the definitions for the CKR framework: for a formal and detailed description and for complete examples, we refer to [5] where the current formalization for CKR has been first introduced.

Intuitively, a CKR is a two layered structure: the upper layer consists of a knowledge base $\mathfrak{G}$ containing (1) *meta-knowledge*, i.e. the structure and properties of contexts of the CKR, and (2) *global (context-independent) knowledge*, i.e., knowledge that applies to every context; the lower layer consists of a set of (local) contexts that contain (locally valid) facts and can refer to what holds in other contexts.

Syntax. In order to separate the elements of the meta-knowledge from the ones of the object knowledge, we build CKRs over two distinct vocabularies and languages. The meta-knowledge of a CKR is expressed in a DL language containing the elements that define the contextual structure. A *meta-vocabulary* is a DL vocabulary Γ containing the sets of symbols for *context names* **N**; *module names* **M**; *context classes* **C**, including the class Ctx; *contextual relations* **R**; *contextual attributes* **A**; and for every attribute $A \in$ **A**, a set D_A of *attribute values* of A. The role mod defined on **N** × **M** expresses associations between contexts and modules. Intuitively, modules represent pieces of knowledge specific to a context or context class; attributes describe contextual dimensions (e.g. time, location, topic) identifying a context (class). The *meta-language* $\mathcal{L}_\Gamma$ of a CKR is a DL language over Γ (where, formally, the range and domain of attributes and mod are restricted as explained above).

The knowledge in contexts of a CKR is expressed via a DL language $\mathcal{L}_\Sigma$, called *object-language*, based on an object-vocabulary Σ. The expressions of the object language are evaluated locally to each context, i.e., contexts can interpret each symbol independently. To access the interpretation of expressions inside a specific context or context class, we extend $\mathcal{L}_\Sigma$ to $\mathcal{L}_\Sigma^e$ with *eval expressions* of the form $eval(X, C)$, where X is a concept or role expression of $\mathcal{L}_\Sigma$ and C is a concept expression of $\mathcal{L}_\Gamma$ (with C $\sqsubseteq$ Ctx). Intuitively, $eval(X, C)$ can be read as "the interpretation of X in all the contexts of type C".

On the base of previous languages, we define a *Contextualized Knowledge Repository (CKR)* as a structure $\mathfrak{K} = \langle \mathfrak{G}, \{K_m\}_{m \in M} \rangle$ where: (i) $\mathfrak{G}$ is a DL knowledge base over $\mathcal{L}_\Gamma \cup \mathcal{L}_\Sigma$; (ii) every K_m is a DL knowledge base over $\mathcal{L}_\Sigma^e$, for each module name $m \in$ **M**. The knowledge in a CKR can be expressed by means of any DL language: in this paper, we consider $\mathcal{SROIQ}$-RL (defined in [5]) as language of reference. $\mathcal{SROIQ}$-RL is a restriction of $\mathcal{SROIQ}$ syntax corresponding to OWL RL [9]. $\mathfrak{K}$ is a $\mathcal{SROIQ}$-RL CKR, if $\mathfrak{G}$ and all K_m are knowledge bases over the extended language of $\mathcal{SROIQ}$-RL where eval-expressions can only occur in left-concepts and contain left-concepts or roles.

Semantics. The model-based semantics of CKR basically follows the two layered structure of the framework. A *CKR interpretation* is a structure $\mathfrak{I} = \langle \mathcal{M}, \mathcal{I} \rangle$ s.t.: (i) $\mathcal{M}$ is a DL interpretation of $\Gamma \cup \Sigma$ (respecting the intuitive interpretation of Ctx as the class of all contexts); (ii) for every $x \in$ Ctx$^\mathcal{M}$, $\mathcal{I}(x)$ is a

DL interpretation over Σ (with same domain and interpretation of individual names of $\mathcal{M}$). The interpretation of ordinary DL expressions on $\mathcal{M}$ and $\mathcal{I}(x)$ in $\mathfrak{I} = \langle \mathcal{M}, \mathcal{I} \rangle$ is as usual; *eval* expressions are interpreted as follows: for every $x \in \mathsf{Ctx}^{\mathcal{M}}$, $eval(X, \mathsf{C})^{\mathcal{I}(x)} = \bigcup_{e \in \mathsf{C}^{\mathcal{M}}} X^{\mathcal{I}(e)}$, i.e. the union of all elements in $X^{\mathcal{I}(e)}$ for all contexts e in $\mathsf{C}^{\mathcal{M}}$.

A CKR interpretation $\mathfrak{I}$ is a *CKR model* of $\mathfrak{K}$ iff the following conditions hold: (i) for $\alpha \in \mathcal{L}_{\Sigma} \cup \mathcal{L}_{\Gamma}$ in $\mathfrak{G}$, $\mathcal{M} \models \alpha$; (ii) for $\langle x, y \rangle \in \mathsf{mod}^{\mathcal{M}}$ with $y = \mathsf{m}^{\mathcal{M}}$, $\mathcal{I}(x) \models \mathsf{K_m}$; (iii) for $\alpha \in \mathfrak{G} \cap \mathcal{L}_{\Sigma}$ and $x \in \mathsf{Ctx}^{\mathcal{M}}$, $\mathcal{I}(x) \models \alpha$. Intuitively, while the first two conditions impose that $\mathfrak{I}$ verifies the contents of global and local modules associated to contexts, last condition states that global knowledge has to be propagated to local contexts.

Materialization calculus. Reasoning inside a CKR has been formalized in form of a materialization calculus. In particular, the calculus proposed in [5] is an adaptation of the calculus presented in [8] in order to define a reasoning procedure for deciding instance checking in the structure of a $\mathcal{SROIQ}$-RL CKR. As we discuss in following sections, this calculus provides the formalization for the definition of rules for the implementation of CKR based on RDF named graphs and forward SPARQL rules.

Intuitively, the calculus is based on a translation to datalog: the axioms of the input CKR are translated to datalog atoms and datalog rules are added to such translation to encode the global and local inferences rules; instance checking is then performed by translating the ABox assertion to be verified as a datalog fact and verifying whether it is entailed by the CKR program. The calculus, thus, has three components: (1) the *input translations* $I_{glob}, I_{loc}, I_{rl}$, where given an axiom α and $\mathsf{c} \in \mathbf{N}$, each $I(\alpha, \mathsf{c})$ is a set of datalog facts or rules: intuitively, they encode as datalog facts the contents of input global and local DL knowledge bases; (2) the *deduction rules* P_{loc}, P_{rl}, which are sets of datalog rules: they represent the inference rules for the instance-level reasoning over the translated axioms; and (3) the *output translation* O, where given an axiom α and $\mathsf{c} \in \mathbf{N}$, $O(\alpha, \mathsf{c})$ is a single datalog fact encoding the ABox assertion α that we want to prove to be entailed by the input CKR (in the context c).

We briefly present here the form of the different sets of translation and deduction rules: tables with the complete set of rules can be found in [5].
(i) $\mathcal{SROIQ}$-*RL translation*: Rules in $I_{rl}(S, \mathsf{c})$ translate to datalog facts $\mathcal{SROIQ}$-RL axioms (in context c). E.g., we translate atomic concept inclusions with the rule $A \sqsubseteq B \mapsto \{\mathtt{subClass}(A, B, \mathsf{c})\}$. The rules in P_{rl} are the deduction rules corresponding to axioms in $\mathcal{SROIQ}$-RL: e.g., for atomic concept inclusions we have

$$\mathtt{subClass}(y, z, c), \mathtt{inst}(x, y, c) \rightarrow \mathtt{inst}(x, z, c)$$

(ii) *Global and local translations*: Global input rules of I_{glob} encode the interpretation of Ctx in the global context. Similarly, local input rules I_{loc} and local deduction rules P_{loc} provide the translation and rules for elements of the local object language. In particular for *eval* expressions in concept inclusions, we have the input rule $eval(A, \mathsf{C}) \sqsubseteq B \mapsto \{\mathtt{subEval}(A, \mathsf{C}, B, \mathsf{c})\}$ and the corresponding deduction rule (where g identifies the global context):

$$\texttt{subEval}(a, c_1, b, c), \texttt{inst}(c', c_1, g), \texttt{inst}(x, a, c') \rightarrow \texttt{inst}(x, b, c)$$

(iii) *Output rules*: The rules in $O(\alpha, c)$ provide the translation of ABox assertions that can be verified to hold in context c by applying the rules of the final program. For example, atomic concept assertions in a context c are translated by $A(a) \mapsto \{\texttt{inst}(a, A, c)\}$.

Given a CKR $\mathfrak{K} = \langle \mathfrak{G}, \{K_m\}_{m \in M} \rangle$, the translation to its datalog program $PK(\mathfrak{K})$ proceeds in four steps:

1. the *global program* $PG(\mathfrak{G})$ for $\mathfrak{G}$ is translated by applying input rules I_{glob} and I_{rl} to $\mathfrak{G}$ and adding deduction rules P_{rl};
2. Let $\mathbf{N}_{\mathfrak{G}} = \{c \in \mathbf{N} \mid PG(\mathfrak{G}) \models \texttt{inst}(c, \texttt{Ctx}, g)\}$. For every $c \in \mathbf{N}_{\mathfrak{G}}$, we define the knowledge base associated to the context as

$$K_c = \bigcup \{K_m \in \mathfrak{K} \mid PG(\mathfrak{G}) \models \texttt{triple}(c, \texttt{mod}, m, g)\}$$

3. We define each *local program* $PC(c)$ for $c \in \mathbf{N}_{\mathfrak{G}}$ by applying input rules I_{loc} and I_{rl} to K_c and adding deduction rules P_{loc} and P_{rl}.
4. The final *CKR program* $PK(\mathfrak{K})$ is then defined as the union of $PG(\mathfrak{G})$ with all local programs $PC(c)$.

We say that $\mathfrak{K}$ *entails* an axiom α in a context $c \in \mathbf{N}$ if the elements of $PK(\mathfrak{K})$ and $O(\alpha, c)$ are defined and $PK(\mathfrak{K}) \models O(\alpha, c)$. We can show (see [5]) that the presented rules and translation process provide a sound and complete calculus for instance checking for $\mathcal{SROIQ}$-RL CKR.

3   CKR Implementation on RDF

We recently presented a prototype [5] implementing the forward reasoning procedure over CKR expressed by the materialization calculus. The prototype accepts RDF input data expressing OWL-RL axioms and assertions for global and local knowledge modules: these different pieces of knowledge are represented as distinct named graphs, while contextual primitives have been encoded in a RDF vocabulary. The prototype is based on an extension of the Sesame RDF Framework[1] and structured in a client-server architecture: the main component, called *CKR core* module and residing in the server-side part, exposes the CKR primitives and a SPARQL 1.1 endpoint for query and update operations on the contextualized knowledge. The module offers the ability to compute and materialize the inference closure of the input CKR, add and remove knowledge and execute queries over the complete CKR structure.

The distribution of knowledge in different named graphs asks for a component to compute inference over multiple graphs in a RDF store, since inference mechanisms in current stores usually ignore the graph part. This component has been realized as a general software layer called *SPRINGLES*[2]. Intuitively, the layer provides methods to demand a closure materialization on the RDF store

---

[1] http://www.openrdf.org/
[2] *SParql-based Rule Inference over Named Graphs Layer Extending Sesame.*

data: rules are encoded as named graphs aware SPARQL queries and it is possible to customize both the input ruleset and the evaluation strategy. The general form of SPRINGLES rules is the following:

```
:<rule-name> a spr:Rule ;
  spr:head """ <graph pattern>""" ;
  spr:body """ <sparql query>""" .
```

`<graph-pattern>` is an RDF (named) graph that can contain a set of variables, which are bounded in the SPARQL query of the body. The body of a rule is a SPARQL query that is evaluated. The result of the evaluation of the rule body is a set of bindings for the variables that occurs in the rule head. For every such a binding the corresponding statement in the head of the rule is added to the repository.

In our case, the ruleset basically encodes the rules of the presented materialization calculus. As an example, we present the rule dealing with atomic concept inclusions:

```
:prl-subc a spr:Rule ;
  spr:head """ GRAPH ?mx { ?x rdf:type ?z } """ ;
  spr:body """ GRAPH ?m1 { ?y rdfs:subClassOf ?z }
               GRAPH ?m2 { ?x rdf:type ?y }
               GRAPH sys:dep { ?mx sys:derivedFrom ?m1,?m2 }
               FILTER NOT EXISTS
                 { GRAPH ?m0 { ?x rdf:type ?z }
                   GRAPH sys:dep { ?mx sys:derivedFrom ?m0 } } """ .
```

where prefix `spr:` corresponds to symbols in the vocabulary of SPRINGLES objects and `sys:` prefixes utility "system" symbols used in the definition of the rules evaluation plan. Intuitively, when the condition in the body part of the rule is verified in graphs ?m1 and ?m2, the head part is materialized in the inference graph ?mx. Note that in the formulation of the rule we work at the level of knowledge modules (i.e. named graphs). Note that the body of the rules contains a "filter" condition, which is a SPARQL based method to avoid the duplication of conclusions: the FILTER condition imposes a rule to be fired only if its conclusion is not already present in the context.

The rules are evaluated with a strategy that basically follows the same steps of the translation process defined for the calculus. The plan goes as follows: (i) we compute the closure on the graph for global context $\mathfrak{G}$, by a fixpoint on rules corresponding to P_{rl}; (ii) we derive associations between contexts and their modules, by adding dependencies for every assertion of the kind $\mathsf{mod}(\mathsf{c},\mathsf{m})$ in the global closure; (iii) we compute the closure the contexts, by applying rules encoded from P_{rl} and P_{loc} and resolving *eval* expressions by the metaknowledge information in the global closure.

4   Experimental Evaluation

In this section we illustrate the experiments we performed to assess the performance of the CKR prototype and their results. We begin by presenting the method we used to create the synthetic test sets that we generated for such evaluation.

Table 1. Percentages of generated axioms

TBox axiom	%
$A \sqsubseteq B$	50%
$A \sqsubseteq \neg B$	20%
$A \sqsubseteq \exists R.\{a\}$	10%
$A \sqcap B \sqsubseteq C$	5%
$\exists R.A \sqsubseteq B$	5%
$A \sqsubseteq \forall R.B$	5%
$A \sqsubseteq \leqslant 1R.B$	5%

ABox axiom	%
$A(a)$	40%
$R(a, b)$	40%
$\neg R(a, b)$	10%
$a = b$	5%
$a \neq b$	5%

RBox axiom	%
$R \sqsubseteq T$	50%
$\text{Inv}(R, S)$	25%
$R \circ S \sqsubseteq T$	10%
$\text{Dis}(R, S)$	10%
$\text{Irr}(R)$	5%

Generation of synthetic test sets. In order to create our test sets, we developed a simple generator that can output randomly generated CKRs with certain features. In particular, for each generated CKR, the generator takes in input: (1) the number n of contexts (i.e. local named graphs) to be generated; (2) the dimensions of the signature to be declared (number m of base classes, l of properties and k of individuals); (3) the axiom size for the global and local modules (number of global TBox, ABox and RBox axioms and number of TBox, ABox and RBox axioms per context); (4) optionally, the number of additional local *eval* axioms and the number of individuals to be propagated across contexts. Intuitively, the generation of a CKR proceeds as follows:

1. The contexts (named : c0, ... , : cn) are declared in the global context named graph and are linked to a different module name (: m0, ... , : mn), corresponding to the named graph containing their local knowledge.
2. Base classes (named : A0, ... , : Am), object properties (: R0, ... , : Rl) and individuals (: a0, ... , : ak) are added to the global graph: these symbols are used in the generation of global and local axioms.
3. Then generation of global axioms takes place. We chose to generate axioms as follows, in order to create realistic instances of knowledge bases:
   – Classes and properties names are taken from the base signature using random selection criteria in the form of (the positive part of) a Gaussian curve centered in 0: intuitively, classes equal or near to : A0 are more probable in axioms than : An.
   – Individuals are randomly selected using a uniform distribution.
   – TBox, ABox and RBox axioms in $\mathcal{SROIQ}$-RL are added in the requested number to the global context module following the percentages shown in Table 1 (note that the reported axioms are normal form $\mathcal{SROIQ}$-RL axioms, as defined in [5]). Such percentages have been manually selected in order to simulate the common distribution in the use of the $\mathcal{SROIQ}$-RL constructs in real knowledge bases.
4. The same generation criteria are then applied in the case of local graphs representing the local knowledge of contexts.
5. If specified, the requested number for *eval* axioms of the form $eval(A, \mathsf{C}) \sqsubseteq B$ and for the set of individuals in the scope of the *eval* operator (i.e. as local members of A) are added to local contexts graphs.

Experimental Setup. Evaluation experiments were carried out on a 4 core Dual Intel Xeon Processor machine with 32Gb 1866MHZ DDR3 RAM, standard S-ATA

(7.200RPM) HDD, running a Linux RedHat 6.5 distribution. We allocated 6Gb of memory to the JVM running the SPRINGLES web-app (i.e. the RDF storage and inference prototype), while 20Gb were allocated to the utility program managing the upload, profiling and cleaning of the test repositories. In order to abstract from the possible overhead for the repository setup, the tests have been averaged over multiple runs of the closure operation for each CKR.

The tests were carried out on different CKR rulesets in order to study their applicability in practical reasoning. The rulesets are limitations to the full set of rules and evaluation strategy presented in previous sections, in particular:

- *ckr-rdfs-global:* inference is only applied to the global context (no local reasoning inside local contexts named graphs). Applies only inference rules for RDFS and for the definition of CKR structure (e.g. association of named graphs for knowledge modules to contexts).
- *ckr-rdfs-local:* inference is applied to the graphs both for global and local contexts. Again, applies only inference rules for RDFS and CKR structure rules.
- *ckr-owl-global:* inference is only applied to the global context, considering all of the inference rules for $\mathcal{SROIQ}$-RL and CKR structure rules.
- *ckr-owl-local:* full strategy defined by the materialization calculus. Inference is applied to the global and local parts, using all of the (global and local) $\mathcal{SROIQ}$-RL and CKR rules.

More in details, application of RDFS rules corresponds to the limitation of OWL RL closure step only to the inference rules for subsumption on classes and object properties.

TS1: scalability evaluation. The first experiments we carried out on the CKR prototype had the task to determine the (average) inference closure time with respect to the increase in number of contexts and their contents: with reference to the research questions in the introduction, this first evaluation aimed at answering question **RQ1**.

Using the CKR generator tool, we generated the set of test CKRs shown in Table 2: we call this test set *TS1*. Intuitively, TS1 contains sets of CKRs with an increasing number of contexts, in which CKRs have an increasing number of axioms. We note that no *eval* axioms were added to TS1 knowledge bases.

We ran the CKR prototype on 3 generations of TS1 also varying the reasoning regime among the rulesets detailed above: the different generation instances of TS1 are necessary in order to reduce the impact of special cases in the random generation. The results of the experiments on TS1 are reported in Table 3. In the table, for each of the generated CKRs (referred by number of contexts and number of base classes in the first two columns), we show the number of total asserted triples in column *Triples* (averaged on the 3 versions of TS1). The following columns list the results of the closure for each of the rulesets: for a ruleset, we list the (average) total number of triples (asserted + inferred), the inferred triples and the (average) time in milliseconds for the closure operation. The value *timedout* in the measures indicates that the closure operation exceeded 30 minutes (1.800.000 ms.).

Table 2. Test set TS1

Contexts	Classes	Roles	Indiv.	Global KB			Local KBs			Total axioms
				TBox	RBox	ABox	TBox	RBox	ABox	
1	10	10	20	10	5	20	10	5	20	70
1	50	50	100	50	25	100	50	25	100	350
1	100	100	200	100	50	200	100	50	200	700
1	500	500	1000	500	250	1000	500	250	1000	3.500
1	1000	1000	2000	1000	500	2000	1000	500	2000	7.000
5	10	10	20	10	5	20	10	5	20	210
5	50	50	100	50	25	100	50	25	100	1.050
5	100	100	200	100	50	200	100	50	200	2.100
5	500	500	1000	500	250	1000	500	250	1000	10.500
5	1000	1000	2000	1000	500	2000	1000	500	2000	21.000
10	10	10	20	10	5	20	10	5	20	385
10	50	50	100	50	25	100	50	25	100	1.925
10	100	100	200	100	50	200	100	50	200	3.850
10	500	500	1000	500	250	1000	500	250	1000	19.250
10	1000	1000	2000	1000	500	2000	1000	500	2000	38.500
50	10	10	20	10	5	20	10	5	20	1.785
50	50	50	100	50	25	100	50	25	100	8.925
50	100	100	200	100	50	200	100	50	200	17.850
50	500	500	1000	500	250	1000	500	250	1000	89.250
50	1000	1000	2000	1000	500	2000	1000	500	2000	178.500
100	10	10	20	10	5	20	10	5	20	3.535
100	50	50	100	50	25	100	50	25	100	17.675
100	100	100	200	100	50	200	100	50	200	35.350
100	500	500	1000	500	250	1000	500	250	1000	176.750
100	1000	1000	2000	1000	500	2000	1000	500	2000	353.500

In order to analyze the results, the behaviour of the prototype for each of the rulesets has been plotted to graphs, shown in Figure 1. Each of the series represents a set with a fixed number of contexts (1 to 100) and each point a CKR. The x axis represents the number of asserted triples, while the y axis shows the time in milliseconds; the red horizontal line depicts the 30 minutes limit for timeout. To better visualize the behaviour of the series, we plotted a trend line for each of the series: the lines represent an approximation of the data trend calculated by polynomial regression[3].

Some conclusions can be derived from these data and graphs: the first most evident fact is that the reasoning regime strongly impacts the scalability of the system. Thus, in practical cases the choice of a naive application of the full OWL RL ruleset might not be viable, in presence of large local datasets: on the other hand, if expressive reasoning inside contexts is not required, scalability can be enhanced by relying on the RDFS rulesets (or, in general, by carefully tailoring the ruleset to the required expressivity).

By analyzing the graphs and the approximations, it is also possible to observe that the system shows a different behaviour depending on the different reasoning regimes. In the case of *ckr-rdfs-global* and *ckr-owl-global*, the results suggest that the management of named graphs does not add overhead to the reasoning in the global context. This can be also seen by checking Table 3: for a similar number of inferred triples the separation across different graphs does not influence the reasoning time. For example, this is visible for cases with similar y values of

---

[3] Average R^2 value across all approximations is $\geq 0,993$.

Table 3. Scalability results for test set TS1

Ctx.	Cls.	Triples	ckr-rdfs-global Total	Inf.	Time	ckr-owl-global Total	Inf.	Time	ckr-rdfs-local Total	Inf.	Time	ckr-owl-local Total	Inf.	Time
1	10	208	228	20	222	234	26	326	249	41	291	298	90	868
1	50	1079	1165	87	221	1288	209	518	1351	272	323	1918	839	4596
1	100	2165	2398	233	260	2666	501	943	2687	521	346	3803	1638	15916
1	500	10549	11870	1321	846	13293	2743	22930	14833	4284	2461	22828	12278	556272
1	1000	20981	23600	2619	1528	25957	4976	95957	29993	9012	4644	timedout	timedout	timedout
5	10	644	685	41	176	698	54	226	780	136	193	1470	826	11721
5	50	3124	3259	135	190	3330	205	341	4134	1010	522	9874	6750	328107
5	100	6201	6450	249	254	6675	475	962	8845	2645	1258	31615	25414	913617
5	500	30928	31994	1066	719	33025	2097	23109	44987	14059	7819	timedout	timedout	timedout
5	1000	61691	64363	2672	1491	66661	4969	106967	95636	33945	16291	timedout	timedout	timedout
10	10	1149	1216	66	165	1225	76	202	1427	278	541	6141	4992	448249
10	50	5620	5782	163	210	5895	275	460	8008	2388	1392	timedout	timedout	timedout
10	100	11058	11353	295	281	11865	807	1745	16315	5257	2986	timedout	timedout	timedout
10	500	56578	57836	1258	910	59052	2474	33643	86821	30243	17375	timedout	timedout	timedout
10	1000	112824	115273	2449	2030	117666	4842	114443	173938	61113	36647	timedout	timedout	timedout
50	10	5509	5780	271	208	5785	276	256	7003	1494	2167	timedout	timedout	timedout
50	50	26327	26676	348	323	26795	467	825	35640	9312	14598	timedout	timedout	timedout
50	100	52037	52543	506	603	52749	713	2384	78439	26402	21461	timedout	timedout	timedout
50	500	259810	261355	1546	2025	262722	2913	41973	416088	156278	299504	timedout	timedout	timedout
50	1000	520276	523082	2807	4350	525702	5426	214434	827451	307176	397110	timedout	timedout	timedout
100	10	10658	11171	513	242	11181	523	279	12916	2258	1865	timedout	timedout	timedout
100	50	51709	52347	638	442	52461	752	1241	73639	21930	31003	timedout	timedout	timedout
100	100	103341	104035	694	531	104259	918	2784	145788	42447	47179	timedout	timedout	timedout
100	500	514497	516316	1819	3469	517567	3070	87325	844215	329718	774657	timedout	timedout	timedout
100	1000	1028233	1031367	3135	7835	1033725	5492	394881	1674765	646532	1018616	timedout	timedout	timedout

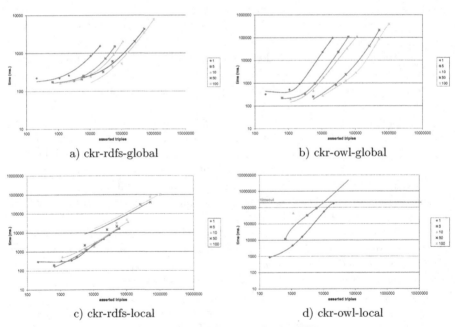

a) ckr-rdfs-global

b) ckr-owl-global

c) ckr-rdfs-local

d) ckr-owl-local

Fig. 1. Scalability graphs for TS1

the graph (e.g. the case for 1000 classes in series for 1 and 5 contexts, in both rulesets). In the case of *ckr-rdfs-local*, the graphs show that local reasoning clearly influences the total inference time. In particular, at the growth of number of contexts, the behaviour tends to be linear in the number of asserted triples. While the data we have on *ckr-owl-local* are more limited, this behaviour seems to be confirmed by the trend lines. On the other hand, OWL local reasoning seems to influence the reasoning time with respect to the RDFS case: informally, this can be seen in the graph by the larger time overhead across points with a similar number of asserted triples (i.e. on the same x values) but a higher number of contexts.

TS2 and TS3: knowledge propagation evaluation. The second set of experiments we carried out was aimed at answering question **RQ2**: we wanted to establish the cost of knowledge propagation among contexts, with respect to an increasing number of connections (i.e. *eval* expressions) across contexts. To this aim, we generated two test sets, called *TS2* and *TS3* structured as follows:

- TS2 is composed by 100 CKRs, each of them with 100 contexts. Except for the triples needed for the definition of the contextual structure, both the global and local knowledge bases contain no randomly generated axioms. The CKRs inside TS2 are generated with an increasing number of contexts connections through *eval* axioms (from no connections to the case of "fully connected" contexts). In particular, for $n = 100$ contexts and k connections, in each context c_i we add axioms of the kind:

$$\text{eval}(D_0, \{c_{i+1(mod\ n)}\}) \sqsubseteq D_1, \ \ldots, \ \text{eval}(D_0, \{c_{i+k(mod\ n)}\}) \sqsubseteq D_1$$

Moreover, in each context we add a fixed number of instances (10 in the case of TS2) of the local concept D_0, that will be propagated through contexts and added to local D_1 concepts by the inference rules for the above *eval* expressions.

- TS3 analogously contains 100 CKRs of 100 contexts and again no randomly generated global or local axioms. Differently from TS2, TS3 contains no *eval* axioms and the connections across contexts are simulated by having multiple versions of D_0 (namely $D_{0\text{-}0}, \ldots, D_{0\text{-}99}$) to represent the local interpretation of the concept. Thus, for $n = 100$ contexts and k connections, in each context c_i we add axioms of the kind $D_{0\text{-}j} \sqsubseteq D_1$ for $j \in \{i+1(mod\ n), \ldots, i+k(mod\ n)\}$. Also, not only we add to c_i the 10 local instances of $D_{0\text{-}i}$, but we also "pre-propagate" instances of each $D_{0\text{-}j}$ by explicitly adding them to the knowledge of c_i.

We remark that the way of expressing "contextualized symbols" used in TS3 has been discussed and compared to the CKR representation in [1].

We ran the CKR prototype for 5 independent runs on TS2 and TS3, only considering *ckr-owl-local* ruleset. An extract of the results of experiments on the two test sets is reported in Table 4: CKRs in the two sets are ordered with respect to the number of relations across contexts; for each CKR, the numbers of asserted, total and inferred triples are shown, followed by the (average) closure

Table 4. Knowledge propagation results (extract) for test set TS2 and TS3

	TS2				TS3			
Related	Triples	Total	Inf.	Time	Triples	Total	Inf.	Time
0	2803	3305	502	276	2803	3305	502	299
4	4703	9205	4502	893	11703	16205	4502	577
9	6703	16205	9502	1564	22703	32205	9502	1017
14	8703	23205	14502	2245	33703	48205	14502	1450
19	10703	30205	19502	2932	44703	64205	19502	1960
24	12703	37205	24502	3467	55703	80205	24502	2580
29	14703	44205	29502	4196	66703	96205	29502	3154
34	16703	51205	34502	4847	77703	112205	34502	4099
39	18703	58205	39502	5987	88703	128205	39502	4645
44	20703	65205	44502	6223	99703	144205	44502	5488
49	22703	72205	49502	6878	110703	160205	49502	6456
54	24703	79205	54502	7689	121703	176205	54502	7545
59	26703	86205	59502	8547	132703	192205	59502	8205
64	28703	93205	64502	9076	143703	208205	64502	9159
69	30703	100205	69502	9640	154703	224205	69502	10335
74	32703	107205	74502	10711	165703	240205	74502	10992
79	34703	114205	79502	11223	176703	256205	79502	11879
84	36703	121205	84502	14611	187703	272205	84502	13088
89	38703	128205	89502	12846	198703	288205	89502	13912
94	40703	135205	94502	14999	209703	304205	94502	15064
99	42703	142205	99502	14107	220703	320205	99502	15799

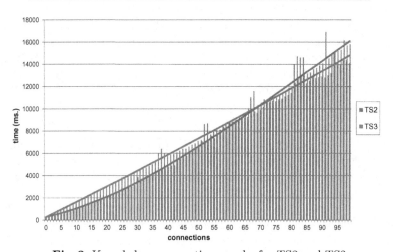

Fig. 2. Knowledge propagation graphs for TS2 and TS3

time in milliseconds. To facilitate the analysis of the results, we plotted such data in histograms in Figure 2. The x axis represents the number of local connections, while the y axis shows the time in milliseconds. Again, to better visualize the behaviour of the series, we plotted a trend line for each of the series, calculated by polynomial regression[4].

From the graph of TS2, we can note that knowledge propagation cost depends linearly on the number of connections: from the data in Table 4 we can calculate that the average increase in closure time for k local connections (for each context) w.r.t. the base case of 0 connections amounts to $(51,2 \cdot k)\%$. The comparison with TS3 confirms the compactness of a contextualized representation of symbols (cfr.

---

[4] Average R^2 value across the two approximations is $\geq 0,989$.

findings in [1]): in fact, note that for an equal number of connections, the number of inferences in both TS2 and TS3 cases is equal, but TS3 always require a larger number of asserted triples. Also, the graph clearly shows that TS3 grows more than linearly: for a small number of connections the knowledge propagation in TS2 requires more inference time (14,9% more, on average), but with the growth of local connections (at $\sim 68\%$ of number of contexts) the cost of TS3 local reasoning surpasses the propagation overhead.

TS4 and TS5: modularization evaluation. The third set of experiments we carried out on the prototype aimed at answering question **RQ3**: we want to verify the effects of modularizing knowledge across global and local modules. We generated two test sets, called *TS4* and *TS5* structured as follows:

- *TS4* is composed by sets of RDFS CKRs with an increasing number of contexts, in which CKRs have an increasing number of axioms and without *eval* axioms (i.e. similar to TS1).
  Paired to TS4, we generated the testset *TS4-flat* that contains a "flat" version of CKRs in TS4: intuitively, every CKR of TS4-flat has a single context c_0 where all the knowledge content of local contexts is represented. In the case of local axioms, the local meaning of symbols is preserved by duplication of symbols: for example, if $A \sqsubseteq B$ appears in context c_1 in TS4, then in the corresponding CKR of TS4-flat the axiom $A_{c1} \sqsubseteq B_{c1}$ appears in the single context c_0. In the case of global logical axioms, the same principle is used: all the global axioms have to be duplicated for each of the contexts in order to preserve the local inferences. Thus, if $A \sqsubseteq B$ appears in the global context of a CKR with n contexts in TS4, then in TS4-flat the axiom is duplicated as $A_{ci} \sqsubseteq B_{ci}$ for $i \in \{0, \ldots, n-1\}$ and added to the global context.
- *TS5* and *TS5-flat* follow the same generation of TS4 and TS4-flat, but no logical axioms (other than the metaknowledge axioms representing the structure of the CKR) are added to the global context.

In this experiment, to generate the "context based" testsets TS4 and TS5 we followed the same generation criteria of the testset for scalability: in practice, TS4 corresponds to the rows for 5, 10, 50 and 100 contexts (for 10, 50, 100 and 500 classes) in Table 2, while TS5 corresponds to the same rows but with zero TBox, RBox and ABox global axioms. Similarly to TS3, the transformation of contextualized axioms to their "flat" counterpart corresponds to the transformations discussed in [1].

We ran the CKR prototype on 3 generations of TS4 / TS4-flat and TS5 / TS5-flat only considering the *ckr-rdfs-local* ruleset. The results of the experiments are reported in Table 5. To analyze the results, in Figure 3 we plotted to graphs a comparison between the contextualized and flat versions of TS4 and TS5. In the histograms, we compare side to side the time in milliseconds for the closure computation in the contextualized and flat versions of the CKRs: each graph represents the set of CKRs for a different number of contexts and each bar represents a CKR in the testset.

Some conclusions can be derived from these results and graphs. First of all, the TS4-flat always require a larger number of asserted triples than TS4 (on

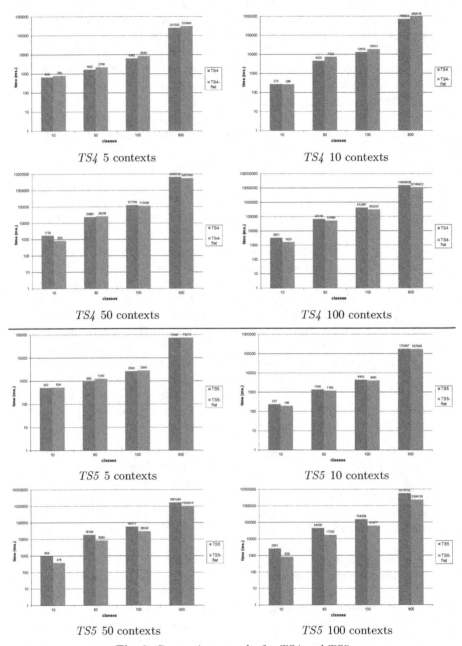

Fig. 3. Comparison graphs for TS4 and TS5

Table 5. Knowledge modularization results for test set TS4 and TS5

Ctx.	Cls.	TS4 Triples	Total	Inf.	Time	TS4-flat Triples	Total	Inf.	Time	TS5 Triples	Total	Inf.	Time	TS5-flat Triples	Total	Inf.	Time
5	10	433	654	221	658	597	940	343	795	394	537	144	507	315	439	124	524
5	50	2111	5534	3423	1642	3053	8012	4958	2180	1919	3700	1782	939	1597	3359	1762	1230
5	100	4206	17000	12794	6392	6125	23556	17430	8540	3814	9870	6056	2644	3193	9229	6036	2840
5	500	20846	281904	261058	257303	30719	360929	330210	313450	19038	112063	93025	72697	15969	108975	93005	73275
10	10	787	1218	431	276	1111	1677	566	269	754	1029	275	237	572	802	230	196
10	50	3817	11423	7605	4526	5648	18985	13337	7322	3646	7078	3432	1340	2878	6265	3387	1183
10	100	7593	31667	24074	12916	11278	45020	33742	18513	7235	16204	8969	4403	5771	14694	8924	3991
10	500	37894	550818	512924	708663	56556	753205	696649	990518	36051	218604	182553	175457	28896	211404	182508	167809
50	10	3662	5766	2104	1725	5132	8224	3092	825	3626	5090	1464	959	2586	3805	1219	378
50	50	17571	52647	35077	23987	26501	78800	52298	26258	17409	36336	18928	18199	13196	31879	18683	8382
50	100	34923	160876	125953	127185	52813	228621	175808	113558	34644	89633	54988	56311	26459	81202	54743	29500
50	500	173983	2803972	2629989	6436152	264315	3611292	3346977	5457590	172343	1112437	940093	1681244	132499	1072347	939848	1025014
100	10	7239	11198	3959	3301	10558	15889	5331	1623	7214	10210	2996	2651	5125	7626	2501	829
100	50	34810	99832	65023	66149	52390	153218	100828	51688	34574	71361	36787	44056	26088	62381	36292	17252
100	100	69112	319866	250754	412487	104152	479977	375825	300257	68867	182419	113552	154258	52326	165384	113057	61077
100	500	344530	5340904	4996374	15066628	523229	7243808	6720579	10749422	342563	2258220	1915657	5579152	261973	2177134	1915162	2306128

average, $47,2\%$ more). This does not hold for TS5: however, it can be shown that by leaving out the declaration of signature in each local context in TS5, then the number of local asserted triples is equal in TS5-flat. On the other hand, note that, while in TS4 this induces an increase of $\sim 29,4\%$ in inferred triples in the flat version, in TS5-flat the number of inferred triples is always around 5 triples per context less than the TS5 version: it can be shown that by keeping the same CKR context structure in the flat version (i.e. maintaining the other "empty" contexts) the numbers of inferred triples in the TS5 and TS5-flat versions become equal.

By comparing the graphs of TS4 and TS4-flat we find that the advantage of modularization of the global context is evident with a lower number of contexts, but it is surpassed by the overhead of context management for a larger number of contexts: on average, for 5 context CKRs, the reasoning in the flat versions is $27,2\%$ slower and $35,5\%$ for 10 contexts; on the other hand, for 50 contexts the contextualized version is $32,2\%$ slower and $52,2\%$ for 100 contexts. The fact that the initial advantage in the contextualized version is due to the modularization of the global context is shown by the graphs for TS5: for 5 context CKRs the reasoning in flat version is comparable to the contextualized version (only $10,6\%$ slower); for 10 contexts the contextualized version is $12,2\%$ slower, while $106,3\%$ for 50 contexts and $167,4\%$ for 100 contexts. We remark that the kind of compactness advantage given by the modularization of global context is similar to the case of associating modules to context classes: in fact, the global knowledge part can be seen as a module associated to the context class of all contexts. This suggests that the advantage in modularization shown by TS4 can be augmented by enlarging the number of modules associated to context classes and the number of their axioms.

5   Conclusions and Future Works

In this paper we provided a first evaluation for the performance of the RDF based implementation of the CKR framework. In the first experiment we evaluated the scalability of the current version of the prototype under different reasoning regimes. The second experiment was aimed at evaluating the cost of intra-context knowledge propagation and its relation to its simulation by "reification" of contextualized symbols. Finally, in the last experiment we evaluated the effects of the modularization of global and local knowledge offered by our framework.

Some further experimental evaluations can be interesting to be carried out over our contextual model. One of these regards the study of the effects of the modularization for different levels of connection across contexts: intuitively, we want to verify the hypothesis that distributing knowledge across a larger number of contexts is convenient when the coupling between contexts is low. The experimental results should be also compared to a theoretical study on the complexity of CKR reasoning (possibly by extending our previous work in this regard [3]).

With respect to the current CKR implementation, the scalability experiments clearly showed that the current naive strategy (defined by a direct translation of the formal calculus) might not be suitable for a real application of the full reasoning to large scale datasets. In this regard, we are going to study different evaluation strategies and optimizations to the current strategy and evaluate the results with respect to the naive case. One of such possible optimizations can regard a "pay-as-you-go" strategy, in which inference rules are activated only for constructs that are recognized in the local language of a context.

References

1. Bozzato, L., Ghidini, C., Serafini, L.: Comparing contextual and flat representations of knowledge: a concrete case about football data. In: K-CAP 2013, pp. 9–16. ACM (2013)
2. Bozzato, L., Eiter, T., Serafini, L.: Contextualized knowledge repositories with justifiable exceptions. In: DL 2014. CEUR-WP, vol. 1193, pp. 112–123. CEUR-WS.org (2014)
3. Bozzato, L., Homola, M., Serafini, L.: ExpTime reasoning for contextualized $\mathcal{ALC}$. Tech. Rep. TR-FBK-DKM-2012-1, Fondazione Bruno Kessler, Trento, Italy (2012). http://dkm.fbk.eu/technologies/technical-report
4. Bozzato, L., Homola, M., Serafini, L.: Towards more effective tableaux reasoning for CKR. In: DL 2012. CEUR-WP, vol. 824, pp. 114–124. CEUR-WS.org (2012)
5. Bozzato, L., Serafini, L.: Materialization calculus for contexts in the semantic web. In: DL 2013. CEUR-WP, vol. 1014. CEUR-WS.org (2013)
6. Khriyenko, O., Terziyan, V.: A framework for context sensitive metadata description. IJSMO **1**(2), 154–164 (2006)
7. Klarman, S.: Reasoning with Contexts in Description Logics. Ph.D. thesis, Free University of Amsterdam (2013)
8. Krötzsch, M.: Efficient inferencing for OWL EL. In: Janhunen, T., Niemelä, I. (eds.) JELIA 2010. LNCS, vol. 6341, pp. 234–246. Springer, Heidelberg (2010)
9. Motik, B., Fokoue, A., Horrocks, I., Wu, Z., Lutz, C., Grau, B.C.: OWL 2 Web Ontology Language Profiles. W3C recommendation, W3C, October 2009. http://www.w3.org/TR/2009/REC-owl2-profiles-20091027/

10. Serafini, L., Homola, M.: Contextualized knowledge repositories for the semantic web. J. of Web Semantics 12 (2012)
11. Straccia, U., Lopes, N., Lukácsy, G., Polleres, A.: A general framework for representing and reasoning with annotated semantic web data. In: AAAI 2010. AAAI Press (2010)
12. Tanca, L.: Context-Based data tailoring for mobile users. In: BTW 2007 Workshops, pp. 282–295 (2007)
13. Udrea, O., Recupero, D., Subrahmanian, V.S.: Annotated RDF. ACM Trans. Comput. Log. 11(2), 1–41 (2010)

Different Types of Conflicting Knowledge in AmI Environments

Martin Homola[1]([✉]) and Theodore Patkos[2]

[1] Comenius University in Bratislava, Mlynská dolina, Bratislava, Slovakia
homola@fmph.uniba.sk
[2] FORTH-ICS, Heraklion, Greece

Abstract. We characterize different types of conflicts that often occur in complex distributed multi-agent scenarios, such as in Ambient Intelligence (AmI) environments, and we argue that these conflicts should be resolved in a suitable order and using the most appropriate conflict resolution strategies for each individual conflict type. Our analysis shows that conflict resolution in AmI environments and similar multi-agent domains is a complex process, spanning through different levels of abstraction. The agents deployed in such environments need to handle conflicts with coordination and with certain level of agreement. We consecutively point out how this problem is currently handled in the relevant AmI literature.

Keywords: Ambient intelligence · Conflicts · Classification · Resolution

1 Introduction

Ambient Intelligence (AmI) [12,33] is a challenging application domains for multi-agent systems. Conceived in the nineties with the aim to accommodate the ever increasing penetration of interconnected mobile devices into our everyday life, it soon triggered a shift in computing – one towards developing more pervasive and sensor-rich environments, often referred to as smart spaces. Research in AmI places the human user in the centre of attention, aiming at creating intelligent environments with the ability to adapt to human preferences, serve their needs and goals, and communicate with their inhabitants utilizing novel means. This paradigm implies a seamless medium of interaction, advanced networking technology, and efficient knowledge management, in order to deploy spaces that are aware of the characteristics of human presence and the diversities of personalities, being also capable to respond intelligently and proactively to the users' needs.

Application domains of smart spaces span from ambient assisted living and health-care monitoring to smart home and office automation [26]. An essential step towards exhibiting responsive behavior and providing meaningful assistance to the inhabitants is to automate the recognition and understanding of the users' current state of affairs, deliberate on it, and complement it with supportive action.

The progress in sensing technology has provided a great variety of devices with rich capabilities that can monitor diverse features related to the human

© Springer International Publishing Switzerland 2015
P. Lambrix et al. (Eds.): EKAW 2014 Satellite Events, LNAI 8982, pp. 52–63, 2015.
DOI: 10.1007/978-3-319-17966-7_5

users and the environment. Of course, the complexity and interdependence of contextual data that characterize certain activities can neither be directly acquired from sensors nor can be derived through statistical reasoning alone [21]. Many user actions, such as the process of making coffee, pre-assume a significant extent of commonsense and domain knowledge with respect to their causal effects and ramifications. In addition, their compositions, often referred to as situations, have rich structural and temporal aspects, such as duration, frequency and subsumption relations.

To facilitate the programming of AmI environments, the abstraction of autonomous software agents is used. These agents control the embedded computing devices that populate smart spaces in an attempt to assess and even influence current and future situations. This often requires for these autonomous entities to cooperate, in order to exchange information about the state of the world and perform collaborative actions that best support the users' needs. As a consequence, such complex scenarios result in conflicts among agents, that need to be recognized and resolved so that the overall system exhibits a coherent behavior [20].

In this paper, we look at the knowledge architecture of such systems and analyse the different types of conflicts that the agents may face: sensory input, context, domain and background knowledge, goal, and action conflicts. We argue that such conflicts should be resolved in a suitable order and using strategies appropriate for each given type. Moreover, conflicts cannot always be resolved by the agents independently; a certain level of consensus and agreement on conflict resolution needs to be pursued. We consecutively take a look on the current body of work in the AmI literature in light of our above mentioned classification of conflicts. We point out how the problem of conflict resolution is handled at different levels, and what the future possible directions with respect to this problem are.

The paper proceeds as follows. Sect. 2 introduces the main notion and challenges that characterize smart spaces. Sect,3 discusses the different types of conflicts that have been identified and introduces a new category that plays an important role in the implementation of such systems. Sect. 4 studies existing methodologies in the field and analyses to what extent different types of conflicts can be accommodated by each of them. Conclusions then follow in Sect. 5.

2 Ambient Intelligence

Zelka et al. [33] and later Aarts [1] devised the requirements, based on which AmI systems should be:

1. *embedded* within the environment: users do not need to be concerned with their operation,
2. *context-aware:* they are able to recognize the user and the situation,
3. *personalized:* able serve different users according to their own needs,
4. *adaptive:* they can change in response to the environment and user's actions,
5. *anticipatory:* they should understand the user's needs and act upon them proactively and not just in response to user's request.

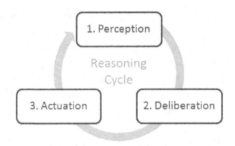

Fig. 1. Reasoning cycle of autonomous devices in smart spaces

As a multitude of devices serving diverse purposes are typically installed in smart spaces, it is reasonable to assume that the agents may be rather heterogeneous in their implementation. Particularly, their cognitive skills may range from simple reactive agents whose behavior is based on the most recent sensor readings, to complex knowledge-based and deliberative agents that perform elaborate reasoning in order to infer relevant context, make estimates over the users' intentions, and communicate and negotiate with the other agents in collaborative manner. Abstracting from unnecessary implementation details, we can generally assume such agents to possess at least the following components:[1]

- A knowledge base of some sort, comprising as a distinguished part the *context model* of the current situation respective to the agent, and possibly some additional background and domain knowledge. However, each agent may keep track of different aspects of the world and represent them differently from the other agents.
- A set of *goals* the agent is able to follow to serve its purpose, from which it selects some subset, depending on the current perceived context.
- Either some predefined plans of *actions* to execute to achieve each goal or the ability to plan the actions accordingly when needed.
- Some means to *communicate* with other agents with the aim to exchange knowledge and cooperate (e.g., messages, queries, bridge rules, etc.).

It should be remarked that in AmI systems the general aim of an agent is to perceive and accommodate the goals of the users and to help them in carrying out actions to achieve these goals. For this reasons, users are likewise often modelled as goal-driven acting agents. This metaphor is indeed useful when studying AmI environments as a whole, however one must keep in mind that there is a distinction between the goals of an agent and goals of a user.

An abstract loop that can characterize the basic internal reasoning phases carried out by an agent is shown in Fig. 1. It involves the phases of perception,

---

[1] We take a pragmatic abstraction from the classical BDI agent architecture [19]: beliefs are stored in the knowledge base, desires are mapped as goals, and intentions allow the agent to map the current situation into a subset of goals to follow and actions to execute.

deliberation and actuation. This cycle is triggered by specific sensory inputs that the agent is monitoring (or the lack of them) and captures the ability to both deliberate about how best to *interpret changes* that occur in the dynamically changing world, as well as to *make decisions* about the most appropriate course of actions that needs to be taken to support the users' activities. While many approaches have been proposed to study each phase alone, recent studies (e.g., [5,17]) argue about the need for a seamless integration of the tasks of perception, recognition and acting in a coherent loop, in order to synthesize support services in smart environments with proper and verifiable behavior.

In addition to its dynamic nature, the aspect of heterogeneity is an equally challenging factor for developing AmI services. Agents operating in smart spaces may have different reasoning skills, obtain access to distinct knowledge repositories, local or shared, and evaluate incoming information based on different trust criteria. A real-world smart system needs to respect the fact that the way context is inferred by each involved agent is not an objective process. Being highly distributed, these environments produce information that can be interpreted in a totally different manner by the various intelligent agents; and it is not uncommon for the agents to end up having incoherent and conflicting views of the current context.

3   Conflicting Knowledge

3.1   Conflicts Taxonomy of Resendes at al.

The importance of dealing with conflicts has been noted by other researchers working in AmI [11,15,20]. Resendes et al. [20] analyze different types of conflicts that may arise in AmI systems and organize them into a taxonomy, as listed in Table 1.

Table 1. Taxonomy of conflicts [20]

Dimension	Source	Intervenients	Detection time	Solvability
Possible types	resource application policy role	single user user vs. user user vs. space	a priori when it occurs a posteriori	conflict avoidance conflict resolution acknowledge inability acknowledge occurrence

The authors identify four basic broad categories of conflicts, which are dubbed *dimensions*, in order to stress their orthogonality, i.e., the fact that one conflict can be independently classified with respect to each of them. The *source* dimension indicates where/how each conflict originates – it may be the case that users (or applications) are conflicting over some resource allocation, or it is not possible to execute some action due to policy, or there are conflicting user profiles. Following the *intervenients* dimension, there might be conflicting intentions within a single user, between multiple users, or between user and the space. The *detection time* dimension sorts conflicts into those that are (can be) detected a priori, at the time they occur, or only a posteriori. Finally, the *solvability* dimension indicates at which level can conflicts be resolved – before they happen (i.e., to avoid them), immediately when they happen, or after some delay, in which case they are further split into those conflicts which cannot be resolved at all and those which cannot be resolved due to being detected too late.

3.2 The Knowledge Type Dimension

The taxonomy of Resendes et al. is arguably very useful. In addition to this classification, though, and considering the agent architecture of AmI systems, it appears to us that conflicts should also be categorized based on the different types of knowledge in which they appear. This is due to the fact that each type of knowledge is processed differently, and in a different point of the agents reasoning cycle depicted in Fig. 1. This classification can be seen as yet another dimension, orthogonal to the previously discussed four, which we propose to add into the taxonomy of Resendes et al., as shown in Table 2 and described next:

Table 2. The knowledge type dimension of conflicts

Dimension	Knowledge type
Possible types	sensory input context domain/background goal action

Sensory input conflict: if a conflicting reading of some sensors appears. This type may refer to multiple readings of the same or similar sensors or it may be the result of different sensors, whose outputs are mutually exclusive (the agents know that these outputs cannot occur at the same time). The conflict may arise within a single agent, but it may also be distributed between more than one agent (each containing part of the conflicting readings). The latter option may subsequently cause a contextual conflict.

For example, an agent may have access to an indoor light intensity sensor reporting that the light is on, while it may also have access to a camera placed within the same room and with some basic image-processing it may be able to observe that the lights are off. Or, the same user's presence may be reported from two different locations in the same time.

Contextual conflict: if two (or more) agents are part of the same situation, their models of the world may be conflicting, implying, e.g., a different location, or perceived activity of the user, etc. This type of conflict may be caused by a previous unnoticed sensory input conflict, but also by a different evaluation of the situation.

For example, one agent may understand the location of a certain user to be the kitchen, while another agent may understand the very same user's location to be the bedroom. This is a simpler form of a contextual conflict, related to sensory processing which can often be resolved more easily (e.g., by comparing or refreshing the sensor information). A more complex form of a contextual conflict may arise when one agent evaluates the user's current activity as cooking, and another agent evaluates the same user's current activity as cleaning the kitchen. Resolving the latter type of contextual conflicts may be more challenging.

Domain and background knowledge conflict: domain   and   background knowledge refer to the information the agent possesses and uses, in order to carry out its tasks and fulfill its purpose.

For instance, a calendar scheduling agent associated with a user records information about months in a year, days in a week, working days, holidays, etc. This is the knowledge respective to the domain of the agent's tasks. To contrast this with contextual knowledge, the fact that Monday follows Sunday is part of unchanging domain knowledge, respective to the calendar domain, while the current date and time, first day of week are in reality contextual knowledge, which changes from situation to situation. It is apparent, that conflicts in domain and background knowledge should occur less frequently in AmI systems, in comparison to the remaining four kinds of conflicts discussed here.

Conflicts in these types of knowledge, if they occur, may require a different kind of solution. In contrast with contextual information which is dynamic and changing, domain and background knowledge are often considered unchanging and fully specified (to the extent required by the application). Hence, redesign of the agent's knowledge base by its creator may be required, rather than resolving the conflict in an automatic manner.

Note that background knowledge plays an important role in detection of sensory and contextual conflicts. Given the case in which the same user's location is detected in two different locations – this is only perceived as a conflict because of the background knowledge that any user cannot be present at two different locations at the same time.

Goal conflict: if two (or more) agents are part of the same situation, their models of the world are compatible, but they have mutually conflicting goals. Note that we do not consider it a goal conflict if agents in the same situation have conflicting goals but also incompatible models of the world. The latter is really a contextual conflict (it is quite natural to have different goals in different situations).

For an example of a goal conflict consider two autonomous agents that are responsible for adjusting the ambient environment conditions for two distinct users located in the same room. One user may have the preference of 18°C, while the other may have the preference of 22°C. If the current ambient temperature is 20°C, one of the agents may set a goal to lower the temperature, while the other may set a goal to increase it.

Action conflict: if two (or more) agents share a compatible model of the world, and a compatible set of goals, however, they decide to undertake a conflicting course of actions to carry our their goals.

For example, given the situation in which the user's activity is perceived as cleaning the kitchen while it is detected that the stove is on, one of the agents sharing the common goal to ensure the user's safety, may decide that the most appropriate action is to warn the user, while a different agent may be able to remotely control the stove and hence it decides to the turn it off. While both plans are sound, if executed simultaneously the user might be confused. Clearly, the agents should resolve the situation by joint coordination of the next action.

3.3   Discussion

It should be noted that there is a difference between the knowledge type dimension and the source dimension, as according to Resendes at al. [20] the source refers to the medium over which the conflict is under dispute and not necessarily to the origin of the information that causes the conflict.

Compared with the classic BDI architecture, the proposed knowledge type dimension is more fine gained: the agent's representation of sensory inputs, context, and domain/background knowledge are all different types of beliefs. As we argued, it is important to distinguish between them because they are resolved differently, and in different time. For instance, together with the two additional knowledge types they can be sorted on the scale from lower to higher level of knowledge: (a) sensory input, (b) contextual, domain and background knowledge, (c) goals, and (d) actions, in the respective order. Distinguishing between these five types is important also due to the following conjecture: solving conflicts in a lower level knowledge can reduce and may possibly prevent occurrence of further conflicts in the higher levels of knowledge. For example, if two agents have a conflict in the contextual knowledge, that is, their interpretation of the situation in which they both participate is not compatible (e.g., they may have conflicting information about location) – if the conflict is resolved at this level, it is less likely that the agents will come up with conflicting goals and consequently action plans.

4   Towards Implementing Smart Environments

A plethora of methodologies and algorithms has been proposed for the implementation of smart spaces, in order to address issues related to the acquisition, representation and inference of the knowledge that the different autonomous entities rely on during their operation (relevant surveys involve [2,4,5,26,30,32]). Conflicts emerge inevitably; in this section, we overview the methodologies that have been applied to resolve conflicts at each level of abstraction and identify their main strong and weak points. As it will become clear, different features are needed in each case, constituting the selection of one approach as a holistic solution to deal with knowledge conflicts unfeasible. Synergies and hybrid approaches present the most prominent direction in future research.

4.1   Conflicts over Sensory and Low-Level Contextual Knowledge

The first step of the cycle presented in Fig. 1 denotes information obtained through sensing mechanisms. The vast volumes of data produced in sensor-rich spaces is most typically processed by so called *data-driven approaches*. These are characterized by the adoption of a probabilistic and statistical view of information and widely rely on the enormous impact of machine learning techniques in real-world applications.

A distinctive characteristic of data-driven algorithms is their capacity to model uncertainty. Conflicts over sensory inputs due to unexpected sensors malfunction or related to the recognition of low-level context caused by interleaved user activities, have been approached with models, such as based on multiple naive Bayesian networks [13], hidden Markov models [27], and others.

The ability to learn from datasets is a big leverage of data-driven approaches for deciding how best to resolve conflicts, but can also become their main point of weakness. Their performance is largely dependent on the availability of big amounts of – labeled or unlabeled – training data, often compromising their scalability capacity. Moreover, due to the pragmatic difficulty to monitor the behavior of humans for a long period of time while they perform everyday activities, or to the inability to accurately train a system for exceptional behaviors, such as a heart attack, the models produced exclusively from data-driven techniques are often prone to domain-dependent performance.

4.2 Conflicts over High-Level Context and Domain/Background Knowledge

Although quantitatively identifiable patterns can help in resolving sensory conflicts, as well as certain types of low-level contextual conflicts, higher-level context and background knowledge require richer representation models and commonsense information, that is not easily obtained through sensing. As the second step in Fig. 1 shows, appropriate reasoning and deliberation mechanisms are needed. The majority of approaches applied for this purpose are based on so called *knowledge-based* techniques that model the rules of inference from first principles, rather than learned from raw data.

Knowledge-based approaches typically rely on the formal specifications of their syntax and semantics and exploit symbolic modeling and logic-based reasoning techniques. The expressive power, along with the capacity to verify the correctness of a modelled conceptualization, and to draw conclusions from it, are their key advantages. A multitude of formal methodologies have been proposed over the years to resolve conflicts on the symbolic level. Among them, ontology-based models are arguably the most popular ones for implementing AmI systems.

Techniques investigating ontology evolution and debugging are relevant in this respect [7]. The former refers to the process of modifying an ontology in response to a certain change in the domain or its conceptualization, trying to prevent conflicts from appearing in the ontology during the evolution process. Ontology debugging addresses conflicts after they have appeared in the knowledge base. Works in ontology debugging are not only dealing with inconsistencies and incoherencies, but also with *invalidities*, which are violations of one or more custom validity rules that express application- or domain-specific requirements on the underlying ontology [24].

Ontology languages have rich and formal semantics that enables them to express complex knowledge using a wide set of primitives. The studies in [22] and [28], based on OWL 2 DL and OWL DL respectively, are indicative of how expressive, sound and decidable algorithms can be applied in context-aware systems to detect inconsistencies, infer activities and reproduce knowledge. Although a multitude of pervasive computing systems have applied ontologies in modeling and reasoning on context knowledge (e.g., [16,18,31]), most of them aim to mitigate the generation of conflicts by relying on centralized solutions, whereas only few try to explicitly incorporate a solution for resolving conflicts about context within a distributed environment [8,9,29].

One serious limitation and a key reason for the superiority of data-driven approaches over ontology-based ones, is the limited support for temporal reasoning by ontology-based languages [23]. In addition, the inherent uncertainty of the information that exists in ubiquitous domains is difficult to handle purely at the symbolic level. While context recognition with respect to coherent incoming information is what most of the aforementioned studies are focusing on, the resolution of information that is conflicting, especially in distributed systems, has not been extensively considered so far. Indeed, most Semantic Web-based approaches deal with the problem of context disambiguation up to the point of acknowledging that certain parameters can be regarded as unknown. Due to the openness of background knowledge, conflicts at this level in particular are even harder to handle. Ontology debugging techniques can be applied, but ofter human intervention cannot be avoided.

4.3   Conflicts over Goals and Actions

User activity and situation awareness only pose one step towards the implementation of intelligent environments. An equally crucial objective for the success of these systems is to enable their components to be *adaptive* to the recognized situation, and support *decision making* on daily and exceptional situations, in order to enhance users' experience. These requirements eventually lead to the other two types of conflicts defined in the previous section, namely goal and action conflicts. As the various smart entities need to interact and negotiate with one another, individually or collectively, in order to make decisions and synchronize their actions, conflicts emerge at the actuation level as well. Despite the availability of methodologies in the field of multi-agent systems, this topic only recently started to attract attention in the research of smart spaces (see, e.g., [3,6,14]).

Data-driven methods are currently the mainstream choice for smart space applications, even though a multitude of recent studies justify the attention that knowledge-based approaches have attracted over the last years [5,32]. Yet, experience shows that both lines of investigation suffer from limitations that restrict the former to the lower levels of data abstraction and the latter to high-level knowledge. In order to handle the identification and resolution of conflicts in complex situations, a seamless integration of methodologies in all levels is essential. For that reason, much of the current research attempts to unravel the potency of hybrid models [10,21,25].

5   Conclusion

The pragmatic challenges faced in implementing real-world intelligent environments forces the methodologies deployed to relax most of the simplifying assumptions that are usually applied in controlled domains. The existence of conflicts is among the most important challenges, due to the interactions among a multitude of diverse autonomous entities that operate in such environments. The implications of such conflicts affect the performance of smart systems in many respects. In this paper, we attempted a clear characterization of conflicts brought about at the different mental levels of agents, i.e., on their beliefs, goals and actions.

For the time being, only few approaches can offer a holistic and effective solution to the problem of developing a real-world smart infrastructure, handling conflicts at various levels. Yet, the importance of a coherent treatment can provide prominent results. As evidenced by Pecora et al. [17], inference, sensing, and actuation must operate in close collaboration, in order to manage an effective integration of the cognitive capabilities of an intelligent system, to be both context-aware and proactive.

With a deeper understanding of the different conflict types and their inherent characteristics, each conflict can properly be addressed at its given level by the most effective means. It is therefore our opinion that hybrid combinations of methodologies may likely provide the substrate for the materialization of future smart spaces.

Acknowledgments. This work resulted from the Slovak–Greek bilateral project "Multi-context Reasoning in Heterogeneous environments", registered on the Slovak side under no. SK-GR-0070-11 with the APVV agency and co-financed by the Greek General Secretariat of Science and Technology and the European Union. It was further supported from the Slovak national VEGA project no. 1/1333/12. Martin Baláž and Martin Homola are also supported from the APVV project no. APVV-0513-10.

References

1. Aarts, E., Harwig, R., Schuurmans, M.: Ambient intelligence. In: Denning, P.J. (ed.) The Invisible Future: The Seamless Integration of Technology into Everyday Life. McGraw-Hill Companies, New York (2001)
2. Aggarwal, J., Ryoo, M.: Human activity analysis: A review. ACM Computing Surveys 43(3), 16:1–16:43 (2011)
3. Bikakis, A., Antoniou, G.: Defeasible contextual reasoning with arguments in ambient intelligence. IEEE Transactions on Knowledge and Data Engineering 22(11), 1492–1506 (2010)
4. Bikakis, A., Patkos, T., Antoniou, G., Plexousakis, D.: A survey of semantics-based approaches for context reasoning in ambient intelligence. In: Constructing Ambient Intelligence - Am I 2007 Workshops Darmstadt, Germany, November 7–10, 2007 Revised Papers. vol. 11, pp. 14–23 (2008)
5. Chen, L., Khalil, I.: Activity recognition: Approaches, practices and trends. In: Activity Recognition in Pervasive Intelligent Environments, Atlantis Ambient and Pervasive Intelligence, vol. 4, pp. 1–31. Atlantis Press (2011)

6. Ferrando, S.P., Onaindia, E.: Defeasible argumentation for multi-agent planning in ambient intelligence applications. In: Proceedings of the 11th International Conference on AutonomousAgents and Multiagent Systems, AAMAS 2012, vol. 1, pp. 509–516 (2012)
7. Flouris, G., Manakanatas, D., Kondylakis, H., Plexousakis, D., Antoniou, G.: Ontology change: Classification and survey. Knowledge Engineering Review (KER 2008) 26(2), 117–152 (2008)
8. Fuchs, F., Hochstatter, I., Krause, M., Berger, M.: A metamodel approach to context information. In: 3rd IEEE Conference on Pervasive Computing and Communications Workshops (PerCom 2005 Workshops), March 8–12, pp. 8–14. IEEE Computer Society (2005)
9. Gu, T., Pung, H.K., Zhang, D.Q.: A service-oriented middleware for building context-aware services. Journal of Network and Computer Applications 28(1), 1–18 (2005)
10. Helaoui, R., Riboni, D., Niepert, M., Bettini, C., Stuckenschmidt, H.: Towards activity recognition using probabilistic description logics. Activity Context Representation: Techniques and Languages, AAAI Technical Report WS-12-05 (2012)
11. Henricksen, K., Indulska, J.: Modelling and using imperfect context information. In: Proceedings of the Second IEEE Annual Conference on Pervasive Computing and Communications Workshops (PerComW 2004), pp. 33–37 (2004)
12. Information Society Technologies Advisory Group (ISTAG): Ambient Intelligence: from vision to reality (2003)
13. Lu, C.H., Fu, L.C.: Robust location-aware activity recognition using wireless sensor network in an attentive home. IEEE Transactions on Automation Science and Engineering 6(4), 598–609 (2009)
14. Munoz, A., Botia, J.A., Augusto, J.C.: Intelligent decision-making for a smart home environment with multiple occupants. Computational Intelligence in Complex Decision Systems, Atlantis Computational Intelligence Systems 2, 325–371 (2010)
15. Ortega, A.M., Blaya, J.A.B., Clemente, F.J.G., Pérez, G.M., Skarmeta, A.F.G.: Solving conflicts in agent-based ubiquitous computing systems: A proposal based on argumentation. In: Agent-Based Ubiquitous Computing, vol. 1, pp. 1–12. Atlantis Press (2010)
16. Patkos, T., Chrysakis, I., Bikakis, A., Plexousakis, D., Antoniou, G.: A reasoning framework for ambient intelligence. In: Konstantopoulos, S., Perantonis, S., Karkaletsis, V., Spyropoulos, C.D., Vouros, G. (eds.) SETN 2010. LNCS, vol. 6040, pp. 213–222. Springer, Heidelberg (2010)
17. Pecora, F., Cirillo, M., Dell'Osa, F., Ullberg, J., Saffiotti, A.: A constraint-based approach for proactive, context-aware human support. Journal of Ambient Intelligence and Smart Environments (JAISE) 4(4), 347–367 (2012)
18. Preuveneers, D., Van den Bergh, J., Wagelaar, D., Georges, A., Rigole, P., Clerckx, T., Berbers, Y., Coninx, K., Jonckers, V., De Bosschere, K.: Towards an extensible context ontology for ambient intelligence. In: Markopoulos, P., Eggen, B., Aarts, E., Crowley, J.L. (eds.) EUSAI 2004. LNCS, vol. 3295, pp. 148–159. Springer, Heidelberg (2004)
19. Rao, A.S., Georgeff, M.P.: Modeling rational agents within a BDI-architecture. In: KR 1991, pp. 473–484 (1991)
20. Resendes, S., Carreira, P., Santos, A.C.: Conflict detection and resolution in home and building automation systems: a literature review. Journal of Ambient Intelligence and Humanized Computing 5(5), 699–715 (2014)

21. Riboni, D., Bettini, C.: COSAR: hybrid reasoning for context-aware activity recognition. Personal and Ubiquitous Computing **15**(3), 271–289 (2011)
22. Riboni, D., Bettini, C.: OWL 2 modeling and reasoning with complex human activities. Pervasive and Mobile Computing **7**(3), 379–395 (2011)
23. Riboni, D., Pareschi, L., Radaelli, L., Bettini, C.: Is ontology-based activity recognition really effective? In: Ninth Annual IEEE International Conference on Pervasive Computing and Communications, PerCom 2011, Workshop Proceedings, pp. 427–431. IEEE (2011)
24. Roussakis, Y., Flouris, G., Christophides, V.: Declarative repairing policies for curated KBs. In: Proceedings of the 10th Hellenic Data Management Symposium (HDMS 2011) (2011)
25. Roy, P.C., Giroux, S., Bouchard, B., Bouzouane, A., Phua, C., Tolstikov, A., Biswas, J.: A possibilistic approach for activity recognition in smart homes for cognitive assistance to alzheimer's patients. In: Activity Recognition in Pervasive Intelligent Environments, Atlantis Ambient and Pervasive Intelligence, vol. 4, pp. 33–58. Atlantis Press (2011)
26. Sadri, F.: Ambient intelligence: A survey. ACM Computing Surveys **43**(4), 36:1–36:66 (2011)
27. Singla, G., Cook, D.J., Schmitter-Edgecombe, M.: Recognizing independent and joint activities among multiple residents in smart environments. Journal of Ambient Intelligence and Humanized Computing **1**(1), 57–63 (2010)
28. Springer, T., Turhan, A.Y.: Employing description logics in ambient intelligence for modeling and reasoning about complex situations. Journal of Ambient Intelligence and Smart Environments **1**(3), 235–259 (2009)
29. Tan, J.G., Zhang, D., Wang, X., Cheng, H.S.: Enhancing semantic spaces with event-driven context interpretation. In: Gellersen, H.-W., Want, R., Schmidt, A. (eds.) PERVASIVE 2005. LNCS, vol. 3468, pp. 80–97. Springer, Heidelberg (2005)
30. Yang, Q.: Activity recognition: linking low-level sensors to high-level intelligence. In: Boutilier, C. (ed.) Proceedings of the 21st International Joint Conference on Artificial Intelligence, pp. 20–25 (2009)
31. Ye, J., Coyle, L., Dobson, S., Nixon, P.: Ontology-based models in pervasive computing systems. The Knowledge Engineering Review **22**(4), 315–347 (2007)
32. Ye, J., Dobson, S., McKeever, S.: Situation identification techniques in pervasive computing: A review. Pervasive and Mobile Computing **8**(1), 36–66 (2012)
33. Zelkha, E.: The future of information appliances and consumer devices. In: Palo Alto Ventures, Palo Alto, California (1998) (unpublished document)

Summary of the Workshop
on Educational Knowledge Management

Inaya Lahoud[1(✉)] and Lars Ahrenberg[2]

Department of Computer science, University of Galatasaray, Istanbul, Turkey
clahoud@gsu.edu.tr
Department of Computer and Information Science, Linköping University, Linköping, Sweden
lars.ahrenberg@liu.se

The first edition of the workshop Educational Knowledge Management[1] (EKM 2014) was held at the 19th International Conference on Knowledge Engineering and Knowledge Management (EKAW). The workshop took place in the city of Linköping, Sweden, on the 24th of November 2014. The workshop was organized by Inaya Lahoud and Lars Ahrenberg.

The interest in Knowledge Engineering and Knowledge Management for the educational domain has been growing in recent years. This can be seen in the series of conferences organized by the International Educational Data Mining Society and in papers discussing the role of knowledge management in higher education. As education is increasingly occurring online or in educational software, resulting in an explosion of data, new techniques are being developed and tested, aiming for instance to improve educational effectiveness, determine the key factors to the success of educational training, support basic research on learning, or manage educational training by satisfying the needs of a community, local industry, or professional development.

The event aimed to bring together researchers, academic and professional leaders, consultants, and practitioners, from the domain of semantic web, data mining, machine learning, linked data, and natural language processing to discuss and share experiences in the educational area.

Each submission was reviewed by two members of the EKM program committee.[2] Following the reviewers' recommendations, three full papers were accepted for presentation at the workshop. One paper was selected to be included in the Springer volume. This paper presents a case study of Multiple Choice Question (MCQ) generation based on an ontology created by an educator with no prior experience in ontology building. As the authors, Tahani Alsubait, Bijan Parsia, and Uli Settler, we believe this is a promising technique, in particular when the ontology can be used for many years or in several courses. The resulting questions were evaluated in terms of their generation cost, usefulness, quality, and difficulty of questions according to reviewers' ratings and reviewers' performance.

Ivan Srba and Maria Bielikova, the authors of the second paper in the EKM workshop, present the Question Answering Community and the importance of applying QA systems in the educational domain to resolve problems such as assisting students

---

[1] http://www.ida.liu.se/conferences/IWEKM14/
[2] http://www.ep.liu.se/ecp_home/index.en.aspx?issue=104

© Springer International Publishing Switzerland 2015
P. Lambrix et al. (Eds.): EKAW 2014 Satellite Events, LNAI 8982, pp. 64–65, 2015.
DOI: 10.1007/978-3-319-17966-7_6

in the learning process. In this paper, the authors presented and analysed three scenarios on how users improve their knowledge in QAC. The third paper, written by Monticolo Davy, Chang Tk and Inaya Lahoud, presents an ideas management system based on ontology and a multi-agents system. The aim of this system is to store, annotate and reuse ideas generated during the creativity workshop "48 hours to generate ideas" organized by the engineering school of innovation of the University of Lorraine.

As Chairs of this workshop, we would like to thank everybody that has been involved in the organization of EKM 2014.

Generating Multiple Choice Questions From Ontologies: How Far Can We Go?

Tahani Alsubait$^{(\boxtimes)}$, Bijan Parsia, and Uli Sattler

School of Computer Science, The University of Manchester,
Manchester, United Kingdom
{alsubait,bparsia,sattler}@cs.man.ac.uk

Abstract. Ontology-based Multiple Choice Question (MCQ) generation has a relatively short history. Many attempts have been carried out to develop methods to generate MCQs from ontologies. However, there is still a need to understand the applicability of these methods in real educational settings. In this paper, we present an empirical evaluation of ontology-based MCQ generation. We examine the feasibility of applying ontology-based MCQ generation methods by educators with no prior experience in ontology building. The findings of this study show that this is feasible and can result in generating a reasonable number of educationally useful questions with good predictions about their difficulty levels.

1 Introduction

Automatic question generation is a relatively new field and dimension within the broad concept of technology-aided assessment. It potentially offers educators some help to ease the burden and reduce the cost of manual assessment construction. In terms of time, it is reported that assessment development requires considerable time [9,18,20]. In terms of cost, it is estimated that the cost of developing one question for a high-stake test can range from $1,500 to $2,000 [19]. More importantly, in terms of quality, as many as 40% of manually constructed questions can fail to perform as intended when used in assessments [11]. This has motivated many researchers to develop automated methods to generate assessment questions. Many of these methods have focused on the generation of Multiple Choice Questions (MCQs) which are typically used in high-stake testing.

Ontologies are machine-processable artefacts that can formally describe the main notions of a specific domain. Recent advancements in ontology languages and ontology tools have created an interest in ontology-based MCQ generation. Various attempts have been made to generate MCQs from ontologies [3,17,24,25]. However, little is known about how useful these MCQs are when used in real educational settings.

© Springer International Publishing Switzerland 2015
P. Lambrix et al. (Eds.): EKAW 2014 Satellite Events, LNAI 8982, pp. 66–79, 2015.
DOI: 10.1007/978-3-319-17966-7_7

We present a new case study for using ontology-based MCQ generation in real educational settings. The purpose of the study is to evaluate the feasibility of using ontology-based MCQ generators by instructors who have no prior experience in ontology development. Rather than using an existing ontology, we examine the case where a new ontology is required to be build from scratch. We estimate the cost of question generation including the cost of building a new ontology by a novice ontology developer (e.g., the instructor in this case). We also evaluate the quality of the generated questions and the accuracy of the generator's predictions about the difficulty of the generated questions.

2   Background

An MCQ item is an assessment tool which is made up of the following parts: 1) A stem, 2) A key and 3) Some distractors. The stem is a statement that introduces a problem to the student. The key is simply the correct answer. A number of incorrect, yet plausible, answers are called the distractors. The number of optimal distractors for MCQs remains debatable [12].

An ontology is a set of axioms which can be either terminological or assertional. Terminological axioms describe relationships between concepts. Assertional axioms describe relationships between individuals and concepts or between individuals and roles. Description Logics (DL) ontologies have formal semantics [7]. In this sense, an ontology is a logical theory which implies that implicit knowledge can be inferred from the explicitly stated knowledge. For a detailed overview of ontologies, the reader is referred to [7].

3   Related Work

Prior to exploring the large body of research related to ontology-based question generation methods, we need to understand the basic/optional components associated with those methods. These components are:

3.1   Source Preparation

Before being able to generate questions, a suitable source ontology must be prepared. Gavrilova et al. [10] present a 5-step strategy aimed at developing teaching ontologies. The stages are: 1) Glossary development, 2) Laddering, 3) Disintegration, 4) Categorisation and 5) Refinement. Sosnovsky et al. [21] present a case study for utilising the above 5-step strategy to develop an ontology for the domain of C programming. In this paper, we have developed a similar procedure to build an ontology but we do not follow the same order of steps. For example, a glossary was used continuously to ensure that the ontology is covering the most interesting concepts in the domain under consideration.

3.2   Item Generation

The next step of generation is to generate an assessment item or part of it (e.g., distractors) from the developed ontology. For example, Mitkov et al. [16] have developed an approach to automatically generate MCQs using NLP methods. They also make use of ontologies to generate distractors that are similar to the correct answer. They report on experimenting with different similarity measures for the purpose of distractor generation.

Zitko et al. [25] proposed templates and algorithms for automatic generation of MCQs from ontologies. They generate a random set of distractors for each questions. Papasalouros et al. [17] constrain the set of distractors to some neighbours of the correct answer in the ontology.

Williams [24] presents a prototype system for generating mathematical word problems from ontologies based on predefined logical patterns. The proposed method makes use of data properties in general ontologies. The data properties are used to replace certain place holders in the predefined patterns.

3.3   Characterisation

Some methods of ontology-based question generation vary the characteristics of the generated questions (e.g., their difficulty). For instance, Williams [24] proposes to vary the difficulty of mathematical problems by introducing/removing distractor numerical values and varying sentence complexity and length. Alsubait et al. [1–3] propose to vary the difficulty of MCQs by varying the similarity between the key and distractors.

3.4   Presentation

To enhance the readability of automatically generated questions, Williams [24] extends the use of SWAT[1] natural language tools to verbalise ontology terms which are used in the generated questions. For example, "has a height of" can be derived from the data property "has_height". Similarly, Papasalouros et al. [17] use simple natural language generation techniques to transform the generated questions into English sentences.

3.5   Post Evaluation

Mitkov et al. [16] present an evaluation study of automatically generated MCQs in real testing settings. Classical test theory (CTT) has been used for the statistical analysis of students results. In particular, they study the following properties: (i) item difficulty, (ii) discrimination between good and poor students and (iii)

---

[1] http://swat.open.ac.uk/tools/

usefulness of distractors. They also compare manual and automatic methods of MCQ generation and report that automated methods perform better than manual methods of test items in terms of time without compromising quality. Item response theory (IRT) [15] has been used by Sumita et al. [22] to analyse their automatically generated language proficiency tests. While Mitkov et al. [16] used item analysis methods to evaluate the generated questions, Sumita et al. [22] incorporated these methods as part of the generation process.

In an earlier study [3], the authors evaluated a large set of multiple-choice questions which have been generated from three different ontologies. The evaluation was carried out using an automated solver which simulates a student trying to answer these questions. The use of the automated solver facilitated the evaluation of the large number of questions. The findings of this study show that it is feasible to control the difficulty of questions by varying the similarity between the key and distractors. A more recent study [5] in which the authors recruit a group of students in real testing settings confirms the results of the study carried earlier using the automated solver.

4 Ontology-Based MCQ Generation in Practice

Introduction to Software Development in Java is a self-study course run by the School of Computer Science at the University of Manchester. It aims to ensure that students enrolled in Masters programs in the school have a thorough grasp of fundamental programming concepts in Java. Topics covered in this course include: object-oriented basics, imperative programming, classes, inheritance, exception handling, collections, stream and file I/O. The course material is delivered online via Moodle. As with any self-study course, students enrolled in this course need a series of self-assessments to guide them through their learning journey.

4.1 Materials and Methods

Equipment Description. The following machine was used for the experiments in this paper: Intel Quad-core i7 2.4GHz processor, 4 GB 1333 MHz DDR3 RAM, running Mac OS X 10.7.5. In addition to the following software: OWL API v3.4.4 [14] and FaCT++ [23].

Building the Ontology. An ontology that covers the contents of the course has been built by an instructor who has an experience in Java but with no huge familiarity with materials of this course. In this case, the instructor had no prior experience in building ontologies. The online course material covers both fundamental concepts (i.e., terminological knowledge) and practical Java examples (i.e., procedural knowledge). Only terminological knowledge is suitable to be modelled in ontologies. This type of knowledge is typically a vital part of education in general and of assessment in particular. It is regarded as the basic level in Bloom's taxonomy of learning objectives [8]. The development of the ontology has gone through the following steps:

- The instructor has been introduced to basics of ontology development in an initial meeting which lasts for 2 hours. This included a brief hands-on tutorial on using *Protégé* 4 ontology editor. Further online materials [13] were forwarded to the instructor to familiarise herself on building and dealing with ontologies.
- The instructor built an initial version of the ontology. She went through the first 6 modules of the course, extracted and added to the ontology any encountered concepts and finally established links between the added concepts. This took a total of 10 hours and 15 minutes spread over 6 days. This has resulted in a total of 91 classes, 44 object properties and 315 axioms.
- A two-hours feedback session took place to highlight weak points in this version of the ontology. The instructor reported that, as the number of classes and relations increased, it got very hard to maintain the same level of understanding of the current state of the ontology.
- The second version of the ontology took 5.5 hours to build. The resulting ontology has a total of 91 classes, 38 object properties and 331 axioms. The main task was to restructure the ontology according to the received feedback. The decrease in the number of object properties is due to merging those object properties which had very similar meaning but different names. The increase in the number of axioms can be partially explained by the fact that the instructor was advised to assert negative facts in the ontology whenever and wherever possible. In addition, some concepts were re-categorised (e.g., declared as a subclass of another exiting class).
- To ensure that the ontology covers the main concepts of the domain, the instructor was advised to consult a glossary of Java-related terms which is part of the online course material. Adding new terms from the glossary in suitable positions in the ontology took a total of 10 hours over 4 days. The resulting ontology has a total of 319 classes, 107 object properties, 213 annotation assertion axioms and 513 logical axioms. The DL expressivity of the resulting ontology is $\mathcal{ALCHQ}$ which allows conjunctions, disjunctions, complements, universal restrictions, existential restrictions, qualified number restrictions and role hierarchies. For more information and examples on Description Logics, the reader is referred to [7].

Generating Questions. We follow the same question generation strategies described in [5] to generate multiple choice questions from ontologies. The first step of question generation is to compute the pairwise similarity for all the classes in the ontology using the similarity measures described in [6]. These similarity measures have been shown to be highly correlated with human similarity measurements [6]. The intuition behind using similarity measures as part of question generation is that varying the similarity between the key and distractors can make it possible to vary the difficulty of the generated questions [4]. In other words, increasing the difficulty to distinguish the correct answer among the given answers makes the question harder.

As an example for the question generation process, let us take a look at a small part of the Java ontology which is shown below:

$$ObjectCode \sqsubseteq ProgramCode,$$
$$RealMachineCode \sqsubseteq ObjectCode,$$
$$VirtualMachineCode \sqsubseteq ObjectCode,$$
$$JavaByteCode \sqsubseteq VirtualMachineCode,$$
$$RealMachineCode \sqsubseteq \exists hasFundamentalFeature.FastProgramExecution,$$
$$VirtualMachineCode \sqsubseteq \exists hasFundamentalFeature.PlatformIndependence,$$
$$VirtualMachineCode \sqsubseteq \exists hasFundamentalFeature.Portability$$

One of the questions that can be generated from the above example is: "*What does Real machine code has as a fundamental feature?*". The correct answer to this question according to the above ontology is "*Fast program execution*", i.e., the filler of the existential restriction axiom. To generate plausible distractors, the generator automatically chooses the concepts that share some similarities with the correct answer. To generate a difficult question, the generator selects the distractors that are the most similar to the key. To generate an easy question, the distractors are selected such that they are less similar than the distractors needed for a difficult question but they must share some commonalities with the key to make them plausible. For the above ontology, the distractors are: "*Platform independence*" and "*Portability*". The common feature in this case is that they are all used as fillers for the same property. To calculate the exact value of the similarity between two concepts, the generator takes into account all the axioms in the Java ontology which is not fully shown above. For more details about the similarity computation process, the reader is referred to [6]. Note that the generator can generate some questions and later discard them due to lack of sufficient number of distractors. For example, the question "*Which of the following is a virtual machine code?*" can be answered correctly by "*Java byte code*". According to the above ontology, "*Real machine code*" is a good distractor as it shares at least the two common subsumers '*Object code*" and

'*Program code*". However, one distractor is not sufficient to construct a question and therefore the question was discarded.

A total of 428 questions have been generated from the Java ontology. Then questions with less than 3 distractors have been excluded (resulting in 344 questions). Questions in which there is an overlap between the stem and the key have been filtered out (resulting in 264 questions). This step was necessary to ensure that there are no word clues in the stem that could make the correct answer too obvious. Previous attempts to generate MCQs from ontologies have identified this as a possible problem [5]. In this study, we filter out questions in which there is a shared word of more than three characters between the stem and key. This does not apply to questions in which the shared word is also present in the distractors. Finally, questions which can be described as redundant and that are not expected/recommended to appear in a single exam were manually excluded (e.g., two questions which have slightly different stems but the the same set of answers or vice versa). This step was carried out only to get a reasonable number of questions that can be reviewed in a limited time. The resulting questions are 65 questions in total. Among these are 25 easy questions and 40 difficult questions.

Reviewing Questions. Three reviewers have been asked to evaluate the 65 questions using the web interface shown in Figure 1. All the reviewers have experience in both the subject matter (i.e., programming in Java) and assessment construction. The reviewers have been randomly numbered as Reviewer 1, Reviewer 2 and Reviewer 3 with Reviewer 2 being the ontology developer. For each question, the reviewer is asked to first attempt to answer the question. Next, the reviewer is asked to rate the difficulty of the question by choosing one of the options 1) Too easy, 2) Reasonably easy, 3) Reasonably difficult and 4) Too difficult. Then the reviewer is asked to rate the usefulness of the question by choosing one of the options: (0) not useful at all, (1) useful as a seed for another question, (2) useful but requires major improvements, (3) useful but requires minor improvements or (4) useful as it is. In addition, the reviewer is asked to check whether the question adhere to 5 rules for constructing good MCQs. These rules were gathered from the qualitative analysis of previous reviewer comments in a previous evaluation study [5]. The rules are: R1) The question is relevant to the course content, R2) The question has exactly one key, R3) The question contains no clues to the key, R4) The question requires more than common knowledge to be answered correctly, and R5) The question is grammatically correct.

4.2   Results and Discussion

Total Cost. We report on the cost, in terms of time, of the three phases: 1) ontology building, 2) question generation and 3) question review. The ontology

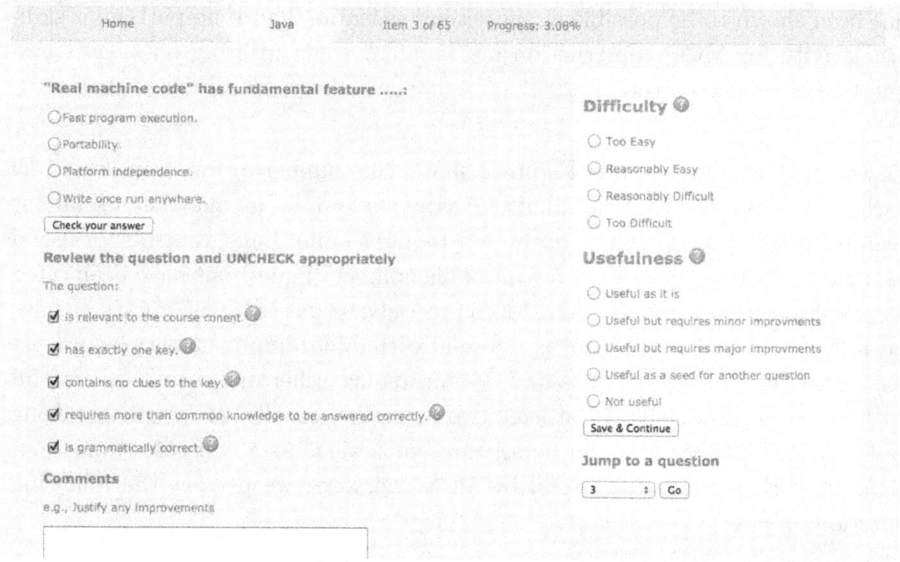

Fig. 1. The reviewing web-interface

took around 25 hours to be built by an instructor who has no prior experience on ontology building and no huge familiarity with the course material used in this study. This cost could have been reduced with an appropriate experience in building ontologies and/or higher familiarity with course content. The generation of a total of 428 questions using the machine described above took around 8 hours including the time required to compute pair-wise similarities. Finally, Reviewers 1, 2 and 3 spent around 43 minutes, 141 minutes, and 56 minutes respectively. We exclude any question for which more than 15 minutes were spent. This indicates that the reviewer was interrupted during the review of that question. In addition, Reviewer 2 reported that she was taking side notes while reviewing each question. For this reason and for other reasons that could interrupt the reviewer, the cost of the reviewing phase should be regarded as a general indicator only.

In terms of cost, it is interesting to compare between two possible scenarios to generate MCQs. The first scenario is where the questions are manually constructed whereas the second scenario utilises ontology-based question generation strategies. The cost of manual generation is expected to be lower than the cost of developing a new ontology added to the cost of question generation and review. However, a few points should be taken into account here. First, in the second scenario, the ontology is expected to be re-used multiple times to generate different sets of questions. Second, the aim is to generate questions with highly accurate predictions about their pedagogical characteristics which has been shown to be possible in the second scenario. Third, no particular skill-s/creativity for MCQ construction are required when utilising ontology-based question generation strategies.

Usefulness of Questions. Figure 2 shows the number of questions rated by each reviewer as: not useful at all, useful as a seed for another question, useful but requires major improvements, useful but requires minor improvements, or useful as it is. As the figure indicates, a reasonable number of questions have been rated as useful by at least one reviewer. More precisely, 63 out of the 65 questions have been rated as either useful as it is or useful with minor improvements by at least one reviewer. And 50 questions have been rated as either useful as it is or useful with minor improvements by at least two reviewers. Finally, 24 questions belong to the same category as rated by all three reviewers. As a concrete example of a question that was rated useful by all 3 reviewers, we present the following question:

Q: ..... refers to "A non-static member variable of a class.":
  (A) Loop variable
  (B) Instance variable (Key)
  (C) Reference variable
  (D) Primitive variable

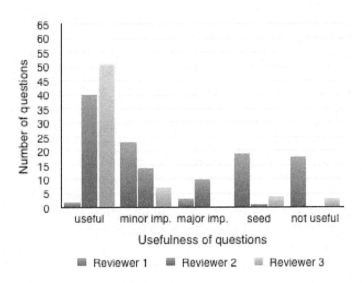

Fig. 2. Usefulness of questions according to reviewers evaluations

Quality of Questions. Adherence to the 5 rules for constructing goof MCQs indicates the quality of the generated questions. Figure 3 shows the number of questions adhering to each rule as evaluated by each reviewer. In general, a large number of questions have been found to adhere to Rules R1, R2 and R4. It can be noticed that only a few questions violate Rule R4 (i.e., no clues rule). Recall that a lexical filter has been applied to the generated questions to filter out questions with obvious word clues. This has resulted in filtering out 80 questions. This means that the lexical filter is needed to enhance the quality of the generated questions. The grammatical correctness rule (R5) was the only rule which got low ratings. According to reviewers' comments, this is mainly due to the lack of appropriate articles (i.e., the, a, an). Dealing with this issue and other presentation/verbalisation issues is part of future work.

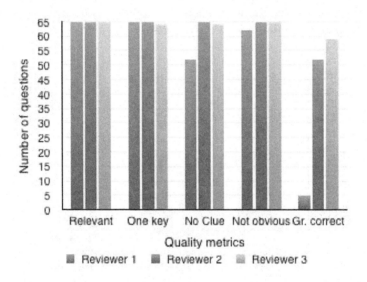

Fig. 3. Quality of questions according to reviewers' evaluations

Difficulty of Questions According to Reviewers' Ratings. Part of the objectives of this study is evaluate the accuracy of predictions made by the questions generation tool about the difficulty of each generated question. To do this, we compare difficulty estimations by each reviewer with tool's predictions. Recall that each reviewer was allowed to select from four options of different difficulty levels (too easy, reasonably easy, too difficult, reasonably difficult). This is to distinguish between acceptable and extreme levels of difficulty/easiness. However, tool's predictions can take only two values (easy or difficult). To study tool-to-reviewers agreements, we only consider the two general categories of difficulty. That is, the four categories of difficulty estimations by reviewers are collapsed into two categories only (easy and difficult). Figure 4 shows the number of questions for which there is an agreement between the tool and at least one, two or three reviewers. As the Figure shows, for a large number of questions (51 out of 65 questions) there has been an agreement between the tool and at least one reviewer. To understand the causes of disagreements, we further categorise the agreements according to the difficulty of questions. Table 1 indicates that the degree of agreement is much higher with easy questions reaching 100% agreements with at least one reviewer. This could mean that the generated distractors for difficult questions were not plausible enough. This has been discussed with the ontology developer because we believe that better distractors could be generated by enriching the ontology. In particular, the ontology developer has indicated that many classes in the ontology have been assigned to a single superclass while they could possibly be assigned to multiple superclasses. Restructuring and enriching the ontology is expected to increase the ability of the tool to generate questions at certain levels of difficulty.

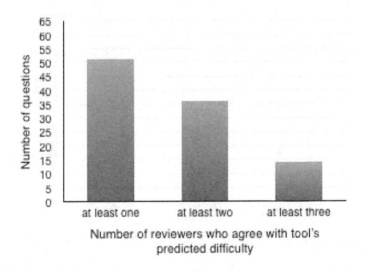

Fig. 4. Difficulty of questions according to reviewers' evaluations

Difficulty of Questions According to Reviewers' Performance. Each reviewer has attempted to solve each question as part of the reviewing process. Interestingly, non of the reviewers has answered all the questions correctly, including the ontology builder who answered 60 questions correctly. The first and third reviewers have correctly answered 55 and 59 questions respectively. This can have different possible explanations. For example, it could be possible that the reviewer have picked a wrong answer by mistake while trying to pick

Table 1. Accuracy of difficulty predictions for easy and difficult questions

	At least 1 reviewer	At least 2 reviewers	At least 3 reviewers
Easy questions	100%	88%	52%
Difficult questions	65%	35%	2.5%
All questions	78.5%	55.4%	21.6%

the key. This has actually happened with the first reviewer who has reported this by leaving a comment on one question. Note also that the third reviewer has reported that in exactly one question there was more than one possible correct answer, see Figure 3. This means that if a reviewer picks an answer other than the one identified by the tool as the correct answer then his/her answer will not be recognised as correct. Figure 5 shows the number of questions answered correctly by at least one, two and three reviewers.

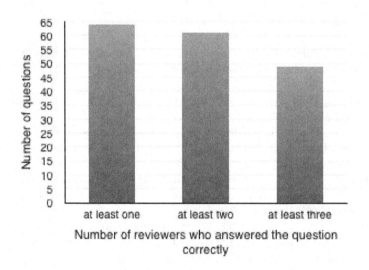

Fig. 5. Difficulty of questions according to reviewers performance

In exactly one question, none of the reviewers answered the question correctly, raising a question about the validity of this question as an assessment tool. The stem part of this question was "Which is the odd one out?". To required task to answer the question is to distinguish between the answers which have a common link (the distractors) and the answer which cannot be linked to the other answers (the key). Although all the reviewers have rated this question as "useful", we believe that it is too difficult and not necessarily very useful as an assessment item.

5   Conclusion and Future Research Directions

We believe that ontology-based MCQ generation has proved to be a useful method for generating quality MCQs. The cost of generation is still considered to be high but is expected to be reduced over continuous uses of the same ontology, especially if a large number of questions is required each time. The main advantage of using the automated method of generation is the ability to estimate the difficulty of the generated questions with high accuracy.

As future work, we aim to administer the generated questions to a group of students in order to see how useful the questions are for the purposes of self-assessments. We also aim to add a verbaliser to the MCQ generator to enhance language accuracy. Finally, we believe that there is a potential in using the developed MCQ generation methods in application other than assessments. For example, we are interested in exploring the applicability of these methods for ontology evaluation and comprehension purposes.

References

1. Alsubait, T., Parsia, B., Sattler, U.: Automatic generation of analogy questions for student assessment: an ontology-based approach. In: ALT-C 2012 Conference Proceedings (2012)
2. Alsubait, T., Parsia, B., Sattler, U.: Mining ontologies for analogy questions: a similarity-based approach. In: OWLED (2012)
3. Alsubait, T., Parsia, B., Sattler, U.: Next generation of e-assessment: automatic generation of questions. International Journal of Technology Enhanced Learning 4(3/4), 156–171 (2012)
4. Alsubait, T., Parsia, B., Sattler, U.: A similarity-based theory of controlling mcq difficulty. In: Second International Conference on e-Learning and e-Technologies in Education (ICEEE), pp. 283–288 (2013)
5. Alsubait, T., Parsia, B., Sattler, U.: Generating multiple choice questions from ontologies: lessons learnt. In: The 11th OWL: Experiences and Directions Workshop (OWLED2014) (2014)
6. Alsubait, T., Parsia, B., Sattler, U.: Measuring similarity in ontologies: how bad is a cheap measure? In: 27th Inernational Workshop on Description Logics (DL-2014) (2014)
7. Baader, F., Calvanese, D., McGuinness, D.L., Nardi, D., Patel-Schneider, P.F.: The Description Logic Handbook: Theory, Implementation and Applications. Cambridge University Press, second edition (2007)
8. Bloom, B.S., Krathwohl, D.R.: Taxonomy of educational objectives: The classification of educational goals by a committee of college and university examiners. Handbook 1. Cognitive domain. Addison-Wesley, New York (1956)
9. Davis, B.G.: Tools for Teaching. Jossey-Bass, San Francisco (2001)
10. Gavrilova, T., Farzan, R., Brusilovsky, P.: One practical algorithm of creating teaching ontologies. In: 12th International Network-Based Education Conference NBE, pp. 29–37 (2005)

11. Haladyna, T.M.: Developing and validating multiple-choice test items. Hillsdale: Lawrence Erlbaum (1994)
12. Haladyna, T.M., Downing, S.M.: How many options is enough for a multiple choice test item? Educational & Psychological Measurement **53**(4), 999–1010 (1993)
13. Horridge, M.: A practical guide to building OWL ontologies using Protégé 4 and CO-ODE tools (edition 1.3.) (2011). http://owl.cs.manchester.ac.uk/tutorials/protegeowltutorial/
14. Horridge, M., Bechhofer, S.: The OWL API: A Java API for working with OWL 2 ontologies. In: Proceedings of the 6th International Workshop on OWL: Experiences and Directions (OWLED) (2009)
15. Miller, M., Linn, R., Gronlund, N.: Measurement and Assessment in Teaching, Tenth Edition. Pearson (2008)
16. Mitkov, R., An Ha, L., Karamani, N.: A computer-aided environment for generating multiple-choice test items, cambridge University Press. Natural Language Engineering **12**(2), 177–194 (2006)
17. Papasalouros, A., Kotis, K., Kanaris, K.: Automatic generation of multiple-choice questions from domain ontologies. In: IADIS e-Learning 2008 conference, Amsterdam (2008)
18. Paxton, M.: A linguistic perspective on multiple choice questioning. Assessment & Evaluation in Higher Education **25**(2), 109–119 (2001)
19. Rudner, L.: Elements of adaptive testing. Implementing the Graduate Management Admission Test Computerized Adaptive Test, pp. 151–165. Springer, New York (2010)
20. Sidick, J.T., Barrett, G.V., Doverspike, D.: Three-alternative multiple-choice tests: An attractive option. Personnel Psychology **47**, 829–835 (1994)
21. Sosnovsky, S., Gavrilova, T.: Development of educational ontology for C-programming. In: Proceedings of the XI-th International Conference Knowledge-Dialogue-Solution, vol. 1, pp. 127–132. FOI ITHEA (2006)
22. Sumita, E., Sugaya, F., Yamamoto, S.: Measuring non-native speakers prociency of english using a test with automatically-generated fill-in-the-blank questions. In: Proceedings of the Second Workshop on Building Educational Applications using Natural Language Processing, Ann Arbor, US, pp. 61–68 (2005)
23. Tsarkov, D., Horrocks, I.: FaCT++ description logic reasoner: System description. In: Furbach, U., Shankar, N. (eds.) Automated Reasoning. LNCS, vol. 4130, pp. 292–297. Springer, Heidelberg (2006)
24. Williams, S.: Generating mathematical word problems. In: 2011 AAAI Fall Symposium Series (2011)
25. Zitko, B., Stankov, S., Rosic, M., Grubisic, A.: Dynamic test generation over ontology-based knowledge representation in authoring shell. Expert Systems with Applications: An International Journal **36**(4), 8185–8196 (2008)

Introduction to VISUAL 2014 - Workshop on Visualizations and User Interfaces for Knowledge Engineering and Linked Data Analytics

Valentina Ivanova[1]([✉]), Tomi Kauppinen[2], Steffen Lohmann[3], Suvodeep Mazumdar[4], Catia Pesquita[5], and Kai Xu[6]

[1] Linköping University, Linköping, Sweden
valentina.ivanova@liu.se
[2] Aalto University, Espoo, Finland
[3] University of Stuttgart, Stuttgart, Germany
steffen.lohmann@vis.uni-stuttgart.de
[4] The University of Sheffield, Sheffield, UK
[5] University of Lisbon, Lisbon, Portugal
[6] Middlesex University, London, UK

Abstract. VISUAL 2014 addressed the challenges in providing knowledge engineers and data analysts with visualizations and well-designed user interfaces to support the understanding of the concepts, data instances and relationships in different domains. The workshop was organized around two tracks: one focused on visualizations and user interfaces for Knowledge Engineering, and the other on Visual Analytics for dynamic and large-scale data. Six contributions were presented at the workshop, which also included an interactive tool demonstration session.

With data continuously generated as a result of daily activities within organizations and new data sources (sensor streams, linked datasets, etc.) introduced within knowledge management, the growth of information is unprecedented. Providing knowledge engineers and data analysts with visualizations and well-designed user interfaces can significantly support the understanding of the concepts, data instances and relationships in different domains.

The development of appropriate visualizations and user interfaces is a challenging task, given the size and complexity of the information that needs to be displayed and the varied backgrounds of the users. Further challenges emerge from technological developments and diverse application contexts. There is no *one size fits all* solution but the various use cases demand different visualization and interaction techniques. Ultimately, providing better visualizations and user interfaces will foster user engagement and likely lead to higher-quality results in different areas of knowledge engineering and linked data analytics.

VISUAL 2014 was collocated with the 19th International Conference on Knowledge Engineering and Knowledge Management (EKAW 2014) that took

© Springer International Publishing Switzerland 2015
P. Lambrix et al. (Eds.): EKAW 2014 Satellite Events, LNAI 8982, pp. 80–82, 2015.
DOI: 10.1007/978-3-319-17966-7_8

place in Linköping (Sweden) on November 24, 2014. The workshop was organized around two tracks. The first addressed visualizations and user interfaces as an integral part of knowledge engineering. As knowledge-based systems and ontologies grow in size and complexity, the demand for comprehensive visualization and optimized interaction also rises. A number of knowledge visualizations have become available in recent years, with some being already well-established, particularly in the field of ontology development. In other areas of knowledge engineering, such as ontology alignment and debugging, although several tools have recently been developed, few have a user interface, and only very seldomly navigational aids or comprehensive visualization techniques.

The second track focused on Visual Analytics, which attempts to address the challenge of analyzing dynamic and large scale data by harmoniously combining the strengths of human processing and electronic data processing. On its own, raw data has little value, but its value and significance is only unleashed when the data is extracted, processed and interpreted. While semi-automated processes result in generating visualizations, humans can use visual processing and interactions to quickly identify trends, patterns and anomalies from large volumes of visual data.

VISUAL 2014 attracted high-quality submissions of different types (both short and full papers). Each manuscript was reviewed by at least three members of the program committee and received an extensive feedback. Six of the submissions were accepted and published as CEUR-WS proceedings volume 1299; one of them was selected and the authors were invited to submit an extended version in this proceedings volume.

A diverse audience consisting of researchers and developers was sharing their experiences and views in lively discussions at the workshop. The accepted submissions were thematically divided and presented in three sessions during the day-long event. Time was dedicated after each session to wrap-up the talks, and for a general discussion after each track where various questions were brought to the attendees attention by the session chairs.

The contributions in the knowledge engineering area addressed issues related to the visualization of complex relationships and structures, as well as current problems in ontology alignment. They were presented in two sessions. The track discussion encompassed various topics, including well-recognized problems like the scalability of visualizations or the representation of ontologies as graph and tree structures. Also less obvious issues were discussed, such as the accessibility of user interfaces or benchmarks for different aspects of visualizations, such as the speed of layout algorithms.

The third session focused on visual approaches to Linked Data and debated the important questions of user studies and visualizations of linked datasets for answering complex queries. The last session was dedicated to tool demonstrations, and everyone was invited to join and present interesting visualizations and user interfaces in a five-minute time frame. A dozen of tools were presented both by the VISUAL organizers and members of the audience. At the end of the day, a closing wrap-up summarized the challenges and the open problems the community is facing.

Further information about the workshop is available at:
http://linkedscience.org/events/visual2014/

OntoViBe 2: Advancing the Ontology Visualization Benchmark

Florian Haag[1], Steffen Lohmann[1]([✉]), Stefan Negru[2], and Thomas Ertl[1]

[1] Institute for Visualization and Interactive Systems, University of Stuttgart,
Universitätsstraße 38, 70569 Stuttgart, Germany
{florian.haag,steffen.lohmann,thomas.ertl}@vis.uni-stuttgart.de
[2] Faculty of Computer Science, Alexandru Ioan Cuza University,
Strada General Henri Mathias Berthelot 16, 700483 Iasi, Romania
stefan.negru@info.uaic.ro

Abstract. A variety of ontology visualizations have been presented in the last couple of years. The features of these visualizations often need to be tested during their development or for evaluation purposes. However, in particular for the testing of special concepts and concept combinations, it can be difficult to find suitable ontologies. We have developed OntoViBe, an ontology covering a wide variety of OWL language constructs for the purpose of testing ontology visualizations. This paper presents OntoViBe 2, which extends the first version by annotations, individuals, anonymous classes, and a module for testing different combinations of cardinality constraints, among others. We describe the design principles underlying OntoViBe 2 and present the supported features in a coverage matrix. Finally, we load OntoViBe 2 with ontology visualization tools and point to some noteworthy aspects of the respective visualizations that become apparent and demonstrate how OntoViBe can be used for testing ontology visualizations.

Keywords: Ontology · Visualization · Benchmark · Evaluation · OWL

1 Introduction

Developing and working with ontologies can be supported by ontology visualizations. Over the past years, a number of visualization approaches geared towards the peculiarities of ontologies have been proposed. Most of the available approaches use node-link diagrams to depict the graph structure of ontologies, while some apply other diagram types like treemaps or nested circles [6,11,14].

During the development of such ontology visualizations, testing with a variety of existing ontologies is required to ensure that the concepts from the underlying ontology language are adequately represented. The same needs to be done to determine the features of an ontology visualization and get an impression of how different ontology language constructs are visually represented. Still, repeatedly loading a set of ontologies that cover a wide variety of language constructs can be a tedious task, even more so as the most common constructs tend to appear

© Springer International Publishing Switzerland 2015
P. Lambrix et al. (Eds.): EKAW 2014 Satellite Events, LNAI 8982, pp. 83–98, 2015.
DOI: 10.1007/978-3-319-17966-7_9

over and over in each of the tested ontologies. In order to help that process with respect to ontologies based on the OWL Web Ontology Language [20], we developed OntoViBe, an Ontology Visualization Benchmark.

Basically, OntoViBe consists of a small set of ontologies that have been designed to incorporate a comprehensive amount of OWL language constructs and systematic combinations thereof. While it is oriented towards OWL 2, it also includes the concepts of OWL 1 due to the complete backwards compatibility of the two ontology languages (i.e., all OWL 1 ontologies are valid OWL 2 ontologies) [21].

As opposed to most other benchmarks found in the computing world, OntoViBe is not meant for testing the scalability of visualizations with respect to the number of elements contained in ontologies, but rather aims for the scope of visualizations in terms of supported features. Related to this, it focuses on the representation of what is usually called the TBox of ontologies (i.e., the classes, properties, datatypes and a few key individuals), while it does not support the testing of ABox information (i.e., larger collections of individuals and data values), which is the focus of most related work.

A first version of OntoViBe was previously introduced [9]. This revised and updated paper presents OntoViBe 2, which advances the first version. In particular, we added annotations to the ontology header and to selected elements of the core ontology. We also added some individuals and anonymous classes in order to provide a more complete set of test cases, as well as a few extra element combinations that may also be useful for testing ontology visualizations. Finally, we complemented the ontologies with two additional modules for testing a minimal case and various combinations of cardinality constraints.

2   Related Work

Several benchmarks for ontology tools have been developed in the past. One well-known example is the Lehigh University Benchmark (LUBM), designed by the SWAT research group of Lehigh University [8]. It consists of three components: 1) an ontology of moderate size and complexity describing concepts and relationships from the university domain, 2) a generator for random instance data that can be scaled up to an arbitrary size, and 3) a set of test queries for the instance data as well as performance metrics.

Since the LUBM benchmark is bound to the university domain, the SWAT research group developed a second benchmark that can be tailored to different domains [22]. It uses a probabilistic model to generate an arbitrary number of instances based on representative data from the domain in focus. As an example, the Lehigh BibTeX Benchmark (LBBM) was created with the probabilistic model and a BibTeX ontology.

Another extension of LUBM has been proposed with the University Ontology Benchmark (UOBM) [15]. UOBM aims to include the complete set of OWL 1 language constructs and defines two ontologies, one being compliant with OWL Lite and the other with OWL DL. Furthermore, it adds several links to the generated instance data and provides related test cases for reasoners.

All these benchmarks focus primarily on performance, efficiency, and scalability, but do not address the visual representation of ontologies. Furthermore, they are mainly oriented towards instance data (the ABox), while systematic combinations of classes, properties, and datatypes (the TBox) are not considered any further. Even though UOBM provides comparatively complete TBox information, it has been designed to test OWL reasoners and not ontology visualizations. This is also the case for JustBench [3], which uses small and clearly defined ontology subsets to evaluate the behavior of OWL reasoners.

In addition, there are some benchmarks addressing specific aspects of ontology engineering. A number of datasets and test cases emerged, for instance, as part of the Ontology Alignment Evaluation Initiative (OAEI) [1]. A related dataset has been created in the OntoFarm project, which provides a collection of ontologies for the task of testing and comparing different ontology alignment methods [19]. An extension of the OntoFarm idea is the MultiFarm project, which offers ontologies translated into different languages with corresponding alignments between them [16]. Overall, the test cases are intended to evaluate and compare the quality and performance of matching algorithms, in the latter case with a special focus on multilingualism.

The W3C Web Ontology Working Group has also developed test cases for OWL 1 [5] and OWL 2 [18]. They are meant to provide examples for the normative definition of OWL and can, for instance, be used to perform conformance checks. However, to the best of our knowledge, there has not been any benchmark particularly addressing the visualization of ontologies before the introduction of OntoViBe.

3   Ontology Visualization Benchmark (OntoViBe)

OntoViBe consists of four modules providing various test cases for ontology visualizations. The two latter modules were added with version 2 of OntoViBe.

1. **Core ontology:**[1] Main module containing most of the ontology elements.
2. **Imported ontology:**[2] Module that is imported by the core ontology. It is required for test cases that contain imported elements.
3. **Minimal ontology:**[3] Module without any elements, annotations, or other OWL concepts, to test a minimal case.
4. **Cardinality ontology:**[4] Module that contains various cardinality restrictions and systematic combinations thereof.

When testing an ontology visualization, the *core ontology*, the *minimal ontology*, and the *cardinality ontology* may be loaded individually. The *imported ontology* complements the *core ontology* and is usually not loaded on its own.

---

[1] http://ontovibe.visualdataweb.org/
[2] http://ontovibe.visualdataweb.org/imported/
[3] http://ontovibe.visualdataweb.org/minimal/
[4] http://ontovibe.visualdataweb.org/cardinalities/

The structure and content of OntoViBe is based on the OWL 2 specifications [21], with the following requirements:

- A wide variety of OWL 2 language constructs must appear. This includes constructs such as class definitions or different kinds of properties, as well as modifiers for these, such as *deprecated* markers.
- Subgraphs that represent compound concepts must appear. This includes small groups of classes that are coupled by particular properties.

Moreover, we tried to keep the overall ontology as small as possible in number of elements. Like this, rather than a mere enumeration of the elements and concepts supported by OWL 2, chances are that the ontology can be completely displayed and grasped "at a single glance" and thereby convey a complete impression of the features supported by the visualization being examined.

OntoViBe was assembled by creating an instance of each of the subgraph structures. Where possible, elements were reused to keep the ontologies small. For instance, to include the OWL element *object property*, a subgraph structure consisting of two classes connected by an object property was added. Hence, two classes were inserted into the ontology, and an object property was defined that uses either of the two classes as its domain and range, respectively. Furthermore, the element *datatype property* needed to appear in the ontology. A compact subgraph structure to express that element consists of a class linked to a datatype property. As the class does not need to have any specific characteristics of its own, one of the two previously inserted classes could be reused.

Other OWL elements were added in a similar fashion to the ontologies. Some of the existing elements were modified to cover all language constructs, combinations, and features that we wanted to consider at least once in the ontologies. For example, some properties were declared as *functional* or *deprecated*. For any language construct that still did not appear in the ontologies, a minimal number of extra elements were added.

Lastly, all elements in the ontologies were named in a self-descriptive manner to allow for an easier interpretation and analysis. For instance, a deprecated class is called `DeprecatedClass`, while the larger of the union classes is called `LargeUnionClass`.

3.1   Exemplary Parts of OntoViBe

Many of the structures could be added in a straightforward way. In some cases, further considerations were required to adequately address the more flexible features of OWL. Where appropriate, excerpts from the ontology in Turtle syntax are shown.

Concepts defined based upon set operators (*unionOf, intersectionOf, complementOf*) come in three variants in version 2 of OntoViBe: One of them uses a set comprising two elements as an example for a small set, while the other features more set elements, usually three (Listing 1.1). Lastly, each set operator is used in one anonymous class to highlight any differences in the representation of anonymous classes.

Listing 1.1. Concepts based upon set operators are featured in two variants, a small set with two elements, and a larger one with more elements.

```
52  this:UnionClass a owl:Class ;
53    rdfs:comment "This is an English comment on a class expression."@en ;
54    owl:unionOf ( this:Class1 this:DeprecatedClass ).
55
56  this:LargeUnionClass a owl:Class ;
57    owl:unionOf ( this:UnionClass other:ImportedClass this:PropertyOwner ).
```

Listing 1.2. OntoViBe 2 contains a few individuals that are used in class definitions based on OWL constructs, such as owl:oneOf.

```
74  this:LargeEnumerationClass a owl:Class ;
75    owl:oneOf ( this:MultiSubclassIndividual2 this:MultiSubclassIndividual3
          this:AnotherIndividual ).
```

Listing 1.3. Individuals are also used for various kinds of assertions.

```
210  _:DifferentIndividualsGroup a owl:AllDifferent ;
211    owl:members ( this:AnotherIndividual this:MultiSubclassIndividual1 this:
          MultiSubclassIndividual2 ).
212
213  this:SameAsMultiSubclassIndividual2 a this:MultiSubclass ;
214    owl:sameAs this:MultiSubclassIndividual2 .
215
216  _:NegativeObjectPropertyAssertion a owl:NegativePropertyAssertion ;
217    owl:sourceIndividual this:MultiSubclassIndividual2 ;
218    owl:assertionProperty this:dummyProperty ;
219    owl:targetIndividual this:AnotherIndividual .
```

For a few of the classes, a small number of individuals have been added in OntoViBe 2. Analogously to the set operators, these have been chosen so the display of classes with a single individual and classes with more than one individual can be examined. Several of the individuals are used in class restrictions, such as owl:oneOf or owl:hasValue (Listing 1.2). Individuals are also used for various kinds of assertions defined in OWL 2 and included in OntoViBe 2 (Listing 1.3).

Furthermore, OntoViBe declares some OWL data ranges (Listing 1.4). Visualizations may or may not represent the exact definitions of these data ranges, but even if they do not, support for datatype properties with custom data ranges needs to be tested. Therefore, custom data ranges are used by some datatype properties in OntoViBe, while common datatypes are used for most other properties (Listing 1.5).

There are also several sets of equivalent classes in OntoViBe. Some of the classes in these sets are deprecated or imported in order to check how these special cases are rendered in the tested visualization.

In ontology visualizations, sets of properties between the same pair of classes (or the same class and literal) pose a particular challenge, as they may lead to overlapping and thus illegible representations. Several of these cases have been

Table 1. Coverage of OntoViBe 2 elements with respect to OWL constructs (*part I*)

"•" indicates that the respective OWL syntax element is included in OntoViBe, while "o" means that an equivalent syntax element is used.

Namespace prefix "a:" denotes elements of the core ontology, while elements from the imported ontology are marked with "b:"

OWL construct	in	PlainClass	DeprecatedClass	Class1	ComplementClass	UnionClass	LargeUnionClass	IntersectionClass	LargeIntersectionClass	DisjointUnionClass	LargeDisjointUnionClass	EnumerationClass	LargeEnumerationClass	AnonymousClassAnchor	anonymousComplementClassProperty	anonymousUnionClassProperty	anonymousIntersectionClassProperty	anonymousEnumerationClassProperty	PropertyOwnerType	PropertyOwner	MultiPropertyOwner	DisjointClass	DisjointClassGroup	Subclass	MultiSubclass	SomeValuesFromClass	AllValuesFromClass	HasValueClass	HasSelfClass	EquivalentDeprecatedClass	EquivalentToDeprecatedClass	EquivalentDeprecatedClassInLargeGroup	EquivalentClassInLargeGroup	Class1Individual	MultiSubclassIndividual1	MultiSubclassIndividual2	MultiSubclassIndividual3	AnotherIndividual	DifferentIndividualsGroup	SameAsMultiSubclassIndividual2	NegativeObjectPropertyAssertion	NegativeDataPropertyAssertion	DivisibleByTwoEnumeration	DivisibleByFiveEnumeration	UnionDatatype	IntersectionDatatype	ComplementDatatype
AllDifferent	•																																							•							
AllDisjointClasses	•																						•																								
AllDisjointProperties	•																																														
Annotation																																															
AnnotationProperty	•																																														
AsymmetricProperty	•																																														
Axiom																																															
Class	•	•	•	•	•	•	•	•	•	•	•	•	•	•	•	•	•	•	•	•	•			•	•	•	•	•	•	•	•	•	•														
DataRange	o																																											o	o	o	o	o
DatatypeProperty	•																																														
DeprecatedClass	o		o																											o		o															
DeprecatedProperty	o																																														
FunctionalProperty	•																																														
InverseFunctionalProperty	•																																														
IrreflexiveProperty	•																																														
NamedIndividual	•																																														
NegativePropertyAssertion	•																																								•	•					
Nothing																																															
ObjectProperty	•														•	•	•	•																													
Ontology	•	•																																													
OntologyProperty																																															
ReflexiveProperty	•																																														
Restriction	•																									•	•	•	•	•																	
SymmetricProperty	•																																														
Thing	•																																														
TransitiveProperty	•																																														
allValuesFrom	•																										•																				
annotatedProperty	•																																														
annotatedSource																																															
annotatedTarget	•																																														
assertionProperty	•																																								•	•					
backwardCompatibleWith	•	•																																													
bottomDataProperty																																															
bottomObjectProperty																																															
cardinality	•			•															•																												
complementOf	•				•										•																																•
datatypeComplementOf	•																																														•
deprecated	•		•																												•	•															
differentFrom	•																																					•									
disjointUnionOf	•									•	•																																				
disjointWith	•																					•																									
distinctMembers																																															
equivalentClass	•																													•	•									•	•					
equivalentProperty	•																																														
hasKey	•																																														
hasSelf	•																												•																		
hasValue	•																											•																			
imports	•																																														
incompatibleWith	•																																														
intersectionOf	•							•	•								•																													•	
inverseOf	•																																														
maxCardinality	•																									•																					
maxQualifiedCardinality																																															
members	•																								•														•								
minCardinality	•																									•																					
minQualifiedCardinality	•																								•																						
onClass																																															
onDataRange																																															
onDatatype																																															
oneOf	•											•	•					•																									•	•			
onProperties																																															
onProperty	•		•																					•	•	•	•	•																			
priorVersion	•	•																																													
propertyChainAxiom	•																																														
propertyDisjointWith	•																																														
qualifiedCardinality																																															
sameAs	•																																							•							
someValuesFrom	•																									•																					
sourceIndividual	•																																									•	•					
targetIndividual	•																																									•						
targetValue	•																																										•					
topDataProperty																																															
topObjectProperty																																															
unionOf	•				•	•										•																													•		
versionInfo	•	•																																													
versionIRI	•	•																																													
withRestrictions																																															

- continued on next page -

Table 2. Coverage of OntoViBe 2 elements with respect to OWL constructs (*part II*)

- continued from previous page -

"•" indicates that the respective OWL syntax element is included in OntoViBe, while "o" means that an equivalent syntax element is used.

Namespace prefix "a:" denotes elements of the core ontology, while elements from the imported ontology are marked with "b:"

Construct	a:standardTypeDatatypeProperty	a:untypedDatatypeProperty	a:customTypeDatatypeProperty	a:unionTypeDatatypeProperty	a:intersectionTypeDatatypeProperty	a:complementTypeDatatypeProperty	a:importedTypeDatatypeProperty	a:classToClassProperty	a:classToUntypedClassProperty	a:untypedClassToClassProperty	a:EquivalentToPropertyOwner	a:EquivalentToSubclass	a:AlsoEquivalentToSubclass	a:cyclicProperty1	HasSelfRestriction	a:cyclicProperty2	a:cyclicProperty3	a:classToClassProperty1	a:classToClassProperty2	a:deprecatedDatatypeProperty	a:deprecatedObjectProperty	a:dummyProperty	a:oppositeDummyProperty	a:equivalentObjectProperty	a:subproperty	a:realProperty	a:equivalentDataProperty	a:anotherEquivalentDataProperty	a:rationalProperty	a:FunctionalAnchor	a:FunctionalProperty	a:functionalProperty	a:inverseFunctionalProperty	a:functionalPropertyAsInverse	a:functionalDatatypeProperty	a:disjointProperty	:DisjointPropertyGroup	b:	b:ImportedClass	b:DeprecatedImportedClass	b:EquivalentImportedClass	b:EquivalentImportedClassInLargeGroup	b:DivisibleByThreeEnumeration	b:importedObjectPropertyWithRange	b:importedObjectPropertyWithDomain	b:importedDatatypeProperty	b:deprecatedImportedObjectProperty	b:deprecatedImportedDatatypeProperty
• AllDifferent																																																
• AllDisjointClasses																																																
• AllDisjointProperties																																					•											
Annotation																																																
AnnotationProperty																																																
• AsymmetricProperty								•																																								
Axiom																																																
• Class								•	•	•																					•								•	•	•							
o DataRange																																					o											
• DatatypeProperty	•	•	•	•	•	•	•														•						•	•	•	•																•		•
o DeprecatedClass																																								o								
o DeprecatedProperty																				o	o																			o							o	o
• FunctionalProperty																															•		•	•	•													
• InverseFunctionalProperty																																	•															
• IrreflexiveProperty																•																																
NamedIndividual																																																
• NegativePropertyAssertion																																																
Nothing																																																
• ObjectProperty								•						•	•			•	•			•	•	•	•	•					•					•								•	•		•	
• Ontology																																								•								
OntologyProperty																																																
• ReflexiveProperty														•																																		
• Restriction															•																																	
• SymmetricProperty								•																																								
• Thing																•																																
• TransitiveProperty																																		•														
• allValuesFrom																																																
annotatedProperty																																																
annotatedSource																																																
annotatedTarget																																																
assertionProperty																																																
• backwardCompatibleWith																																								•								
bottomDataProperty																																																
bottomObjectProperty																																																
• cardinality																																																
• complementOf																																																
• datatypeComplementOf																																																
• deprecated																				•	•																			•							•	•
• differentFrom																																																
• disjointUnionOf																																																
• disjointWith																																																
distinctMembers																																																
• equivalentClass								•	•	•																															•							
• equivalentProperty																								•			•	•																				
• hasKey																																																
• hasSelf															•																																	
• hasValue																																																
• imports																																								•								
• incompatibleWith																																								•								
• intersectionOf																																																
• inverseOf																																	•															
• maxCardinality																																																
maxQualifiedCardinality																																																
• members																																								•								
• minCardinality																																																
minQualifiedCardinality																																																
onClass																																																
onDataRange																																																
onDatatype																																																
• oneOf																																										•						
onProperties																																																
• onProperty														•																																		
• priorVersion																																								•								
propertyChainAxiom																																																
• propertyDisjointWith																																				•												
qualifiedCardinality																																																
• sameAs																																																
someValuesFrom																																																
sourceIndividual																																																
targetIndividual																																																
targetValue																																																
topDataProperty																																																
topObjectProperty																																																
• unionOf																																																
• versionInfo																																								•								
• versionIRI																																								•								
withRestrictions																																																

Listing 1.4. OntoViBe defines custom OWL data ranges.

```
234  this:DivisibleByFiveEnumeration a rdfs:Datatype ;
235    owl:equivalentClass [
236      a rdfs:Datatype ;
237      owl:oneOf ( 5 10 15 20 )
238    ].
```

Listing 1.5. Both custom and common datatypes are used by properties.

```
254  this:standardTypeDatatypeProperty a owl:DatatypeProperty ;
255    rdfs:domain this:PropertyOwner ;
256    rdfs:range xsd:integer .
257
258  this:customTypeDatatypeProperty a owl:DatatypeProperty ;
259    rdfs:domain this:PropertyOwner ;
260    rdfs:range this:DivisibleByFiveEnumeration .
```

considered in OntoViBe. For instance, Listing 1.6 shows two cyclic properties
(i.e., properties whose domain and range are identical) connected to the same
class.

In addition, a few of the ontology elements are provided with labels, to check
how visualizations cope with multilingual labels that may also contain non-
ASCII characters (Listing 1.7). We used the escaped ASCII representation for
all non-ASCII characters, as that maximizes the chances for a good compatibility
with parsers reading the ontology files. We also annotated some elements with
`rdfs:comment` and `dc:description` properties using multilingual text strings
(Listing 1.1 and Listing 1.6).

Finally, we added annotations to the ontology header, including OWL version
information and common Dublin Core metadata (author, title, description, etc.).
A test case where any such metadata is missing is provided by the *minimal
ontology*.

3.2 Coverage and Omissions

To verify that OntoViBe 2 covers most of the concepts defined in the OWL 2
specifications, we provide a coverage matrix (Table 1 and Table 2). It lists all
OWL 2 language constructs (as per the IRIs declared in the OWL 2 Namespace Document [2]) and shows where they are used in OntoViBe 2. Note that
only the elements of the core and imported ontology are included in the coverage matrix, as these are the key modules of OntoViBe 2. The cardinality
module is not included—it has a different purpose and would add a large number of elements to the matrix while covering only two more OWL 2 language
constructs not already included in the *core* and *imported* ontologies, namely
`owl:qualifiedCardinality` and `owl:maxQualifiedCardinality`.

A few OWL elements were intentionally not included in OntoViBe 2, as indicated by the coverage matrix:

Listing 1.6. Sets of properties connected to the same classes allow for testing whether a visualization positions such properties in a non-overlapping way. This example shows two cyclic properties connected to the same class.

```
316  this:cyclicProperty2 a owl:ReflexiveProperty ;
317    rdfs:domain this:MultiPropertyOwner ;
318    rdfs:range this:MultiPropertyOwner ;
319    rdfs:comment "This is an English comment on a property that also has a
               non-English description."@en ;
320    dc:description "Dies ist eine deutsche Beschreibung einer Eigenschaft,
               die auch einen nicht in Deutsch verfassten Kommentar enth\u00E4lt."
               @de .
321
322  this:cyclicProperty3 a owl:ObjectProperty ;
323    rdfs:domain this:MultiPropertyOwner ;
324    rdfs:range this:MultiPropertyOwner .
```

Listing 1.7. Multilingual labels, some of which contain characters from different scripts, exist for a few of the ontology elements.

```
276  this:importedTypeDatatypeProperty a owl:DatatypeProperty ;
277    rdfs:domain this:PropertyOwner ;
278    rdfs:range other:DivisibleByThreeEnumeration ;
279    rdfs:label "imported type datatype property"@en ;
280    rdfs:label "propri\u00E9t\u00E9 d'un type de donn\u00E9es import\u00E9"
               @fr ;
281    rdfs:label "\u4E00\u79CD\u5BFC\u5165\u7C7B\u578B\u7684\u6570\u636E\u7C7B\
               u578B\u6027\u8D28"@zh-Hans .
```

Complex anonymous classes: OntoViBe 2 contains some anonymous classes in combination with set operators, such as *union* and *intersection*. It also features some named classes based on complex class expressions for enumeration types or `owl:allValuesFrom` restrictions. Anonymous classes using these latter class expressions are, however, not included, as this would result in an unnecessarily large and redundant ontology.

Equivalent elements: In cases of syntactically equivalent ways to express statements in OWL, only one way has been integrated into OntoViBe. For instance, deprecation of ontology elements can either be expressed by adding the `owl:deprecated` attribute or by declaring the element as belonging to one of the classes `owl:DeprecatedClass` or `owl:DeprecatedProperty`.

Deprecated elements: Deprecated language constructs of OWL are not used in OntoViBe. An example is `owl:DataRange` that has been deprecated in favor of `rdfs:Datatype` as of OWL 2 [2].

4   Examples of Application

A requirement for applying OntoViBe is that the corresponding tool is capable of interpreting OWL 2 ontologies. For that reason, OntoViBe cannot be processed and visualized by a number of older visualization tools and prototypes. Moreover, we found that some implementations of OWL 2 parsers exhibit technical issues when loading OntoViBe, although OntoViBe is conformant with the OWL 2 specifications, as also confirmed by the validator of the OWL API reference implementation (version 3.4.5) [10]. However, we expect that support for OWL 2 ontologies like OntoViBe will gradually increase in the next years.

In this section, we take a look at a selection of tools that are able to process and visualize OntoViBe 2.[5] We show the visualizations generated by the tools for the *core* and *imported* ontology modules of OntoViBe 2, giving an impression of the supported features. We point out peculiarities of the visualizations and their implementations that become apparent based on OntoViBe 2. By this, we would like to provide some examples of how to use OntoViBe for the qualitative analysis of ontology visualizations.

It should be noted that a comprehensive analysis of ontology visualizations requires additional methods and measures, such as a checklist comprising further evaluation criteria. Those methods are typically not generic but tailored to the type of visualization. For instance, measures for graph visualizations of ontologies could include the number of edges and edge crossings. However, such quantitative analyses are outside the scope of this work.

4.1 VOWL

The Visual Notation for OWL Ontologies (VOWL) has been developed as a means to both obtain a structural overview of OWL ontologies and recognize various attributes of ontology elements at a glance [14]. It has been implemented in two different tools, a plugin for the ontology editor Protégé [13] and a responsive web application called WebVOWL [12], which provides a more complete implementation of the VOWL 2 specification than the Protégé plugin. Figure 1 has been created with version 0.3.3 of WebVOWL (and version 0.1.4 of its OWL2VOWL converter).[6]

Visualizing OntoViBe 2 with WebVOWL shows some typical characteristics of VOWL visualizations, such as equivalent classes being represented in a single node with a double border, other special elements being multiplied in the visualization (e.g., `owl:Thing`), or text in brackets below the labels indicating attributes such as *functional* or *deprecated*.

However, custom data ranges are not fully visualized in VOWL 2, as can be seen by the respective datatype nodes (on the right hand side of Figure 1) that display only the names of the data ranges (e.g., "Divisib..." for `DivisibleByFiveEnumeration`) but no more information. In addition, the custom data ranges are represented by classes (e.g. "DivisibleByFiv..." for `DivisibleByFiveEnumeration`, on the left) that are connected via set operators representing other datatypes of OntoViBe (e.g., `UnionDatatype`).

---

[5] In contrast to our earlier paper on OntoViBe [9], the ontology visualization SOVA is not included, as it failed to parse OntoViBe 2. In addition, we replaced the hierarchical OWLViz visualization with the UML-based visualization of OWLGrEd.

[6] The interactive WebVOWL visualization of OntoViBe is available at http://vowl. visualdataweb.org/webvowl/#ontovibe.

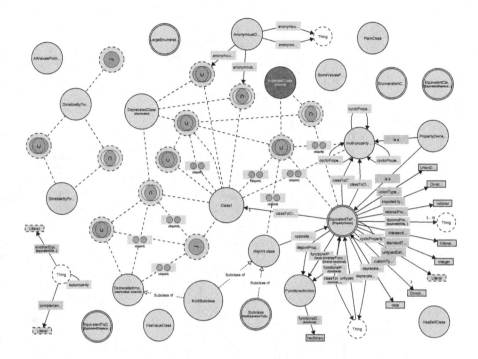

Fig. 1. OntoViBe 2 visualized with WebVOWL 0.3.3 [12]

4.2   OWLGrEd

OWLGrEd [4] uses a UML-based diagram to visualize OntoViBe 2, as shown
in Figure 2.[7] It therefore features some UML-specific visualization attributes
in contrast to the VOWL visualization, such as the typical class notation of
UML listing datatype properties linked to the class in this case. OWLGrEd also
includes annotations (e.g., comments) in the visualization, whereas WebVOWL
lists such details in a separate part of the user interface (not shown in Figure 1).
However, annotations and datatype properties are removed from the visualization when switching to the Compact Diagram Mode provided by OWLGrEd.

Links and restrictions of classes and individuals are displayed with a variety
of graphical features. As becomes evident from the large number of interlinked
elements in OntoViBe 2, not all of the connection lines in OWLGrEd are helpful
for understanding relationships in the ontology. Many of them are routed in
a suboptimal way (even after some manual adjustment of the automatically
generated layout), so that it is hard to follow and distinguish an individual
connection line. This does not change in the Compact Diagram Mode, either.

---

[7] The desktop and online edition of OWLGrEd are available at http://owlgred.lumii.
lv. Figure 2 has been created with the desktop edition (version 1.6.0), since the
online edition failed to load OntoViBe 2.

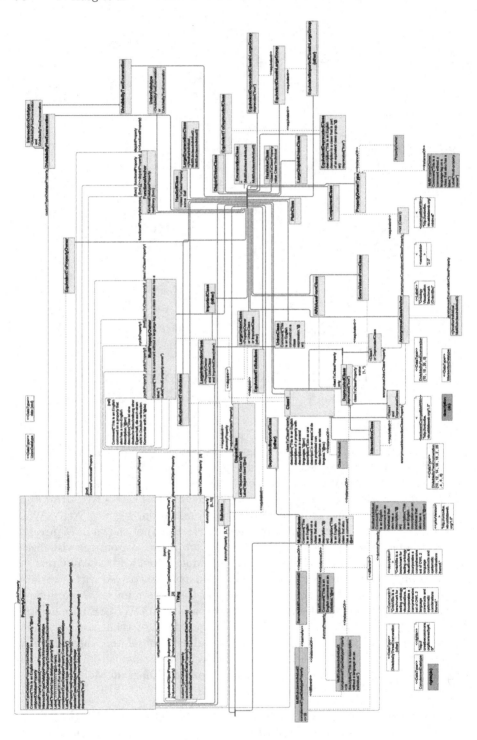

Fig. 2. OntoViBe 2 visualized with OWLGrEd 1.6.0 [4]

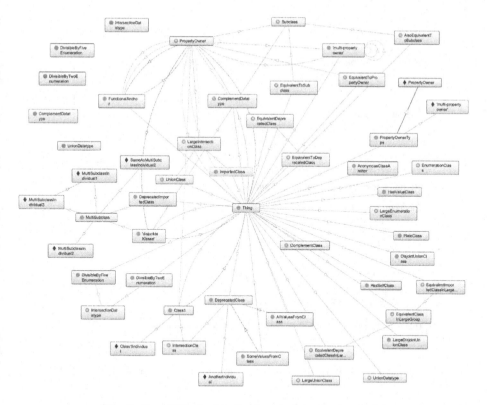

Fig. 3. OntoViBe 2 visualized with OntoGraf 1.0.3 [7]

On the other hand, the question which kinds of items (classes, individuals, etc.) and how many of them are contained in the ontology can be quickly answered based on the different colors, and further information on each element can be directly found in the visualization. In particular, this means that even the custom data range definitions and ontology annotations defined by OntoViBe 2 are clearly indicated in the visualization.

4.3   OntoGraf

OntoGraf [7] is a visualization plugin included in the default installation of the Protégé desktop edition. The visualization of Figure 3 has been created with version 1.0.3 of the plugin that comes with Protégé 5.0.0. OntoGraf depicts the classes, individuals, and custom data ranges of OntoViBe 2 as nodes that are linked by properties. The type of each node is indicated by a colored symbol, the type and direction of each property by a colored directed edge.

Overall, the visualization contains several edge crossings, which reduce its readability. A large number of these edges result from the fact that all implicit subclass relations to owl:Thing are depicted in the visualization. However, it is also visible that OntoGraf copes well with cyclic properties applied to the same

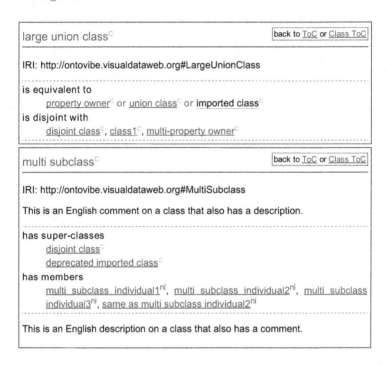

Fig. 4. Excerpt of the HTML document for OntoViBe 2 generated by LODE 1.2 [17]

class, as these are depicted in a non-overlapping way (see class `MultiProperty-Owner` in the upper right of Figure 3).

In contrast to VOWL and OWLGrEd, less information is shown in the visualization. While additional details about the elements, such as IRIs and annotations, are provided in tooltips, important information is missing. For instance, there are neither representations for anonymous classes nor for set operators or cardinalities and other property restrictions. Like in VOWL, only the names of the custom data ranges are shown, but no additional information is visible. Finally, it is unclear from the visualization which of the elements belong to the *core ontology* and which are from the *imported ontology*.

4.4   LODE

LODE is a documentation generator for ontologies [17]. While LODE does not provide a visual representation, the output after processing OntoViBe 2 can be examined in a similar fashion. Features that get apparent in the HTML-based excerpt shown in Figure 4[8] include the transformation of the camel-cased element names into separate words (e.g., `DeprecatedClass` becomes "deprecated

---

[8] The excerpt has been created with version 1.2 of LODE that is available as an online service at http://www.essepuntato.it/lode.

class"), and the lists of superclasses, members, equivalent, and disjoint classes. Annotations, such as comments and descriptions, are also added to the generated HTML document.

5   Conclusion

Based on the OWL 2 specifications, we have developed OntoViBe, a benchmark for testing ontology visualizations. We did not focus on scalability, execution time, or other common benchmark goals, but rather on feature completeness and flexibility in terms of combinations of elements with regard to the OWL 2 specifications. Since OWL may further evolve in the future, OntoViBe needs to keep being updated accordingly. Generally, we hope that our experiences from the development of OntoViBe can benefit other projects, including benchmark data models beyond the task of ontology visualization.

References

1. Ontology Alignment Evaluation Initiative. http://oaei.ontologymatching.org
2. The OWL 2 Schema Vocabulary (2009). http://www.w3.org/2002/07/owl.rdf
3. Bail, S., Parsia, B., Sattler, U.: JustBench: a framework for OWL benchmarking. In: Patel-Schneider, P.F., Pan, Y., Hitzler, P., Mika, P., Zhang, L., Pan, J.Z., Horrocks, I., Glimm, B. (eds.) ISWC 2010, Part I. LNCS, vol. 6496, pp. 32–47. Springer, Heidelberg (2010)
4. Bārzdiņš, J., Bārzdiņš, G., Čerāns, K., Liepiņš, R., Sproģis, A.: UML style graphical notation and editor for OWL 2. In: Forbrig, P., Günther, H. (eds.) BIR 2010. LNBIP, vol. 64, pp. 102–114. Springer, Heidelberg (2010)
5. Carroll, J.J., Roo, J.D.: OWL web ontology language test cases (2004). http://www.w3.org/TR/owl-test/
6. Dudáš, M., Zamazal, O., Svátek, V.: Roadmapping and navigating in the ontology visualization landscape. In: Janowicz, K., Schlobach, S., Lambrix, P., Hyvönen, E. (eds.) EKAW 2014. LNCS, vol. 8876, pp. 137–152. Springer, Heidelberg (2014)
7. Falconer, S.: OntoGraf (2010). http://protegewiki.stanford.edu/wiki/OntoGraf
8. Guo, Y., Pan, Z., Heflin, J.: LUBM: A benchmark for OWL knowledge base systems. Web Semantics 3(2–3), 158–182 (2005)
9. Haag, F., Lohmann, S., Negru, S., Ertl, T.: OntoViBe: an ontology visualization benchmark. In: International Workshop on Visualizations and User Interfaces for Knowledge Engineering and Linked Data Analytics (VISUAL 2014), vol. 1299, pp. 14–27. CEUR-WS (2014)
10. Horridge, M., Bechhofer, S.: The OWL API: A java API for OWL ontologies. Semantic Web 2(1), 11–21 (2011)
11. Katifori, A., Halatsis, C., Lepouras, G., Vassilakis, C., Giannopoulou, E.: Ontology visualization methods - a survey. ACM Computing Surveys 39(4), 10:1–10:43 (2007)
12. Lohmann, S., Link, V., Marbach, E., Negru, S.: WebVOWL: Web-based visualization of ontologies. In: Lambrix, P., et al. (eds.) EKAW 2014 Satellite Events. LNAI, pp. 154–158. Springer (2015). doi:10.1007/978-3-319-17966-721

13. Lohmann, S., Negru, S., Bold, D.: The ProtégéVOWL plugin: ontology visualization for everyone. In: Presutti, V., Blomqvist, E., Troncy, R., Sack, H., Papadakis, I., Tordai, A. (eds.) ESWC 2014 Satellite Events. LNCS, pp. 395–400. Springer, Heidelberg (2014)

14. Lohmann, S., Negru, S., Haag, F., Ertl, T.: VOWL 2: user-oriented visualization of ontologies. In: Janowicz, K., Schlobach, S., Lambrix, P., Hyvönen, E. (eds.) EKAW 2014. LNCS, vol. 8876, pp. 266–281. Springer, Heidelberg (2014)

15. Ma, L., Yang, Y., Qiu, Z., Xie, G.T., Pan, Y., Liu, S.: Towards a complete OWL ontology benchmark. In: Sure, Y., Domingue, J. (eds.) ESWC 2006. LNCS, vol. 4011, pp. 125–139. Springer, Heidelberg (2006)

16. Meilicke, C., García-Castro, R., Freitas, F., Van Hage, W.R., Montiel-Ponsoda, E.: Ribeiro De Azevedo, R., Stuckenschmidt, H., Šváb Zamazal, O., Svátek, V., Tamilin, A., Trojahn, C., Wang, S.: MultiFarm: A benchmark for multilingual ontology matching. Web Semantics 15, 62–68 (2012)

17. Peroni, S., Shotton, D., Vitali, F.: The live OWL documentation environment: a tool for the automatic generation of ontology documentation. In: ten Teije, A., Völker, J., Handschuh, S., Stuckenschmidt, H., d'Acquin, M., Nikolov, A., Aussenac-Gilles, N., Hernandez, N. (eds.) EKAW 2012. LNCS, vol. 7603, pp. 398–412. Springer, Heidelberg (2012)

18. Smith, M., Horrocks, I., Krötzsch, M., Glimm, B.: OWL 2 web ontology language conformance (second edition) (2012). http://www.w3.org/TR/owl2-conformance/

19. Šváb, O., Svátek, V., Berka, P., Rak, D., Tomášek, P.: OntoFarm: towards an experimental collection of parallel ontologies. In: Poster Track of ISWC 2005 (2005)

20. W3C: OWL - semantic web standards (2004). http://www.w3.org/2004/OWL/

21. W3C OWL Working Group: OWL 2 web ontology language document overview (second edition) (2012). http://www.w3.org/TR/owl2-overview/

22. Wang, S.-Y., Guo, Y., Qasem, A., Heflin, J.: Rapid benchmarking for semantic web knowledge base systems. In: Gil, Y., Motta, E., Benjamins, V.R., Musen, M.A. (eds.) ISWC 2005. LNCS, vol. 3729, pp. 758–772. Springer, Heidelberg (2005).

Posters

The Semantic Lancet Project: A Linked Open Dataset for Scholarly Publishing

Andrea Bagnacani[1], Paolo Ciancarini[1,2], Angelo Di Iorio[1],
Andrea Giovanni Nuzzolese[2], Silvio Peroni[1,2(✉)], and Fabio Vitali[1]

[1] Department of Computer Science and Engineering,
University of Bologna, Bologna, Italy
andrea.bagnacani@studio.unibo.it,
{paolo.ciancarini,angelo.diiorio,silvio.peroni,fabio.vitali}@unibo.it
[2] Semantic Technology Laboratory, ISTC-CNR, Rome, Italy
andrea.nuzzolese@istc.cnr.it

Abstract. In this poster we introduce the *Semantic Lancet Project*, whose goal is to make available rich data about scholarly publications and to provide users with sophisticated services on top of those data.

Keywords: Data reengineering and enhancement · Linked open data · Scholarly data · Semantic lancet project · Semantic publishing · SPAR ontologies

1 Introduction

The availability of rich open (linked) data about scholarly data opens the way to novel applications for a large spectrum of users. The knowledge management of scholarly products is an emerging research area, and involves different users such as authors (for gathering personal repositories of papers), publishers (for constructing repositories of assets from venues), institutions and funding agencies (for ranking research assets). Even if there is interest in publishing such data as Linked Open Data (LOD), the current landscape is fragmented: some projects focus on bibliographic data (e.g., Nature Publishing Group LOD Platform[1]), others on authorship data (e.g., DBLP++[2]), others on citations (e.g., OpenCitation corpus [2,4]).

In this poster we introduce the *Semantic Lancet Project*, whose goal is to make available rich scholarly data and to provide users with sophisticated services on top of those data. The structure of the paper is as follows: Section 2 introduces our project, while Section 3 sketches out some future works.

---

[1] http://www.nature.com/developers/documentation/linked-data-platform/
[2] http://dblp.l3s.de/dblp++.php

© Springer International Publishing Switzerland 2015
P. Lambrix et al. (Eds.): EKAW 2014 Satellite Events, LNAI 8982, pp. 101–105, 2015.
DOI: 10.1007/978-3-319-17966-7_10

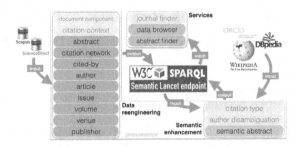

Fig. 1. The overall structure of the Semantic Lancet Project. The blurry blocks (e.g., *document component, citation type, journal finder*) are currently under development.

2   Semantic Lancet Project

The *Semantic Lancet Project* (http://www.semanticlancet.eu) is focused on building a Linked Open Dataset of scholarly publications. The aim of the project is twofold. On the one hand, we want to develop a series of scripts that allow us to produce proper RDF data compliant with the *Semantic Publishing and Referencing (SPAR) Ontologies* (http://www.sparontologies.net). On the other hand, we want to make publicly-available a rich RDF triplestore[3] (accompanied by a SPARQL endpoint) and a series of services built upon it starting from the data made available from Elsevier – while preparing the whole infrastructure in order to facilitate the future managing of data coming from other publishers. We have already converted and published on the Semantic Lancet triplestore all the data concerning the Journal of Web Semantics[4] (367 articles, 80920 RDF statements). The framework of the Semantic Lancet Project, summarised in Fig. 1, is composed basically by three macro sections, that we briefly introduce as follows[5].

Data reengineering. The data reengineering section is the one responsible of the translation of the raw data coming from the Science Direct and Scopus[6] repositories into RDF. Even if this could seem a duplication of the same data, gathering data from both repositories is a required action since some of the data in Scopus may be missing (e.g., there is no DOI specified for some articles) or wrong (e.g., the issue number of a certain article is zero) while they may be complete and correct in Science Direct, and vice versa. Such a 'twofold' approach improves the quality of the imported data[7].

---

[3] The triplestore we are currently using is Fuseki.

[4] http://www.journals.elsevier.com/journal-of-web-semantics

[5] The *provenance* module included in Fig. 1 is still under development.

[6] Science Direct (http://sciencedirect.com); Scopus (http://www.scopus.com).

[7] From a preliminary analysis performed considering 10 different journals coming from different academic disciplines, we decided to use Science Direct as base repository and Scopus for addressing incorrectness/missing in data.

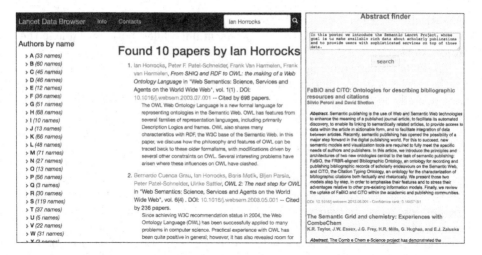

Fig. 2. The Semantic Lancet data browser (left) and abstract finder (right)

Basically, two kinds of data are requested by using the API made available by Elsevier[8]: those referring to metadata of articles and those concerning the full text of articles. The collected data are processed by a chain of scripts, one for each block of the data reengineering section shown in the left side of Fig. 1; each script retrieves all the data of interest and convert them into proper SPAR-based RDF statements.

Semantic enhancement. The following step of our workflow consists of enriching the dataset with more semantic data, that can be exploited for sophisticated end-user applications. On the one hand, some of these data are derived from the content of the papers by extracting semantic features from unstructured or semi-structured text and representing them as RDF [1]. On the other hand, the other data are the result of further refinement of the existing dataset.

Currently we have implemented a module for generating *semantic abstracts*. The generation of semantic abstracts relies mainly on FRED[9][3], which is a tool that implements deep machine reading methods based on Discourse Representation Theory, Linguistic Frames, and Ontology Design Patterns. FRED allows us to derive an OWL representation of the natural language sentences contained in the abstract, as well as to retrieve entities (e.g., DBpedia resources) that are cited in the abstracts.

Services. The framework is completed by a set of services for accessing, making sense and exploiting the (semantic) information available in the dataset. This part is shown in the top of Fig. 1 and consists of an extensible set of modules. Each module is independent from the others, it is built on top of the underlying

---

[8] http://www.developers.elsevier.com/devcms/content-apis

[9] http://wit.istc.cnr.it/stlab-tools/fred

semantically-enriched data, and it provides particular functionalities to the user. We have currently implemented two experimental modules, both available in the project website: the *data browser* and the *abstract finder*.

The *data browser* (cf. Fig. 2, on the left) is an interactive and user-friendly interface, with autocompletion and incremental loading of content, that allows users to easily access authors and their papers. The solution we propose is to hide the intrinsic complexities of the data and of the underlying technologies, giving users an higher-level view over the dataset content. The tool, in fact, does not show directly the entities stored in the dataset but groups those entities in more abstract "objects" that are finally shown to the users. A paper, for instance, is internally modelled according to the SPAR model, thus according to FRBR [5], and is defined in terms of Work, Expression(s), Manifestation(s) and Item(s). The dataset items are transparent to the user (though are available to software agents) who only deals with the concept of "paper". The same happens for properties: there is no distinction between object properties and data properties visible to the user. That distinction is in the dataset, and can be browsed on demand, but is fully hidden by default. Users, in fact, are not expected to master directly the Semantic Web technologies.

The *abstract finder* allows us to retrieve relevant papers according to their textual abstract as well as to the related *semantic abstract* – i.e., by exploiting the semantic information about concepts, events, roles and named entities produced during the *semantic enhancement* step. This tool works in two phases. First, it creates a *semiotic index* of the semantic abstracts with respect to the related taxonomy of types defined within them – that are aligned to WordNet synsets and DBpedia resources. In this way we can index the papers according to the textual content of their abstracts as well as the concepts represented in that content. Finally, a simple interface (cf. Fig. 2, on the right) allows users to query for papers having similar abstracts to the text specified as input.

3   Conclusions

In this poster we presented the *Semantic Lancet Project*, which aims at making available rich scholarly data and at providing users with sophisticated services on top of those data. There are other services we can build on our dataset in the future, once extended with more journals and kinds of data – e.g., citation contexts, citation functions, authors' affiliations and documents' internal components. In addition, some refinements are still under development, such as the disambiguation of authors' names and the inclusion of provenance information.

Acknowledgments. We would like to thank Elsevier for granting access to Scopus and ScienceDirect APIs.

References

1. Gangemi, A.: A comparison of knowledge extraction tools for the semantic web. In: Cimiano, P., Corcho, O., Presutti, V., Hollink, L., Rudolph, S. (eds.) ESWC 2013. LNCS, vol. 7882, pp. 351–366. Springer, Heidelberg (2013). doi:10.1007/978-3-642-38288-824
2. Peroni, S., Gray, T., Dutton, A., Shotton, D.: Setting our bibliographic references free: towards open citation data. Journal of Documentation **71**(2), (2015). doi:10.1108/JD-12-2013-0166
3. Presutti, V., Draicchio, F., Gangemi, A.: Knowledge extraction based on discourse representation theory and linguistic frames. In: ten Teije, A., Völker, J., Handschuh, S., Stuckenschmidt, H., d'Acquin, M., Nikolov, A., Aussenac-Gilles, N., Hernandez, N. (eds.) EKAW 2012. LNCS, vol. 7603, pp. 114–129. Springer, Heidelberg (2012). doi:10.1007/978-3-642-33876-212
4. Shotton, D.: Open citations. Nature **502**(7471) (2013). doi:10.1038/502295a
5. IFLA Study Group on the FRBR. Functional Requirements for Bibliographic Records (2009). http://www.ifla.org/publications/functional-requirements-for-bibliographic-records

Personalised, Serendipitous and Diverse Linked Data Resource Recommendations

Milan Dojchinovski[(✉)] and Tomas Vitvar

Web Intelligence Research Group, Faculty of Information Technology,
Czech Technical University in Prague, Prague, Czech Republic
{Milan.Dojchinovski,Tomas.Vitvar}@fit.cvut.cz

Abstract. Due to the huge and diverse amount of information, the actual access to a piece of information in the Linked Open Data (LOD) cloud still demands significant amount of effort. To overcome this problem, number of Linked Data based recommender systems have been developed. However, they have been primarily developed for a particular domain, they require human intervention in the dataset pre-processing step, and they can be hardly adopted to new datasets. In this paper, we present our method for personalised access to Linked Data, in particular focusing on its applicability and its salient features.

Keywords: Personalisation · Recommendation · Linked data · Semantic distance · Similarity metric

1 Introduction

Due to the huge and diverse amount of information, the actual access to a piece of information in the Linked Open Data (LOD) cloud still demands significant amount of effort. To overcome this problem, number of Linked Data based recommender systems have been developed. However, they have been primarily developed for a particular domain (e.g., music or videos), they require human intervention in the dataset pre-processing step, and they can be hardly adopted to other datasets.

In our related EKAW 2014 research paper [3], we described in detail our method for "personalised access to Linked Data". In this paper, we focus on its usage in different domains and datasets, and its salient features. Section 2 describes the resource recommendation workflow. Section 3 presents a resource recommendation case study from the Web services domain. Finally, Section 4 highlights its salient features.

2 Linked Data Resource Recommendation

The prototype of our method implements the workflow depicted in Figure 1. It starts with (i) Linked Data datasets and user profiles import, followed by

© Springer International Publishing Switzerland 2015
P. Lambrix et al. (Eds.): EKAW 2014 Satellite Events, LNAI 8982, pp. 106–110, 2015.
DOI: 10.1007/978-3-319-17966-7_11

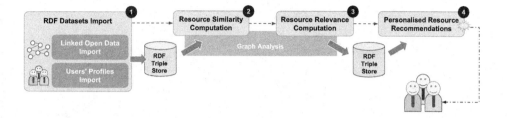

Fig. 1. Overview of the resource recommendation workflow

(ii) graph based data analysis, and ends with (iii) generation of personalised Linked Data resource recommendations.

RDF Datasets Import. First, it is necessary to identify one or more datasets which contain the resources of interest. The datasets can be single domain datasets such as GeoNames, or multi-domain datasets such as DBpedia. It is also necessary to provide users' profiles information which encodes users' activities and their relations to other people and resources. According to the statistics as of April 2014 [5], 48% of all datasets in the LOD cloud are datasets providing social information such as people profiles data and social relationships among them. Note that the RDF data is imported and analysed in its original form. In other words, we do not perform any domain-dependent selection or filtering of the information. For comparison, the movie recommender described in [1] uses only a subset of the information, defined as a set of RDF properties.

Graph Analysis. Our resource recommendation method is based on the collaborative filtering technique and it recommends resources from users with interests in similar resources. To measure the user similarity, we perform graph based analysis of the users' RDF context graphs. To this end, we introduce a novel domain–independent semantic resource similarity metric, which takes into account the *commonalities* and *informativeness* of the shared resources. Our assumption is that the more information two resources share, the more similar they are. And second, the more informative resources they have in common, the more similar they are. The resources informativeness is primarily incorporated to differentiate informative shared resources from non-informative (e.g., *owl:Thing* or *skos:Concept*).

    Figure 2 illustrates computation of similarity between two users, *Alfredo* and *mlachwani*. The users have 6 resources in common, which convey different amount of information content. According to our assumption, resources with high graph degree value convey less information content, than resources with lower graph degree. Considering the whole Linked Web APIs dataset, the Facebook API with node degree of 418, is more informative and carries more similarity information than the Twitter API, with node degree of 799. Facebook API is characterised with a lower degree due to its lower usage in mashups, leading to a lower number of incident links.

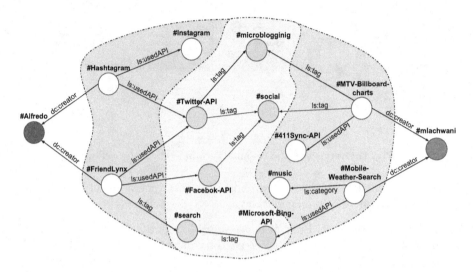

Fig. 2. Excerpt from the Linked Web APIs dataset with resource context graphs with context distance of 3

Personalised Resource Recommendations. The similarities between the resources representing users are then used to compute the relevance of each resource candidate. For a user requester, the method first computes the *connectivity* between each similar user (i.e., a user similar with the user requester) and each resource candidate. The connectivity is computed as the amount of gained information between the similar user and the resource candidate. The final relevance score aggregates the user similarity scores and the connectivity scores for the resource candidate. Finally, the method returns the top-n most relevant resources for the user requester.

3   Case Study: Recommendation of Linked Web APIs

In this section we show a resource recommendation case study on the Linked Web APIs dataset [2], which provides RDF representation of the Pro- grammableWeb.com service repository as of April 24th 2014. The datasets pro- vides descriptions for 11,339 Web APIs, 7,415 mashups and 5,907 users.

Step 1: Identification of Requesters and Items of Interest. We start with identification of resources representing requesters and resources represent- ing items of interest. In our case, requesters are users represented with the *foaf:Person* class and items of interests are Web APIs represented with the *wl:Service* class. If we want to develop a music recommendation system for recommendation of artists and bands, it will be necessary to specify the class describing those resources of interest. In DBpedia those are resources of type *dbpedia:MusicalArtist* and *dbpedia:Band*.

Step 2: Data Analysis. Next, the method computes the similarities between resources representing users (i.e., *foaf:Person*) and computes the relevance of each resource candidate for each user. In this step, the resource information content is also computed and considered.

Step 3: Generate Resource Recommendations. Finally, the method can generates a list of top-n most relevant resources for the user requester.

4   Salient Features

Serendipitous and Diverse Recommendations. For any recommender system it is important to accommodate the difference between the individuals in order to produce accurate, while at the same time serendipitous and diverse recommendations. The results from our evaluation [3] show that our method satisfy these requirements and also outperforms the traditional personalised collaborative filtering methods and non-personalised methods.

Adaptability. One drawback of the existing Linked Data based recommendation systems [1,4] is their applicability on different datasets due to the metric used for computation of the resource similarity. The metrics used in [1,4] are not suitable for computation of similarities between resources in datasets (i.e., the Linked Web APIs dataset), where the graph distance between the resources is more than two. In comparison, our method can be easily adapted to any dataset by setting the size of the resource context. In datasets, where the users in the RDF graph are close to each other, will require setting lower distance, while in datasets where the users are far, will require higher distance. Choosing small context distance in datasets where the users are far from each other, can possibly lead to no overlap of the resource context graphs, and no similarity evidenced.

Cross-Dataset and Domain Recommendations. As shown in Section 2, without any restrictions our method can consume and benefit from one or more Linked Data datasets from different domains, and at the same time produce resource recommendations for these domains and datasets. In contrast, the methods presented in [1,4] use only subsets of Linked Data datasets, which need to be defined in advance for the particular domain.

Acknowledgments. This work was supported by the Grant Agency of the Czech Technical University in Prague, grant No. SGS14/104/OHK3/1T/18. We also thank to Programmableweb.com for supporting this research.

References

1. Di Noia, T., et al.: Linked open data to support content-based recommender systems. In: Proceedings of the 8th International Conference on Semantic Systems, I-SEMANTICS 2012, pp. 1–8. ACM, New York (2012)
2. Zaremba, M., Dojchinovski, M., Kuchar, J., Vitvar, T.: Personalised graph-based selection of web APIs. In: Cudré-Mauroux, P., Heflin, J., Sirin, E., Tudorache, T., Euzenat, J., Hauswirth, M., Parreira, J.X., Hendler, J., Schreiber, G., Bernstein, A., Blomqvist, E. (eds.) ISWC 2012, Part I. LNCS, vol. 7649, pp. 34–48. Springer, Heidelberg (2012)

3. Dojchinovski, M., Vitvar, T.: Personalised access to linked data. In: Janowicz, K., Schlobach, S., Lambrix, P., Hyvönen, E. (eds.) EKAW 2014. LNCS, vol. 8876, pp. 121–136. Springer, Heidelberg (2014)
4. Passant, A.: DBrec — Music recommendations using DBpedia. In: Patel-Schneider, P.F., Pan, Y., Hitzler, P., Mika, P., Zhang, L., Pan, J.Z., Horrocks, I., Glimm, B. (eds.) ISWC 2010, Part II. LNCS, vol. 6497, pp. 209–224. Springer, Heidelberg (2010)
5. Schmachtenberg, M., Bizer, C., Paulheim, H.: Adoption of the linked data best practices in different topical domains. In: Mika, P., Tudorache, T., Bernstein, A., Welty, C., Knoblock, C., Vrandečić, D., Groth, P., Noy, N., Janowicz, K., Goble, C. (eds.) ISWC 2014, Part I. LNCS, vol. 8796, pp. 245–260. Springer, Heidelberg (2014)

Spreadsheet-Based Knowledge Acquisition for Facilitating Active Domain Expert Participation

Martina Freiberg[✉], Felix Herrmann, and Frank Puppe

Department of Artificial Intelligence and Applied Informatics,
Institute of Computer Science, University of Würzburg,
Am Hubland, D-97074 Würzburg, Germany
{martina.freiberg,felix.herrmann,frank.puppe}@uni-wuerzburg.de

Abstract. (Poster) We propose a spreadsheet-based knowledge acquisition (KA) approach for lowering the familiarization hurdle and thus increasing the ease of use and user experience for domain experts. Thus, by enabling experts to (mostly) autonomously participate in KA, the approach adds to the overall diversity of today's KA tool landscape.

Keywords: Knowledge engineering · Knowledge acquisition · Domain expert participation · Standard office tools · Spreadsheet software

1 Motivation

Offering a spreadsheet-based knowledge acquisition (KA) method facilitates participation in the development of knowledge-based consultation and documentation systems (KBS) also for domain experts. Potential benefits include: Reducing conceptual knowledge base (KB) errors due to the experts' domain expertise; or rendering overall KBS engineering more efficient as tasks can be distributed between experts and knowledge engineers. We motivate that spreadsheets impose a substantially lower familiarization hurdle on experts in contrast to complex KA tools, e.g., Protégé [4]. We propose a spreadsheet-based KA approach for engineering *rule-based* knowledge bases, and we summarize its integration within an encompassing KBS engineering process. Also, we delineate promising practical experiences in two actual projects.

2 Spreadsheet Based KBS Engineering

We now first summarize spreadsheet-based KA; then, we sketch its integration with an encompassing process for developing ready-to-use KBS artifacts.

Spreadsheet-Based Knowledge Formalization

Knowledge formalization becomes the easier for non-knowledge engineers, the less prescriptions regarding its syntactical representation exist. The risk of errors,

P. Lambrix et al. (Eds.): EKAW 2014 Satellite Events, LNAI 8982, pp. 111–115, 2015.
DOI: 10.1007/978-3-319-17966-7_12

IF		ID	C	Type	QA (Questions-Answers)		Alt	H	H
1	IF			Type	QA (Questions-Answers)	**(a)**	Alt	H	H
2				K					
3				Lzeile				common ACS	stable Angina pectoris
5		LS1		JN	Difficulties with breathing?			P1	P1
6		LS2		JN	Cough?				
7		LS3		JN	Nausea?			P1	P1
8				E	Do you often feel sick or have to throw up?				
9	LS1=Yes			U	Difficulties with breathing				
10				OC	Occurence of breathing difficulties		When do you observe breathing difficulties?		
11				A	Inactive			P2	N2
12				A	Medium strain			N2	P1
13			Atmung	A	Strong strain			N2	P2

Fig. 1. Spreadsheet specification (a) for a medical KB and corresponding final KBS (b)

induced by rather free text input, can be minimized by applying (semi-) automated validation mechanisms of the syntactical correctness of the input. A key advantage of spreadsheets is, that they are one of the most commonly used software types today, and thus can be operated quite intuitively by most computer users. Spreadsheets further offer flexibility and expressiveness; at the same time, an explicit, formal syntax becomes unnecessary for the greater part of 'straightforward knowledge', e.g., scoring or indication rules. Of course, often also the inclusion of more complexly nested rules, or rules building on mathematical functions is necessary—the potential complexity of which can not easily be mapped on a spreadsheet-based input template. Therefore, we also allow the direct entry of complex rule syntax either by the expert, or (in cooperation with) a knowledge engineer. Regarding the input validation, we deliver an adaptable meta-specification with each knowledge spreadsheet that specifies the particular syntax—e.g., which input data is allowed in which column. Thus the specification format can be fine-tuned according to the respective user requirements—e.g., regarding another sequencing of the input columns—adding to the flexibility of the approach. The validation can either be invoked manually by the user from within the knowledge spreadsheet by means of a macro function, thus allowing for immediate in-place validation; further, it is automatically called during the KB compilation process with KnowOF (see next section).

Figure 1 shows an excerpt from a medical consultation KB spreadsheet (a), and the corresponding final KBS in a compact questionnaire style UI (b). Basically, one line in the spreadsheet concerns one specific interview item. The interview item type, e.g., one choice question (OC), question group (U), answer option (A), or explanation (E) are specified in the **Type** column. Interview item texts, e.g., the question wording, are defined in the **QA** column; answers are entered into the lines subsequent to the corresponding question; e.g., line 10–13 define the question *Occurence of breathing difficulties* with answers *Inactive*, *Medium strain*, and *Strong strain*. The **H** columns are used to define the rating

Fig. 2. General workflow from spreadsheet specification to functional KBS artifact

conditions for solutions; thereby, each column defines a distinct solution; the rating value, this solution receives dependent on a defined answer, is entered in the cell where the respective answer line and solution column cross—e.g., line 11 creates the rule IF Occurence of breathing difficulties = Inactive THEN common ACS = P2. Indication mechanisms finally are defined in column **IF**; e.g., item *Difficulties with breathing*, line 9, is indicated for presentation only in case the question with ID *LS1* is answered with yes (which is internally transferred in a formal rule syntax). Apart from that, various more information may be specified: Special question properties, e.g., symptom abstractions; translations for multilingualism of the KBS; or useful meta-information for organizing/documenting the KB development progress, such as comments or markers for work in progress.

Engineering Knowledge-Based Systems with KnowOF & ProKEt
KnowOF is a web application that transforms spreadsheet knowledge specifications into executable [1]*d3web* KBs. By coupling KnowOF with the UI-focussed KBS engineering tool *ProKEt* [2], an all-encompassing process from KA to reviewing a productive KBS artifact is supported (see Figure 2). When creating the spreadsheet, domain experts can arbitrarily validate it manually via a built-in macro functionality, delivered with the spreadsheet template. For reviewing the KB within an actual KBS artifact, the spreadsheet is uploaded to KnowOF. This automatically invokes the EXUP syntactical validator; in the case of success, the returned *.csv* format is transformed into a tailored *.txt* format, based on the formal markup of the d3web knowledge engineering wiki *KnowWE* [1]. Then, the *KnowWE Headless App* compiles a productive *d3web* KB. The direct coupling to ProKEt allows to execute the final KB within several predefined ProKEt KBS UI artifacts for their immediate interactive assessment. This entire upload and transformation process happens quite rapidly, thus it is predestined to be applied in highly iterative, agile development processes.

3   Case Studies

We have made positive and promising experiences with the approach in two actual projects. In a cooperation with the European Hernia Society, the[2]**EuraHS** system is being developed: A smart documentation system for

---

[1] http://www.d3web.de/ (last accessed July 17th., 2014)
[2] www.eurahs.eu (accessed July 17th, 2014)

collecting critical hernia surgery data for later (statistical) evaluation. EuraHS currently consists of about 500 complexly interconnected questions; the KBS then provides the intelligence to display only relevant questions regarding the chosen topical path and level of detail, interactively integrating follow up items, etc. At project start in 2010, KnowOF had not yet been available, resulting in much more workload on the side of the KBS developer, less expert participation, and an overall more cumbersome KA/KBS engineering process. With the availability of spreadsheet-based KA now also domain experts actively participate themselves. In another recently initiated project, an **encompassing consultation KBS for general medicine** is developed, ranging from digesting problems to cardiology. The knowledge is formalized by several medical (Ph.D.) students in a distributed manner. So far, one of the spreadsheet specifications—covering only one portion of the overall KB—has already grown as large as roughly 500 lines and 250 columns, thus representing a huge number of symptoms, diagnoses, and corresponding rules. An excerpt thereof was shown earlier in Figure 1 for exemplifying the spreadsheet specification as well as a possible KBS UI representation.

In both projects, spreadsheet-based KA was welcomed by the medical experts due to their literacy regarding that software type. Also, overviewing the knowledge and coherences only based on the (complex) spreadsheet files so far was rather cumbersome; effortlessly and easily reviewing the KB in a fully functional KBS artifact with an interactive and intelligent UI instead has proven a huge relief. As a result, experts now are more encouraged and motivated to (mostly) autonomously formalize the core knowledge and regularly check the outcome in a realistic implementation themselves.

4   Conclusions

We suggested the benefits of integrating domain experts actively into the KA process by making available the tool *KnowOF* for spreadsheet-based KA. Some efforts regarding KA with tailored electronic documents were published by Molina et al. [3]; yet—in contrast to our approach—their solution is not easily generalizable for diverse domains and further requires a very specialized input format. The feasibility and usefulness of our approach was demonstrated in several case studies. An interesting future research issue is to target the tool also towards entirely different knowledge output formats, e.g., (OWL) ontologies.

References

1. Baumeister, J., Reutelshoefer, J., Puppe, F.: KnowWE: A Semantic Wiki for Knowledge Engineering. Applied Intelligence **35**(3), 323–344 (2011)
2. Freiberg, M., Striffler, A., Puppe, F.: Extensible prototyping for pragmatic engineering of knowledge-based systems. Expert Systems with Applications **39**(11), 10177–10190 (2012)

3. Molina, M., Blasco, G.: KATS: a knowledge acquisition tool based on electronic document processing. In: Motta, E., Shadbolt, N.R., Stutt, A., Gibbins, N. (eds.) EKAW 2004. LNCS (LNAI), vol. 3257, pp. 403–418. Springer, Heidelberg (2004)
4. Noy, N.F., Grosso, W.E., Musen, M.A.: Knowledge-acquisition interfaces for domain experts an empirical evaluation of protege-2000. In: Proceedings of the 12th Internal Conference on Software and Knowledge Engineering. Chicago, USA, July, 5–7, 2000, pp. 5–7 (2000)

From ER Models to the Entity Model

Fausto Giunchiglia, and Mattia Fumagalli[✉]

DISI – University of Trento, Trento, Italy
{fausto.giunchiglia,mattia.fumagalli}@unitn.it

Abstract. In this paper, a new knowledge representation formalism, called the *entity model*, is introduced. This model can be used to address knowledge diversity by making the modeling assumptions of different knowledge representations explicit and by rooting them in a world representation. The entity model can be used to: 1) detect the possible ways in which the diversity appears in ER models and therefore improving their representational adequacy; 2) make the modeling assumptions behind different ER models explicit; 3) combine the different ER models in a unified view, thus enabling data integration.

Keywords: Knowledge representation · Conceptual modeling · Ontological analysis · Semantic heterogeneity · Knowledge diversity

1 Introduction

When we set ourselves for representing the world we have to deal with what we often informally call *diversity*. On one side, many criteria can be found for distinguishing categories of things which can make two representations of the same portion of reality completely incompatible. On the other side, diversity allows us to identify the single items which are needed in order to distinguish the different portions of reality. In the first case, diversity can be conceived as an intrinsic property of our knowledge representation, namely a function of local factors, like needs, beliefs or culture [4]. In the second case, diversity can be conceived as a property of things in the world, namely the characteristic of being distinct.

Diversity in world representations can be reduced to what is often called *semantic heterogeneity*. Semantic heterogeneity is a long-standing problem [5], for which a comprehensive solution still does not exist, that needs to be addressed in different application areas such as resource discovery, data integration, data migration, query translation, peer-to-peer networks, agent communication, schema and ontology matching. For this problem we propose to study semantic heterogeneity as the result of the projection of diversity in the real world into further, possibly diverse, representational choices. In other terms, we want to study the semantic heterogeneity problem as the result of injecting possibly diverse representational choices into the pre-existing real world diversity. To this extent, we propose a new formalism, and a corresponding methodology, called the *entity model*, which represents the real world diversity, and we take the ER model [2] as the formalism used to encode diversity in world representations.

© Springer International Publishing Switzerland 2015
P. Lambrix et al. (Eds.): EKAW 2014 Satellite Events, LNAI 8982, pp. 116–119, 2015.
DOI: 10.1007/978-3-319-17966-7_13

Our work can also be seen as providing an ontological foundation to the ER model. So far, there have been very few attempts at using ontological distinctions for constraining the semantics of a conceptual modelling language. The most complete research in this direction has been made in [6], where an ontological foundation for UML language is proposed. The ER model still needs to be ontologically well-founded. Moreover, as far as we know, there are no attempts to constrain a conceptual modeling language by means of a reference ontology which takes into account the distinction between world diversity and knowledge diversity.

The rest of the paper is structured as follows. Section 2 provides the motivation for our work showing an example of diversity in ER modeling and introducing the relations between the ER models and the entity model. Section 3 gives an explanation of the basic steps for creating the entity model and for rooting different ER models in the entity model.

2   Motivation

One concrete example of how diversity can be conceived as a structural feature of ER modelling is described through Fig. 1.

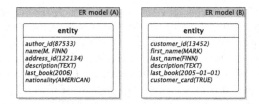

Fig. 1. Different representations for the same portion of reality

The matching of two references extracted from two different datasets (see Fig. 1) raises fundamental ontological and meta-ontological issues, for instance: (i) what entities do we have? (ii) Are these the same entities? (iii) What are the admissible attributes for these entities?

The entity model, taking into account the distinction between diversity in knowledge representation and the real world diversity, provides a model of the world based on the individuation of entities. The key advantage of this representation formalism is that, by rooting diversity of representations in the diversity of the world, we can trace back all the possible sources of diversity and therefore select the possible ways this diversity appears in ER models (Fig. 2). By tracing diversity, it is possible to verify and evaluate the potential of the entity model, which can be used for: improving the ER models representational adequacy; making the modeling assumptions behind different ER models explicit; combining different ER models in a unified view.

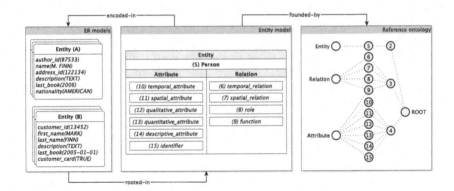

Fig. 2. Rooting the diversity of representations in the diversity of the world

The entity model has a straightforward formalization into the ER model. The set of terms T denoting the entity model basic components can be seen as a triple, $T = <E, R, A>$ [3]. Each term of T can be conceived as belonging to a hierarchy of terms rooted in a reference ontology, which will be grounded on a philosophical theory [1] and will be extended by information derived from different domain of knowledge. The entity model defines the set of *core entities, core attributes* and *core relations*, which are derived from the reference ontology. These core components will constitute the structure to be used for rooting the ER models in the entity model and therefore for tracing diversity. Let us consider the example of Fig. 2. Entities (A) and (B) are derived from the composition of terms denoting entities, relations and attributes. All these terms can be traced back to a core component of the entity model: terms like CUSTOMER and AUTHOR can be traced back to ROLE; terms like LAST_BOOK can be traced back to TEMPORAL_ATTRIBUTE, which may be specified as DATE_OF_PURCHEASE or DATE_OF_CREATION. The entity model will provide a set of *basic grounding constraints* for guiding the modelling choices of the knowledge engineer. For instance, let us assume that according to the entity model all the *entity terms* are those terms α, such that 'x is α' iff α is needed to be x. A term like CUSTOMER should not be considered as an entity term (e.g., *Mark,* may be a CUSTOMER, but it is not needed to be a CUSTOMER for being *Mark*). Moreover, the ER models may provide information for extending the entity model and its reference ontology. For instance, AUTHOR_ID and CUSTOMER_ID may be used to extend the class IDENTIFIER. Consequently, through the entity model it is possible to capture how (A) and (B) reflect different representational choices for describing the same individual and to combine these different representations in a unified view.

3   Our Approach

All the steps (Fig. 3) of the methodology can be grouped into two main processes: a *global process*, or a set of top-down steps, covering (1), (2) and (3), whose output

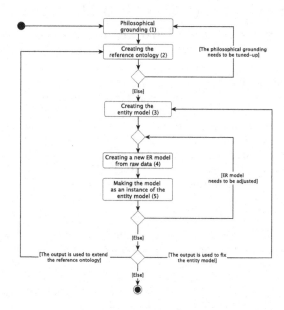

Fig. 3. Form ER models to the entity model

is an encoding of diversity in the real world, and a *local process*, namely a set of bottom-up steps, covering (4) and (5), whose output is an encoding of knowledge diversity, namely an expandable set of ER models. The entity model is generated, updated and extended through both these processes.

Acknowledgements. This research has received funding from the Smart Society Collaborative Project, funded by the European Commission's 7th Framework ICT Programme for Research and Technological Development under the Grant Agreement no. 600854.

References

1. Brentano, F.: On the Several Senses of Being in Aristotle. UC Press (1976)
2. Chen, P.: The entity-relationship model - toward a unified view of data. In: ACM Transactions on Database Systems, pp. 9–36 (1976)
3. Giunchiglia, F., Dutta, B., Maltese, V.: From knowledge organization to knowledge representation. In: ISKO UK (2013)
4. Giunchiglia, F., Maltese, V., Dutta, B.: Domains and context: First steps towards managing diversity in knowledge. Journal of Web Semantics: Science, Services and Agents on the World Wide Web **12–13**, 53–63 (2012)
5. Guarino, N.: The ontological level: revisiting 30 years of knowledge representation. In: Borgida, A.T., Chaudhri, V.K., Giorgini, P., Yu, E.S. (eds.) Conceptual Modeling: Foundations and Applications. LNCS, vol. 5600, pp. 52–67. Springer, Heidelberg (2009)
6. Guizzardi, G.: Ontological foundations for structural conceptual models. In: Telematica Instituut Fundamental Research Series (2005)

xWCPS: Bridging the Gap Between Array and Semi-structured Data

Panagiotis Liakos[1]([⊠]), Panagiota Koltsida[1],
George Kakaletris[1], and Peter Baumann[2]

[1] Athena Research and Innovation Center, Artemidos 6 and Epidavrou,
15125 Maroussi, Greece
{p.liakos,gkakas}@di.uoa.gr, p.koltsida@imis.athena-innovation.gr
[2] Jacobs University Bremen, Campus Ring 1, 28759 Bremen, Germany
p.baumann@jacobs-university.de

Abstract. The ever growing amount of information collected by scientific instruments and the presence of descriptive metadata accompanying them calls for a unified way of querying over array and semi-structured data. We present xWCPS, a novel query language that bridges the path between these two different worlds, enhancing the expressiveness and user-friendliness of previous approaches.

Keywords: Array databases · Query language · Scientific data

1 Introduction

Earth scientists are increasingly overwhelmed by the large volume of data produced during their observations and experiments, e.g., due to the extensive use of sensor arrays. While scientific data conveys a significant diversity of data structures, it is usually multidimensional and complex in nature, it is accompanied with metadata regarding its provenance, and its updates are mostly append-only [1]. Implementing interoperable infrastructures to provide unified access to this kind of data is a challenging problem requiring advances in various domains.

The inefficiency of traditional database management systems (DBMSs) to handle arrays, has led to the development of array DBMSs like rasdaman [2], which close this gap by extending the set of supported data structures of relational databases with multidimensional arrays of unlimited size. This enables the efficient storage of n-D spatiotemporal scientific data generated by satellites, telescopes and sensors. Search, retrieval and processing operations on top of array DBMSs has been enhanced through standards specified by the Open Geospatial Consortium (OGC)[1], which defines directives to implement simple

This research has been partially supported by *EC FP7 Work programme (2007-2013) under grant agreements n. 283610 "European Scalable Earth Science Service Environment (EarthServer)" and n. 262693 "International Network for Terrestrial Research and Monitoring in the Arctic (INTERACT)".*

[1] www.opengeospatial.org

© Springer International Publishing Switzerland 2015
P. Lambrix et al. (Eds.): EKAW 2014 Satellite Events, LNAI 8982, pp. 120–123, 2015.
DOI: 10.1007/978-3-319-17966-7_14

and easy-to-use web-based interfaces. As far as the metadata is concerned, the World Wide Web Consortium (W3C)[2] provides standard definitions, such as XML and XQuery [4], that enable the encoding and querying of semi-structured data.

Our approach aims at interconnecting the aforementioned technological advances to offer a unified way of querying array data and their respective metadata. We propose xWCPS, an innovative query language that combines ideas from previous approaches and evaluate its syntactic power with the use of a running example. In particular, we consider an array database giving access to *coverages*[3] and their accompanying XML metadata, we process as PNG images those that satisfy a certain condition and project their *boundingbox* element.

In Section 2 we discuss the buildings blocks of xWCPS and in Section 3 we present it formally. Section 4 concludes this study.

2   Background and Motivation

The fundamental idea of this work is the merging of two extensively used standards into a unified language, which provides a more expressive way to query array databases. In this section, we discuss the details of the components used as the building blocks of our query language, the XQuery and WCPS languages, and explore their use and limitations.

XQuery. The use of XML data has exploded in recent years and now a colossal amount of information is stored in XML databases or documents in a filesystem. XQuery [4] is a query language designed by the W3C to enable the efficient utilization of this information. It allows the user to select the XML data elements of interest, reorganize and possibly transform them, and return the results in a structure of her choosing. The basic structure of its queries is the FLWOR (pronounced *'flower'*) expression. The acronym derives from the keywords permitted in XQuery expressions, namely for, let, where, order by and return. The first query in Fig. 1 provides a sample XQuery. Suppose we wish to fetch the *boundingbox* element of all the *coverages* that have *'Clay'* as the title for their *lithology* element. This information is part of our descriptive metadata, so we can simply iterate over the names using for, apply our condition with where, and retrieve our results with return after they are ordered using order by. However, XQuery does not provide any means to process the *coverages* as images.

WCPS. The Web Coverage Processing Service (WCPS) Interface Standard is defined by OGC[4] and specifies a language for retrieval and processing of multidimensional geospatial data [3], with rasdaman [2] as the reference implementation. The primary structure of WCPS comprises the for, where, and return

---

[2] http://www.w3.org/

[3] *Coverages* are digital geospatial information representing space/time-varying phenomena.

[4] www.opengeospatial.org

clauses. To illustrate, we continue with our example and process two *coverages* as PNG images with the second query in Fig. 1. WCPS allows the selection of *coverages* by specifying their names, which is very limiting when one wants to query for all the available *coverages*. Moreover, the where clause supports only expressions evaluating criteria regarding the array data. Therefore, the descriptive information is inaccessible through WCPS.

(a)

(b)

```
for $c in /server/coverages/coverage
where $c//lithology/@title = 'Clay'
order by $c
return $c//boundingbox
```

```
for $c in (coverageA,coverageB)
return encode($c, "png")
```

Fig. 1. Sample XQuery (a) and WCPS (b) queries

Motivation. Having briefly discussed XQuery and WCPS, it is now evident that the simple task of our example has no practical solution with existing approaches. One needs to use XQuery to filter the *coverages* and retrieve the metadata part of the results, and then compose a WCPS query with the correct names to fetch the images. The results should be then merged manually. Limitations such as the aforementioned have motivated us to propose xWCPS, a query language able to resolve them effortlessly.

3   xWCPS: A Novel Query Language

The xWCPS query language aims towards merging the path two widely adopted standards, namely XQuery and WCPS, have paved, into a new construct, which enables search on both XML-encoded metadata and OGC *coverages*. Additionally, by using xWCPS as the subsuming language we avoid alienating our targeted users, i.e., those already familiar with WCPS. Our language follows XQuery's FLWOR expression syntax and adds two clauses to WCPS, which along with the increased syntactic power instilled into the ones the two languages share, enables the composition of more expressive queries.

The enriched set of clauses is outlined below. Clauses for and let can appear any number of times in any order. Clauses where and order by are optional, but must appear in the predefined order should they be used.

- for: can create iterator variables holding *coverages* through the WCPS syntax or metadata, which can be *coverages* as well, through the XQuery syntax.
- let: can initialize variables following either of the two syntaxes in the assignment expression. The use of the let clause can greatly reduce repetitiveness, making xWCPS extremely less verbose than WCPS.
- where: can specify criteria on both data and metadata, thus enriching significantly the selecting and filtering capabilities.
- order by: can order the results depending on the expression provided.

– **return**: supports both **XQuery** and **WCPS** expressions and enables the creation of *mixed results*, through a newly defined function, viz. **mixed()**. The current available *mixed* formats are **XML**, **HTML** and **ZIP**.

The query in Fig. 2 illustrates how easy it is to retrieve the desired results of our example with **xWCPS**. We iterate over our desired *coverages* with **for**, apply our condition with **where**, order the results with **order by**, and retrieve both processed images and selected metadata. Cases where conditions on array data are needed as well, or results should be pure **WCPS** or **XQuery**, are also handled by **xWCPS**, as noted above.

```
for $c in /server/coverages/coverage
where $c//lithology/@title = 'Clay'
order by $c
return mixed(encode($c, "png"), xquery($c//boundingbox), "xml")
```

Fig. 2. A sample xWCPS query

In the context of the EarthServer[5] project, we have developed an xWCPS engine, able to parse queries and execute them over cooperating array and XML databases. Our partners, forming a very experienced evaluation team in the earth data domain, have verified the effectiveness of our innovative language.

4   Conclusion

We presented a novel query language which allows seamless integration of multidimensional *coverage* data with metadata for retrieval and processing applications. The merits of **xWCPS**, which are visible through the use case provided, indicate that merging these two different worlds is a very promising direction.

References

1. Ailamaki, A., Kantere, V., Dash, D.: Managing scientific data. Commun. ACM **53**(6), 68–78 (2010)
2. Baumann, P., Dehmel, A., Furtado, P., Ritsch, R., Widmann, N.: The multidimensional database system rasdaman. In: Proc. of the 1998 ACM SIGMOD Int. Conf. on Management of Data, Seattle, Washington, USA, pp. 575–577, Jun 1998
3. Baumann, P.: The OGC web coverage processing service (WCPS) standard. Geoinformatica **14**(4), 447–479 (2010)
4. Chamberlin, D.: XQuery: A query language for XML. In: Proc. of the 2003 ACM SIGMOD Int. Conf. on Management of Dat, San Diego, California pp. 682–682, Jun 2003

---

[5] http://www.earthserver.eu/

Adapting the SEPIA System to the Educational Context

Le Vinh Thai[1,3(✉)], Blandine Ginon[1,2], Stéphanie Jean-Daubias[1,3],
and Marie Lefevre[1,3]

[1] Université de Lyon, CNRS, Lyon, France
{le-vinh.thai,blandine.ginon,
stephanie.jean-daubias,marie.lefevre}@liris.cnrs.fr
[2] INSA-Lyon, LIRIS, UMR5205, F-69621 Villeurbanne cedex, France
[3] Université Lyon 1, LIRIS, UMR5205, F-69622 Lyon, France

Abstract. The SEPIA system allows creating assistance systems that meet
technical assistance needs. In this paper, we aim at the exploitation of SEPIA in
the educational context by confronting it to pedagogical assistance needs. This
exploitation shows the limitations in the SEPIA system: complex description of
rules by pedagogical designers, lack of domain knowledge. Therefore, we present our patterns that facilitate the creation of assistance systems in the educational context and our ideas to allow the exploitation of domain knowledge.

Keywords: User assistance · Education · Pattern · Domain knowledge · ILE

1 Introduction

Users often meet difficulties in handling and using applications: they under-exploit
those applications by ignoring necessary functionalities and they can even abandon
their use. In the educational context, these difficulties, under-exploitation and aban-
donment, can compromise learning when learners use either ILEs (Interactive Learning Environments), or classical applications for learning. Thus, one solution is the
plugging of assistance systems that provide technical assistance to users. This solution
can also be used to provide pedagogical assistance, if it is desired by the pedagogical
designers or teachers but not supported by the target-applications. We identified the
technical and pedagogical assistance needs [2] that an assistance system should meet
in an educational context: handling, use, choice of the activity, learning prerequisites,
explanation on steps, hints, examples, transitional diagnosis…

Currently several systems (e.g. [1] [3]) allow the specification of assistance systems. However, they are specific to a given environment or to Web applications. By
contrast, the SEPIA system [2] proposed in the AGATE project applies an epiphytic
and generic approach. It proposes the setup of assistance systems to very diverse existing target-applications and has the capacity to personalize the assistance according
to user profile, assistance history, user's past actions and state of the target-
application. However, the SEPIA system aims only at technical assistance needs because of its generic characteristic. Thus, in this paper, we explain how we adapt it to
the specific needs of the educational context.

© Springer International Publishing Switzerland 2015
P. Lambrix et al. (Eds.): EKAW 2014 Satellite Events, LNAI 8982, pp. 124–128, 2015.
DOI: 10.1007/978-3-319-17966-7_15

At first, we present the SEPIA system and its possible exploitation in an educational context by presenting its capacities and identifying its limitations. We then present our solutions to adapt SEPIA to the educational context.

2   The SEPIA System

The AGATE (Approach for Genericity in Assistance To complEx tasks) project aims at proposing generic models and unified tools to make possible the setup of assistance systems in various existing applications, that we call *target-applications,* by applying a generic and epiphytic approach. This project led to aLDEAS (a Language to Define Epi-Assistance Systems), a graphical rule language allowing assistance designers to define assistance systems and aMEAS (a Model to Execute aLDEAS Assistance Systems) that explains how an assistance system is executed. The SEPIA system (Specification and Execution of Personalized Intelligent Assistance), the first product of AGATE project, is designed and implemented by operationalizing the aLDEAS language and the aMEAS model. The SEPIA system is composed of two main tools: an assistance editor that allows assistance designers to define assistance systems and a generic assistance engine that executes these assistance systems on the target-applications without disturbing them in order to provide assistance to users. The target-applications supported by actual SEPIA are Windows native applications, Java applications and Web applications.

3   Exploiting SEPIA in the Educational Context

SEPIA is designed and implemented by taking into account the technical assistance needs. However, SEPIA can also meet pedagogical assistance needs. In the educational context, the assistance designer is the pedagogical designer who can be a teacher or a group of teachers and the user is mainly a learner. We tested SEPIA in the pedagogical context of a Human-Computer Interaction course. We created an assistance system (as a set of tutorials) for the handling of Java programing in NetBeans IDE. This experiment showed that students can acquire knowledge thanks to our tutorials. Thus, we can conclude from now that SEPIA is also useful in an educational context [2].

However, we identified several limitations to the use of SEPIA to create pedagogical assistances. Firstly, the pedagogical designers may not be familiar with the description of rules because they are not experts of SEPIA. Therefore, they may waste time in technical work instead of concentrating on the pedagogical work. Secondly, in order to propose a more complex assistance, we need domain knowledge that could be described with SEPIA, but complexly. As an example, a learner can submit different good answers if "X-5" is the solution, the system should identify that "X-4-1" or "X-3-2" are correct answers too. The automatic generation of examples or hints also requires domain knowledge in order to have a more suitable assistance.

4   Adapting SEPIA to Educational Context

In this section, we present our solutions to overcome the limitations of exploiting SEPIA in an educational context: proposition of patterns and integration of domain knowledge in the system. We aim not only at the technical facilitation of assistance systems description, but also at a more natural description for the designers.

Pedagogical assistances can be examples and explanations that consist of the consecutive steps of assistance or tutorials that merge them (as the tutorials we defined for NetBeans). In order to define such assistance, the designers have to create assistance rules with user consultations. This task is more complex if they want to modify the sequence of steps. Therefore, we proposed and implemented a **first pattern** called **"sequence of steps"**. Assistance actions are associated with each step. They can be messages, enhancements, links to resources (web pages, programs...) or actions on the interface of the target-application (e.g. a click on a button). We proposed three modes to realize actions on the interface in this first pattern: automating the actions, waiting for user's actions and waiting for user's confirmation of the actions realization. The use of these modes depends on the pedagogical designer's needs and on SEPIA's capacities to detect and automate the actions on the target-application. In addition, we propose in this pattern the possibility to set up the back, next and finish buttons, in order to allow the final user to see again the previous step, the next step or to finish the sequence of steps. The designers can reuse and easily modify the sequence of steps. With this pattern, the pedagogical designers can concentrate less on description of rules and more on their choice of assistance actions for each step. This pattern is implemented and integrated to SEPIA as one assistance action of the system. The figure Fig. 1 shows a screenshot of this pattern that support three modes to realize actions on the interface.

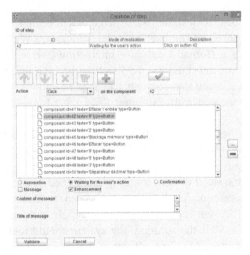

Fig. 1. Screenshot of step creation in the pattern "sequence of steps"

In order to assist more effectively the learner, the designers have to well identify the assistance needs and defining suited assistance rules. The designers first create a set of assistance actions (explanation, examples, hints, etc.) and then have to define conditions to specify how to launch these actions at the right time. We studied the modes of providing assistance in existing educational software: assistance upon the request of the learner, next assistance more detailed or closer to the solution than the previous one... These modes are based on different kind of approaches: proactive, reactive, parameterized and mainly mixed. In SEPIA, the application of these modes is compromised by the capacity of SEPIA (technical capacity, lack of domain knowledge) and the difficulty of the rules description (for example, how to provide easily assistance more and more detailed). Thus, we propose a **second pattern "assistance needs refinement"**. We are defining a tree structure of the assistance steps for this pattern that will be then implemented.

More, the recommendation of activities suitable to learner requires organization of the activities. SEPIA does not support this organization. The designers have to create rules, conditions to identify activities suitable to the learner and create learner consultations to know his choice. These tasks are complex and the number of necessary rules is huge. Thus, we plan to implement a **third pattern** examining researches that concern the **recommendation of activities**. In addition, we will implement ways of visualizing a summary and a monitoring of activities (e.g. through a progression bar).

Finally, we will focus on defining and implementing an **over layer** to SEPIA that allows the system to use **domain knowledge**. We will first have to propose the architecture of this layer. For this purpose, we aim at reusing existing modules that allow pedagogical designers to define different domains knowledge, and at integrating modules of knowledge management specific to a domain (e.g. mathematics).

5   Conclusion

We have presented the exploitation of SEPIA in an educational context. SEPIA has been shown to have a strong potential to create assistance systems in an educational context. However, because of the genericity of our approach, it has some limitations. To overcome these limitations, our solutions concern the proposition of patterns and the integration of domain knowledge in our system. Thanks to these solutions, the pedagogical designers will concentrate mainly on the pedagogical works, but not on technical works. In addition, domain knowledge helps them to create assistance systems that provide more appropriate assistance because these systems will know more precisely the learner's problems and the assistance needs. We will validate these solutions by several experimentations with teachers, and students who will play the role of "pedagogical designers". We will compare the use of SEPIA with and without our solutions (patterns and domain knowledge).

References

1. Dufresne, A., Paquette, G.: ExploraGraph: a flexible and adaptive interface to support distance learning. In: Ed-Media, Victoria, Canada, pp. 304–309 (2000)
2. Ginon, B., Thai, L.V., Jean-Daubias, S., Lefevre, M., Champin, P.-A.: Adding epiphytic assistance systems in learning applications using the SEPIA system. In: Ec-Tel, Graz, Austria (2014)
3. Paquette, G., Pachet, F., Giroux, S., Girard, J.: Epitalk, a generic tool for the development of advisor systems. In: IJAIED, pp. 349–370 (1996)

Demos

An Intelligent Textbook that Answers Questions

Vinay K. Chaudhri$^{(\boxtimes)}$, Adam Overholtzer, and Aaron Spaulding

Artificial Intelligence Center, SRI International, Menlo Park, CA 94025, USA
Vinay.Chaudhri@SRI.COM

Abstract. Inquire Biology is a prototype of a new kind of intelligent textbook that answers students questions, engages their interest, and improves their understanding. Inquire uses knowledge representation of the conceptual knowledge from the textbook and uses inference procedures to answer questions. Students ask questions by typing free-form natural language queries or by selecting passages of text. The system then attempts to answer the question and also generates suggested questions related to the query or selection. The questions supported by the system were chosen to be educationally useful, for example: what is the structure of X?; compare X and Y?; how does X relate to Y? In user studies, students found this question-answering capability to be useful while reading and while doing problem solving. In a controlled experiment, community college students using Inquire Biology outperformed students using either a hard copy or conventional E-book version of the same textbook. While additional research is needed to fully develop Inquire, the prototype demonstrates the promise of applying knowledge representation and question-answering to electronic textbooks.

1 Introduction

Inquire Biology, is a novel electronic textbook that runs on an iPad and embeds a rich biology knowledge representation and reasoning system [1]. Inquire is an outcome of Project Halo [7]. A description of the process of testing the knowledge base used in Inquire and its suggested question mechanism appears as two separate papers in the in-use track of this conference [2,4]. Our demonstration of Inquire at the conference will show how a student could use Inquire while reading a textbook and while doing homework. In this paper, we summarize the key features of Inquire.

Inquire supports traditional electronic book reading features such as navigation, highlighting, and note taking. Beyond these, Inquire employs unique knowledge representation and reasoning features in three ways: (1) Each word in the textbook that has a corresponding representation in the knowledge base is hyperlinked and, when selected, provides summary information generated from the knowledge base. This provides a quick reference as well as a study aid. (2) As a user highlights a section of the textbook, the system suggests questions to the user about the selected knowledge. The answers to some of the suggested questions may be obvious from the reading of the paragraph, but some suggested

© Springer International Publishing Switzerland 2015
P. Lambrix et al. (Eds.): EKAW 2014 Satellite Events, LNAI 8982, pp. 131–135, 2015.
DOI: 10.1007/978-3-319-17966-7_16

The Need for Energy in Active Transport

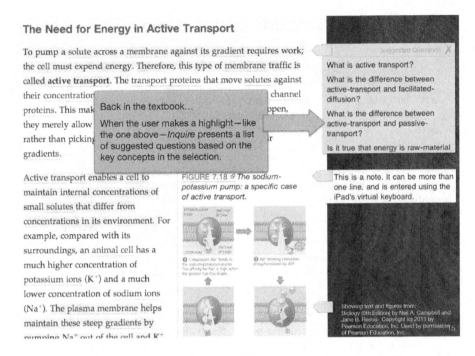

To pump a solute across a membrane against its gradient requires work; the cell must expend energy. Therefore, this type of membrane traffic is called **active transport**. The transport proteins that move solutes against their concentration ... channel proteins. This mak... ppen, they merely allow ... rather than pickin... r gradients.

Back in the textbook...

When the user makes a highlight—like the one above—*Inquire* presents a list of suggested questions based on the key concepts in the selection.

What is active transport?

What is the difference between active-transport and facilitated-diffusion?

What is the difference between active-transport and passive-transport?

Is it true that energy is raw-material

Active transport enables a cell to maintain internal concentrations of small solutes that differ from concentrations in its environment. For example, compared with its surroundings, an animal cell has a much higher concentration of potassium ions (K⁺) and a much lower concentration of sodium ions (Na⁺). The plasma membrane helps maintain these steep gradients by pumping Na⁺ out of the cell and K⁺

FIGURE 7.18 ⊘ *The sodium-potassium pump: a specific case of active transport.*

This is a note. It can be more than one line, and is entered using the iPad's virtual keyboard.

Showing text and figures from: Biology (9th Edition) by Neil A. Campbell and Jane B. Reece. Copyright (c) 2011 by Pearson Education, Inc. Used by permission of Pearson Education, Inc.

Fig. 1. An example use of Inquire in which it suggests questions to the user

questions may require combining the knowledge in the paragraph with knowledge stated elsewhere in the textbook. Students can use the questions to test their reading comprehension or to prepare for an exam. The question suggestion is based on the knowledge that is represented about the paragraph in the knowledge base. (3) Users can pose some classes of questions to Inquire about their misconceptions, and Inquire uses its knowledge base and reasoning to answer those questions.

As an illustration of these features, Figure 1 shows a screenshot of the application in action where the user has selected text and the system has suggested questions based on that text. The user can select one of the suggested questions, potentially edit the question to better suit his or her need, and pose it to the system. An example of the answer returned by the system is shown in Figure 2.

The hyperlinks from the textbook to the knowledge base are created by preprocessing the textbook content. The suggested questions and answers to the users questions are generated at run time by connecting to a knowledge server called AURA [7].

The AURA knowledge server currently has taxonomy for concepts in the Campbell Biology textbook and detailed question-answering rules corresponding to 20 chapters of the book. This knowledge base is manually curated by a team of professional biologists and biology teachers. The team of biologists analyzes each sentence for its relevance to answering questions and then represents it using the

	Glycoprotein	Glycolipid
	What are the differences between a glycoprotein and a glycolipid? DIFFERENCES SIMILARITIES	
definition	A protein with one or more carbohydrates covalently attached to it.	A lipid with covalently attached carbohydrate(s).
type of	molecule amphipathic molecule protein	molecule amphipathic molecule lipid
structure	**subunits** ▫ at least 1 polypeptide ▫ polypeptide ▫ protein domain ▫ monomer ▫ amino acid	**subunits** ▫ hydrocarbon ▫ hydrophobic end

Fig. 2. An example answer produced by Inquire

AURA knowledge entry interface to the extent that it can be represented. Many sentences in the textbook are too difficult to represent because of limitations in either the representation or the knowledge acquisition technology. The knowledge base has been extensively tested by evaluating the quality of the answers the system produces. The current knowledge base has approximately 6,000 concepts and more than 100,000 rules.

The knowledge acquisition capabilities of AURA have been under development for several years, and the underlying technology has been published in several papers [3,5]. AURA uses a knowledge representation language called KM (the Knowledge Machine) that combines an object-oriented representation of knowledge with deductive rules [6]. For the purpose of this paper, it is sufficient to understand that the knowledge captured in AURA can be exported into public domain languages such as Web Ontology Language [9] and Rule Interchange format [8]. AURA also supports a logic level API, enabling external applications to query its knowledge.

SRI evaluated Inquire in a pilot experiment with community college students. There were three experimental conditions: paper textbook (N=23), electronic textbook (N=25), a textbook with knowledge representation and question answering supported by Inquire (N=24). Here, N is the number of students in each group. The students in each group engaged in active reading and problem solving on the topic of membrane structure and function. The problem solving task was comparable to what students might do during an assigned homework. During the evaluation exercise, the students worked on problem solving in an open book format, and at the end of the exercise, answered quiz questions in a closed-book format. We compared the problem solving and quiz scores across the three groups.

The quiz scores of students in Inquire were higher than the scores of the students in the paper textbook (p value=0.05) and electronic textbook group by approximately 10% (p value=0.002). Here, p value is the statistical significance of the test. The mean problem solving score for the Inquire group was higher than both the corresponding score of the paper textbook and electronic textbook groups. The difference between the Inquire group and the electronic textbook group was not statistically significant (p value=0.12), but the difference between the Inquire group and the paper textbook group was significant (p value=0.02). The observed trend is consistent with our hypothesis that Inquire enhances learning by helping students perform better on homework. Although the mean homework score of electronic textbook group was higher than the mean score for the paper textbook group, there was no statistical difference between these conditions (p value=0.52). Similarly, there was no statistical difference between the quiz scores of students under these two conditions (p value=0.18). While the results presented here are encouraging, they are only preliminary. It is unknown if these results will generalize if the students were to study from Inquire over an extended period of time. There was also a lack of control on the ability of the students and how it might affect how much they learned. We also observed that the students in the Inquire group did not get any Ds or Fs suggesting that it may be especially helpful for lower performing students. This result, however, was not statistically significant, and more extensive experimentation is needed to confirm this result.

Acknowledgments. This work has been funded by Vulcan Inc. and SRI International. We thank the members of the AURA development team for their contributions to this work.

References

1. Chaudhri, V.K., Cheng, B., Overholtzer, A., Roschelle, J., Spaulding, A., Clark, P., Greaves, M., Gunning, D.: Inquire Biology: A Textbook that Answers Questions. AI Magazine, 34(3), September 2013
2. Chaudhri, V.K., Clark, P.E., Overholtzer, A., Spaulding, A.: Question generation from a knowledge base. In: Janowicz, K., Schlobach, S., Lambrix, P., Hyvönen, E. (eds.) EKAW 2014. LNCS, vol. 8876, pp. 54–65. Springer, Heidelberg (2014)
3. Chaudhri, V.K., John, B.E., Mishra, S., Pacheco, J., Porter, B., Spaulding, A.: Enabling experts to build knowledge bases from science textbooks. In Proceedings of the 4th International Conference on Knowledge Capture, pp. 159–166. ACM (2007)

4. Chaudhri, V.K., Katragadda, R., Shrager, J., Wessel, M.: Inconsistency monitoring in a large scientific knowledge base. In: Janowicz, K., Schlobach, S., Lambrix, P., Hyvönen, E. (eds.) EKAW 2014. LNCS, vol. 8876, pp. 66–79. Springer, Heidelberg (2014)
5. Clark, P., Chaw, K.B.J., Chaudhri, V.K., Harrison, P., Fan, J., John, B., Porter, B., Spaulding, A., Thompson, J., Yeh, P.: Capturing and answering questions posed to a knowledge-based system. In: Proceedings of the Fourth International Conference on Knowledge Capture (K-CAP), October 2007
6. Clark, P., Porter, B.: Km-the knowledge machine: Users manual. Technical report, Technical report, AI Lab, Univ Texas at Austin (1999). http://www.cs.utexas.edu/users/mfkb/km.html
7. Gunning, D., Chaudhri, V.K., Clark, P., Barker, K., Chaw, S.-Y., Greaves, M., Grosof, B., Leung, A., McDonald, D., Mishra, S., Pacheco, J., Porter, B., Spaulding, A., Tecuci, D., Tien, J.: Project Halo update: Progress toward Digital Aristotle. AI Magazine, Fall 2010
8. Kifer, M.: Rule interchange format: The framework. In: Calvanese, D., Lausen, G. (eds.) RR 2008. LNCS, vol. 5341, pp. 1–11. Springer, Heidelberg (2008)
9. McGuinness, D.L., Van Harmelen, F., et al.: Owl web ontology language overview. W3C Recommendation 10(10) (2004)

SHELDON: Semantic Holistic framEwork for LinkeD ONtology Data

Diego Reforgiato Recupero[1,2]([⊠]), Andrea Giovanni Nuzzolese[1,2],
Sergio Consoli[1,2], Aldo Gangemi[1,2], and Valentina Presutti[1,2]

[1] STLab-ISTC Consiglio Nazionale delle Ricerche, Catania, Italy
[2] LIPN Sorbonne-Cité, Université de Paris-13, Villetaneuse, France
diego.reforgiato@istc.cnr.it

Abstract. SHELDON is a framework that builds upon a machine reader
for extracting RDF graphs from text so that the output is compliant to
Semantic Web and Linked Data patterns. It extends the current human-
readable web by using semantic best practices and technologies in a
machine-processable form. Given a sentence in any language, it provides
different semantic tasks as well as nice visualization tools which make
use of the JavaScript infoVis Toolkit and a knowledge enrichment component on top of RelFinder. The system can be freely used at http://
wit.istc.cnr.it/stlab-tools/sheldon.

1 Introduction

Machine Reading relies on bootstrapped, self-supervised Natural Language Processing (NLP) performed on basic tasks, in order to extract knowledge from
text. SHELDON generates RDF graph representations out of the knowledge
extracted from text by tools dedicated to basic NLP tasks. Such graphs extend
and improve NLP output, and are typically customized for application tasks.
SHELDON includes and extends several components successfully evaluated in
the past [1,4–11]. FRED [4,10], a tool for automatically producing RDF/OWL
ontologies and linked data from text and represents the machine reader capability of SHELDON. The backbone deep semantic parsing is provided by Boxer [2]
which uses a statistical parser (C&C) producing Combinatory Categorial Gram-
mar trees. The basic NLP tasks performed by FRED include: A list of NLP tasks
performed by FRED incudes (i) event detection (FRED uses DOLCE+DnS[1] [3]),
(ii) semantic role labeling with VerbNet[2] and FrameNet roles, (iii) first- order
logic representation of predicate-argument structures, (iv) logical operators scop-
ing, (v) modality detection, (vi) tense representation, (vii) entity recognition
using TAGME[3], (viii) word sense disambiguation using IMS and BabelNet[4].
Also, SHELDON leverages LEGALO [9], a novel method for uncovering the

---

[1] D.U.L. Ontology. http://www.ontologydesignpatterns.org/ont/dul/dul.owl
[2] T.V. project. http://verbs.colorado.edu/mpalmer/projects/verbnet.html
[3] http://tagme.di.unipi.it/
[4] http://babelnet.org/

© Springer International Publishing Switzerland 2015
P. Lambrix et al. (Eds.): EKAW 2014 Satellite Events, LNAI 8982, pp. 136–139, 2015.
DOI: 10.1007/978-3-319-17966-7_17

intended semantics of links by tagging them with semantic relations. LEGALO implements a set of graph pattern-based rules for extracting, from FRED graphs, Semantic Web binary relations that capture the semantics of specific links. The rationale behind is that revealing the semantics of hyperlinks has a high potential impact on the amount of Web knowledge that can be published in machine readable form, keeping the binding with its corresponding natural language source. One more component of SHELDON performs semantic sentiment analysis. It is built on top of SENTILO [6,11], a domain-independent system that performs SA by hybridizing natural language processing techniques and semantic Web technologies. Given an opinion expressing sentence, SENTILO recognizes its holder, detects related topics and subtopics, links them to relevant situations/events referred to by it and evaluates the sentiment expressed. The automatic typing of DBpedia entities is one more component of SHELDON. The related component is based on TIPALO [5], which identifies the most appropriate types for an entity by interpreting its natural language definition. Bibliographic citations are the most used tools of academic communities for linking research, for instance by connecting scientific papers to related works or source of experimental data. One more component of SHELDON implements a strategy for the linking within scientific research articles feature. It is built on top of CITALO [8], a tool to infer automatically the function of citations by means of Semantic Web technologies and NLP techniques. A sentence containing a reference to a bibliographic entity and the CiTO ontology used to describe the nature of citations in scientific research articles are taken as input to infer the function of that citation. Data visualization is also a matter taking into account in SHELDON. Graph and the triple visualization of each component of SHELDON can be shown. An appealing data visualization component built on top of [1] relies on the JavaScript Info-Vis Toolkit. Besides, it is possible to augment the identified relations between detected DBpedia entities using a SHELDON component that is built on top of RelFinder [7]. REST API are provided for each of the SHELDON component. Thus, everyone can build online end-user applications that integrate, visualize, analyze, combine and deduce the available knowledge at the desired level of granularity. The reader notices that end-users of SHELDON are developers and researchers that want to leverage semantics knowledge provided by SHELDON for their final applications.

2   SHELDON at Work

SHELDON 's main interface shows a text box where one can type a sentence in any language and decide which semantic task to perform. The reader notices that that SHELDON will always provide the results in English. The Bing Translation APIS have been used and embedded within SHELDON.

If the used language of the sentence is different than English, then an automatic language detection[5] module will identify the target language. For example, the sentence: *Riva del Garda è una bella città che fa parte dell'Italia* would be

---

[5] That makes use of the Language Identification Engine of Apache Stanbol.

a valid Italian sentence to be processed which would be correctly translated from Italian to English. If the machine reader capability is chosen, SHELDON outputs an RDF graph with several associated information (DBpedia entities, events and situations mapped within DOLCE, WordNet and VerbNet mapping, pronoun resolution). If the SA option is used, for the same sentence SHELDON returns a semantic SA ontology with scores for the positive adjective, *beautiful*, and for the entity *Riva del Garda* which was computed according to the propagation algorithm [11]. If the relation discovery choice is made, SHELDON returns the new (or aligned against existing repositories) relations between DBpedia entities, in our example *Riva del Garda* and *Italy*.

Each DBpedia entity nodes displayed the graphs is clickable in order to automatically assign types in a new LOD-intensive graph. Fig. 1(a), (b) and (c) shows, respectively, the produced output of the machine reader feature, the semantic SA and the produced relations between the DBpedia entities recognized within the sentence. For each of the three main capabilities it is possible to show the complete list of RDF triples that SHELDON outputs by choosing any other view other than the Graphical View item.

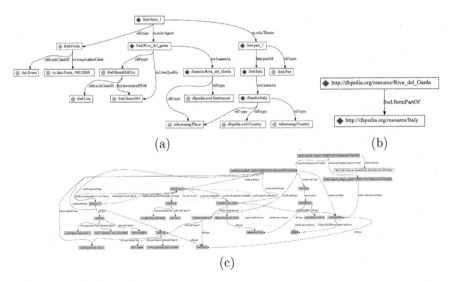

(a)   (b)

(c)

Fig. 1. Machine reader output (a), semantic link identification (b), and semantic SA output (c) for the Italian sentence *Riva del Garda è una bella città che fa parte dell'Italia*

Within the options at the bottom of the produced graphs it is possible to export the graph as images, to see the augmented knowledge for the identified DBpedia entities from SHELDON using a nice GUI built on top of RelFinder and to navigate the graph through a nice visualization tool that builds upon the Semantic Scout [1] and that uses the JavaScript InfoVis Toolkit[6].

---

[6] http://philogb.github.io/jit/

3   Conclusions

We have shown SHELDON[7], a framework that provides several Semantic Web features for a sentence in any language. SHELDON augments the knowledge of entities identified within the sentence and includes appealing visualization tools.

References

1. Baldassarre, C., Daga, E., Gangemi, A., Gliozzo, A.M., Salvati, A., Troiani, G.: Semantic scout: making sense of organizational knowledge. In: Cimiano, P., Pinto, H.S. (eds.) EKAW 2010. LNCS, vol. 6317, pp. 272–286. Springer, Heidelberg (2010)
2. Bos, J.: Wide-coverage semantic analysis with boxer. In: Proceedings of the 2008 Conference on Semantics in Text Processing, STEP 2008, pp. 277–286. Association for Computational Linguistics, Stroudsburg (2008)
3. Gangemi, A.: Whats in a schema?, pp. 144–182. Cambridge University Press, Cambridge (2010)
4. Gangemi, A.: A comparison of knowledge extraction tools for the semantic web. In: Cimiano, P., Corcho, O., Presutti, V., Hollink, L., Rudolph, S. (eds.) ESWC 2013. LNCS, vol. 7882, pp. 351–366. Springer, Heidelberg (2013)
5. Gangemi, A., Nuzzolese, A.G., Presutti, V., Draicchio, F., Musetti, A., Ciancarini, P.: Automatic typing of dbpedia entities. In: Cudré-Mauroux, P., Heflin, J., Sirin, E., Tudorache, T., Euzenat, J., Hauswirth, M., Parreira, J.X., Hendler, J., Schreiber, G., Bernstein, A., Blomqvist, E. (eds.) ISWC 2012, Part I. LNCS, vol. 7649, pp. 65–81. Springer, Heidelberg (2012)
6. Gangemi, A., Presutti, V., Recupero, D.R.: Frame-based detection of opinion holders and topics: A model and a tool. IEEE Comp. Int. Mag. $9(1)$, 20–30 (2014)
7. Heim, P., Hellmann, S., Lehmann, J., Lohmann, S., Stegemann, T.: RelFinder: revealing relationships in RDF knowledge bases. In: Chua, T.-S., Kompatsiaris, Y., Mérialdo, B., Haas, W., Thallinger, G., Bailer, W. (eds.) SAMT 2009. LNCS, vol. 5887, pp. 182–187. Springer, Heidelberg (2009)
8. Iorio, A.D., Nuzzolese, A.G., Peroni, S.: Towards the automatic identification of the nature of citations. In: Castro, A.G., Lange, C., Lord, P.W., Stevens, R. (eds) SePublica. CEUR Workshop Proceedings, vol. 994, pp. 63–74. CEUR-WS.org (2013)
9. Presutti, V., Consoli, S., Nuzzolese, A.G., Recupero, D.R., Gangemi, A., Bannour, I., Zargayouna, H.: Uncovering the semantics of wikipedia wikilinks. In: 19th International Conference on Knowledge Engineering and Knowledge Management (EKAW 2014) (2014)
10. Presutti, V., Draicchio, F., Gangemi, A.: Knowledge extraction based on discourse representation theory and linguistic frames. In: ten Teije, A., Völker, J., Handschuh, S., Stuckenschmidt, H., d'Acquin, M., Nikolov, A., Aussenac-Gilles, N., Hernandez, N. (eds.) EKAW 2012. LNCS, vol. 7603, pp. 114–129. Springer, Heidelberg (2012)
11. Recupero, D.R., Presutti, V., Consoli, S., Gangemi, A., Nuzzolese, A.G.: Sentilo: Frame-based sentiment analysis. Cognitive Computation (2014)

---

[7] The work described in this paper was performed with the support of the PRISMA (PiattafoRme cloud Interoperabili per SMArt-government) project, funded by the MIUR (Ministero dellIstruzione, dellUniversit'a e della Ricerca).

Legalo: Revealing the Semantics of Links

Sergio Consoli[2], Andrea Giovanni Nuzzolese[1][(✉)], Valentina Presutti[1],
Diego Reforgiato Recupero[2], and Aldo Gangemi[1]

[1] STLab, ISTC-CNR, via Nomentana, 56-00161 Rome, Italy
andrea.nuzzolese@istc.cnr.it
[2] STLab, ISTC-CNR, via Gaifami, 18-95126 Catania, Italy

Abstract. Links in webpages carry an intended semantics: usually, they indicate a relation between two things, a subject (something referenced to within the web page) and an object (the target webpage of the link, or something referred to within it). We designed and implemented a novel system, named *Legalo*, which uncovers the intended semantics of links by defining Semantic Web properties that capture its meaning. Legalo properties can be used for tagging links with semantic relations. The system can be used at http://wit.istc.cnr.it/stlab-tools/legalo.

1   Introduction

The ultimate goal of the Semantic Web is to enable intelligent agents to automatically interpret Web content, just like humans do by inspecting it, and assist users in performing a significant number of tasks by relieving their cognitive load. In order to realize this vision the Web has to be populated with machine understandable data.

Most of the Web content consists of natural language text, and current knowledge extraction (KE) tools mainly focus on linking pieces of text to Semantic Web entities (e.g. `owl:sameAs`) by means of named entity recognition (NER) methods and sense tagging (e.g., through `owl:sameAs` and `rdf:type`). Examples are NERD[1] [1], FOX[2], conTEXT[3] [2], Dbpedia Spotlight[4], Stanbol[5].

Although recognizing entities and their types is an important task and such methods address it very well, it is desirable to enrich the Web also with other types of semantic relations, e.g. factual relations, as in Linked Data. A good practice is to embed RDFa annotations within HTML anchor tags for making these relations explicit. This requires the design of binary properties that capture the essential semantics of the relations between two entities. For example, consider the sentence

"John McCarthy invented LISP."

---

[1] http://nerd.eurecom.fr
[2] http://aksw.org/Projects/FOX.html
[3] http://context.aksw.org/app/
[4] http://dbpedia-spotlight.github.com/demo
[5] http://stanbol.apache.org

© Springer International Publishing Switzerland 2015
P. Lambrix et al. (Eds.): EKAW 2014 Satellite Events, LNAI 8982, pp. 140–144, 2015.
DOI: 10.1007/978-3-319-17966-7_18

Let's hypothesize that the term "LISP" is embedded in a href tag, i.e. it is a link. When defining such a link the author is providing a *pragmatic* trace of a semantic relation between a subject and "LISP"; in this case, the subject is "John McCarthy".

Such semantic relations can be simple (intrinsically binary) like in this case: we may represent it by means of a property `invent`. They can be complex (chains of relations); consider for example the sentence:

"The New York Times reported that John McCarthy died."

In this case the relation between "The New York Times" and "John McCarthy" is a chain, involving the act of reporting and the event of John McCarthy's death.

However, in order to use it as RDFa (as well as in many other Linked Data applications) we may need to design a binary property that "summarizes" its meaning.

How can this design be done automatically? We can use the text surrounding links, which, in addition to the pragmatic trace, i.e. a link, provides us with a *linguistic trace* of such semantic relations. In fact, the text within which we include a link usually expresses directly or indirectly its intended semantics. In the above example, the sentence expresses that "The New York Times" "has reported about the death of "John McCarthy". As for this example, our aim is to automatically produce a triple[6] such as:

```
dbpedia:The_New_York_Times legalo:reportDie dbpedia:John_McCarthy
```

Legalo automatically designs a binary semantic property, which captures the essential semantics expressed by a sentence on how entities are related. When possible it aligns the extracted property to an existing semantic Web property.

Legalo is based on a pipeline of components, which has at its core a machine reader, i.e. FRED[7] [3]. FRED transforms natural language text to a formal RDF/OWL graph representation. Legalo implements a set of graph pattern-based rules, and apply them on FRED graphs for producing Semantic Web binary relations that capture the semantics of specific links.

Legalo REST service is available at http://wit.istc.cnr.it/stlab-tools/legalo, where a GUI interface is available serving as a demonstration. A specialized version of Legalo working on Wikipedia links is available at http://wit.istc.cnr.it/stlab-tools/legalo/wikipedia. The theory and method behind Legalo, and its user-based evaluation, is described in the full research paper accepted at the main conference[8].

1.1   The Subject/Object Identification Issue

Generating a semantic property that captures the intended semantics of a link means being able as well to identify the subject and the object of such a property. Subjects and objects can be expressed, in natural language text, by following

---

[6] Prefix `dbpedia:` stands for http://dbpedia.org/page/

[7] http://wit.istc.cnr.it/stlab-tools/fred/

[8] A reference to the full research paper will be included in a possible camera ready.

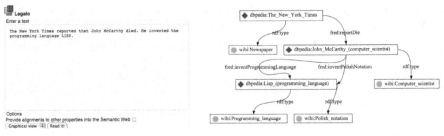

(a) Legalo user interface.   (b) Example of a result of Legalo.

Fig. 1. Legalo user interface 1 and 1(b) an example of result for the sentence "The New York Times reported that John McCarthy died. He invented the programming language LISP".

diverse rhetorical structures, narrative forms, etc. making it hard to identify one and a unique way to identify them in a sentence.

In the context of Legalo, and its specialized Wikipedia version, we implement a number of heuristics based on certain assumptions:

- Legalo works on any "plain" natural language sentence including at least two DBpedia named entities. It detects such entities and assumes that each pair of them is a candidate subject/object pair for a semantic relation; one approach consisted in concatenating all labels of graph entities in the extracted subgraphs belonging to the `fred:` namespace, including the more general types of intermediate nodes. With this strategy, each link was associated to a number of properties resulting from different possible paths, each having different length.
- Legalo-wikipedia is specialized for generating a semantic relation for each `wikiPageWikiLink` triple. Hence the subject/object pair is given by the DBpedia dataset.

Both these approaches have limitations, however in this work our focus is on a method for generating a semantic relation between two given entities, hence these heuristics provide a good approximation. We leave to further research the identification of all possible related subject/object pairs that can be found in a sentence.

2   Legalo Demos

We will show two demos: Legalo and Legalo-wikipedia, respectively.

Legalo. Figure 1 shows the main interface of Legalo. The user can input a sentence in a text field. By clicking on the "Link it" button, the system returns to the user a number of semantic relations that are expressed in the sentence, between DBpedia entities that are there mentioned. The result can be viewed as a graph (as shown in Figure 1(b)) or returned as a RDF serialization[9]

---

[9] Legalo supports six different RDF formats.

For example, consider the sentence

"The New York Times reported that John McCarthy died. He invented
the programming language LISP."

Legalo identifies three dbpedia named entities, i.e. dbpedia:The_New_Times,
dbpedia:John_McCarty, dbpedia:Lisp. Consequently, it generates three semantic relations by applying a relation discovery algorithm, as it is depicted in
Figure 1(b). Additionally, Legalo provides a formalization for all the discovered
properties in terms of domain, range (provided as WiBi[10]) types and OWL2
property chain[11]. The latter is aimed at capturing the intensional meaning of
the property as originally represented by FRED.

Legalo Specialized for Wikipeda Pagelinks. The specialized version of Wikipedia
takes as input a DBpedia entity and retrieves all its associated pagelinks, i.e.
wikiPageWikiLinks triples, returning them in a table, and including their associated sentences[12]. The user can select some or all of them and by clicking on
"Link it!" the system will return a binary property produced for capturing the
essential semantics expressed by the sentence about how the two entities are
related (cf. Figure 2).

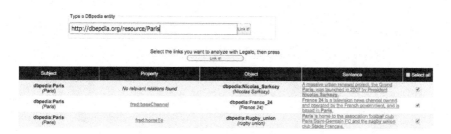

Fig. 2. Legalo-wikipedia demo applied to the entity "Paris"

3   Conclusion

In this demo we show a system, named *Legalo* able to produce Semantic Web
properties that make it explicit the intended meaning of links in webpages. We
implemented two versions of Legalo, one able to work on any natural language
sentence, the other specialized on Wikipedia links. The specialized version is
described in detail and evaluated in a full research paper accepted at the main
conference, while the generalized version is a novel contribution.

---

[10] http://www.wibitaxonomy.org/

[11] Available with any available output format except "Graphical view".

[12] The sentence is the one surrounding the object of the link in the Wikipedia page of
the subject.

References

1. Rizzo, G., Troncy, R., Hellmann, S., Bruemmer, M.: NERD meets NIF: Lifting NLP extraction results to the linked data cloud. In: LDOW, 5th Wks. on Linked Data on the Web, Lyon, France, April 2012
2. Khalili, A., Auer, S., Ngonga Ngomo, A.-C.: conTEXT – lightweight text analytics using linked data. In: Presutti, V., d'Amato, C., Gandon, F., d'Aquin, M., Staab, S., Tordai, A. (eds.) ESWC 2014. LNCS, vol. 8465, pp. 628–643. Springer, Heidelberg (2014)
3. Presutti, V., Draicchio, F., Gangemi, A.: Knowledge extraction based on discourse representation theory and linguistic frames. In: ten Teije, A., Völker, J., Handschuh, S., Stuckenschmidt, H., d'Acquin, M., Nikolov, A., Aussenac-Gilles, N., Hernandez, N. (eds.) EKAW 2012. LNCS, vol. 7603, pp. 114–129. Springer, Heidelberg (2012)

TourRDF: Representing, Enriching, and Publishing Curated Tours Based on Linked Data

Esko Ikkala, Eetu Mäkelä, and Eero Hyvönen[✉]

Semantic Computing Research Group (SeCo), Aalto University, Espoo, Finland
{Esko.Ikkala,Eetu.Makela,Eero.Hyvonen}@aalto.fi
http://www.seco.tkk.fi/

Abstract. Current mobile tourist guide systems are developed and used in separate data silos: each system and vendor tends to use its own proprietary, closed formats for representing tours and point of interest (POI) content. As a result, tour data cannot be enriched from other providers' tour and POI repositories, or from other external data sources — even when such data were publicly available by, e.g., cities willing to promote tourism. This paper argues, that an open shared RDF-based tour vocabulary is needed to address these problems, and introduces such a model, TourRDF, extending the earlier TourML schema into the era of Linked Data. As a test and an evaluation of the approach, a case study based on data about the Unesco World Heritage site Suomenlinna fortress is presented.

1 Problem: Linked Data Standards for Curated Tours

Context-aware mobile tourist guides have been an obvious application for mobile phones as soon as GPS enabled mobile phones went mainstream in 2007. They use recorded or automatically generated spoken commentary (audio guides), maps and multimedia content to inform and guide the user along the tour. Tours are essentially sequences of POIs, either outdoors in nature (e.g., a walking tour in the old town of a city) or indoors in buildings (e.g., a museum tour). POIs associate tangible and intangible cultural assets (e.g., data about a building or information about a historical event) with a place. The main purpose of a (self- or professionally) guided tour is to help the user in finding POIs, and then to provide her with contextualized information about them. Such information about cultural sights, historical persons, places, events, museum objects etc. typically form complex interlinked networks of heterogeneous, distributed data, making Cultural Heritage (CH) a promising application case for Linked Data [3].

Today, a large number of geospatially referenced CH data is openly available in RDF-format via SPARQL endpoints, and systems such as DBpedia Mobile [1] already utilize them. However, there are no standards for representing tours and POIs as Linked Data. As a result, data about tours and POIs is incompatible in different systems, and the data is difficult to share and enrich with related

© Springer International Publishing Switzerland 2015
P. Lambrix et al. (Eds.): EKAW 2014 Satellite Events, LNAI 8982, pp. 145–149, 2015.
DOI: 10.1007/978-3-319-17966-7_19

data. There is also the risk that the content, created by one vendor, is incompatible with new generations of devices and platforms, or becomes obsolete due to bankruptcy. The CH content providers, publishers, and end users would therefore benefit from a standard way of representing tours, and specifications for this, most notably TourML, have already been proposed [5,6]. However, these specifications do not take into account the potential of Linked Data.

This paper presents a solution approach to these issues by introducing an RDF-based vocabulary, TourRDF, for representing curated tours. We first present the model and demonstrate its usage by a tour visualization demo and a map widget for browsing georeferenced data from different sources. Finally, we also show how the Linked Data in our system can be accessed and re-used from the outside as a SPARQL service.

2   TourRDF for Representing Curated Tours

TourRDF vocabulary[1] is based on TourML [6] extending it with the Linked Data dimension. The primary goal of the existing TourML specification is to make sure that the tours created by a museum are compatible with different mobile devices and software systems, but it doesn't offer effective methods for the content providers to link and enrich the content of the tour with external data sources. By offering an easy access to CH data sources via SPARQL endpoints, the Linked Data extension makes it possible for the content provider to produce richer and more contextualized background information on the tour destinations.

The structure of a tour is similar to TourML: the basic building blocks of a tour are *stops* and *connections* between them. Amongst other things, a tour stop has coordinates, and a trigger zone to start the audio descripton, when the user approaches the stop. There are two kinds of stops: navigational stops, that are used to guide the user along the route, and actual stops that include *assets* to be exposed to the end user. The connections have a source and a destination stop, and they can also contain information about the distance or accessibility restrictions between the stops. Modeling the actual path that the user has to follow to get to the next stop is left for the application utilizing TourRDF.

Linked Data annotations are included in the assets. A tour stop can contain references to, e.g., historical persons, events, places, or objects. TourRDF describes only the structure of the tour, and the different assets are modeled using seperate schemas. For example, for the POIs we used the POI schema developed in TravelSampo [4], and for historical events CIDOC CRM was used, as in [2].

3   Case Suomenlinna: Enriching Tours with Linked Data

To test TourRDF, we annotated and georeferenced data about 250 buildings in the Suomenlinna maritime fortress, a Unesco World Heritage Site, located off the

---

[1] Cf. http://vocab.at/page/71qi for documentation how TourRDF is used with example tour data.

coast of Helsinki. The primary data source was the History of Buildings map of Suomenlinna[2]. In addition to basic information, such as coordinates and textual descriptions, 50 POI types, 15 persons, 23 historical events, and 158 keyword IRIs were linked to the buildings. The resulting RDF dataset was published in the Linked Data Finland (LDF) data service[3].

A tour visualization demo[4] was implemented with Google Maps API on top of the LDF SPARQL endpoint. The idea of the demo is to visualize how different linked data sources can be combined to enrich and add more content to tours, not to act as an actual mobile guide. The example tour shown on the Figure 1 is the main tourist route in Suomenlinna, the Blue Route.[5] The tour consists of 42 stops, and each stop consists of one Suomenlinna building (POI). When a map marker is clicked, an info window with a short description, POI type, and keywords (if available) pops out. The *Read more* button there generates a stop info page with links to additional contextual background data. The background data is generated by SPARQL queries to several datasets published in the LDF data service, such as the Finnish History Ontology, Semantic National Biography, and MuseumFinland collections of artifacts.

Fig. 1. Suomenlinna Blue Route represented with TourRDF, with a tour stop selected

4   Browsing Georeferenced Linked Data

To foster reuse of linked tour data, we implemented an annotation tool POI Finder [6]. It is targeted for finding assets for tours represented using TourRDF, but it can also be used with other web-based tour authoring applications, such

---

[2] http://herba.suomenlinna.fi/map/

[3] Cf. http://www.ldf.fi/dataset/poi/ for dataset documentation and the SPARQL end point.

[4] http://www.ldf.fi/dev/tour-demo/

[5] http://www.suomenlinna.fi/en/visitor/plan-your-visit/blue-route/

[6] http://www.ldf.fi/dev/poi-finder/

as IZI.travel[7] or My Tours[8]. There are two main usage scenarios for finding IRIs:
1) browsing and selecting POIs for a tour annotation in an external application,
and 2) enriching existing tour content with related IRI references. POI Finder
is a map widget, which gathers georeferenced RDF data from different openly
available sources (SPARQL endpoints) and visualizes the data using Google
Maps API. Currently RDF data is queried from five sources: Linked Geo Data,
DBPedia, RKY (cultural-historically significant milieu in Finland), Tarinoiden
Helsinki (literature data relating to places) and Suomenlinna dataset.

Fig. 2. POI Finder, 424 POIs near Helsinki city center

Fig. 2 shows POI Finder in action. POIs inside the draggable bounding circle
are rendered on the map. When a map marker is clicked, an info window with
a short description and POI type (if available) pops out. By clicking the *Read
more* button, the POI properties are provived either in HTML and JSON formats
(about the POIs published in the LDF data service) or via dereferenceable URIs
(about other POI sources).

5   Discussion

TourRDF is to our knowledge the first attempt to represent curated tours as
Linked Data. Its goal is to foster interoperability, data reuse, and data enrichment between content providers. In this way, more useful applications for end
users can be created with less costs. Future work includes incorporating more
georeferenced data sources and also information on the relationship between a
tour stop and it's linked data annotations.

---

[7] http://izi.travel/
[8] http://www.mytoursapp.com/

References

1. Becker, C., Bizer, C.: Exploring the geospatial semantic web with DBpedia Mobile. Web Semantics: Science, Services and Agents on the World Wide Web **7**(4), 278–286 (2009)
2. Hyvönen, E., Alonen, M., Ikkala, E., Mäkelä, E.: Semantic National Biography: an event-based approach to publishing life stories as linked data. In: Proceedings of ISWC 2014, Demos and Posters (forth-coming). Springer-Verlag (2014)
3. Hyvönen, E.: Publishing and using cultural heritage linked data on the semantic web. Morgan & Claypool, Palo Alto, CA (2012)
4. Mäkelä, E., Lindblad, A., Väätäinen, J., Alatalo, R., Suominen, O., Hyvönen, E.: Discovering places of interest through direct and indirect associations in heterogeneous sources–the TravelSampo system. In: Terra Cognita 2011: Foundations, Technologies and Applications of the Geospatial Web. CEUR Workshop Proceedings, vol. 798 (2011)
5. Sacher, D., Biella, D., Luther, W.: Towards a versatile metadata exchange format for digital museum collections. Digital Heritage International Congress (DigitalHeritage) **2**, 129–136 (2013)
6. Stein, R., Proctor, N.: TourML: an emerging specification for museum mobile experiences. In: Museums and the Web 2011: Proc. Archieves & Museum Informatics, Toronto (2011)

SUGOI: Automated Ontology Interchangeability

Zubeida Casmod Khan[1,2(✉)] and C. Maria Keet[1]

[1] Department of Computer Science, University of Cape Town,
Cape Town, South Africa
zkhan@csir.co.za, mkeet@cs.uct.ac.za
[2] Council for Scientific and Industrial Research, Pretoria, South Africa

Abstract. A foundational ontology can solve interoperability issues among the domain ontologies aligned to it. However, several foundational ontologies have been developed, hence such interoperability issues exist among domain ontologies. The novel SUGOI tool, *Software Used to Gain Ontology Interchangeability*, allows a user to interchange automatically a domain ontology among the DOLCE, BFO and GFO foundational ontologies. The success of swapping varies due to differences in coverage, and amount of mappings both between the foundational ontologies and the alignment mappings between the domain and the foundational ontology. In this demo we present the tool, and attendees can bring their preferred ontology for interchange by SUGOI, and will be assisted with the analysis of the results in terms of 'good' and 'bad' entity linking to assess how feasible it is to change it over to the other foundational ontology.

1 Introduction

Since over ten years, foundational ontologies (FOs) have been proposed as a component to facilitate interoperability among domain ontologies on the Semantic Web, because they provide common high-level categories so that domain ontologies linked to them are also interoperable [7]. Multiple FOs have been developed in the meantime, however, such as DOLCE, BFO [7], GFO [1], SUMO [9], and YAMATO [8]. This created the problem of semantic conflicts for domain ontologies that are linked to different FOs—if those FOs are indeed really different on crucial components—and raises new questions for ontology engineers, including:

1. If domain ontology O_A is linked to FO O_X, then is it still interoperable with domain ontology O_B that is linked to FO O_Y?
2. Is it feasible to automatically generate links between O_A and O_Y, given O_A is linked to O_X?

To answer these two questions, we developed SUGOI, a *Software Used to Gain Ontology Interchangeability*, which automatically interchanges the FO a domain ontology is linked to. The current version can swap between DOLCE, BFO, and GFO (their mappings have been studied in detail [3,5]); it easily can be extended to handle other FOs, as only new mapping files will have to be provided. SUGOI and a video capture demo demonstrating the online and offline versions of the

© Springer International Publishing Switzerland 2015
P. Lambrix et al. (Eds.): EKAW 2014 Satellite Events, LNAI 8982, pp. 150–153, 2015.
DOI: 10.1007/978-3-319-17966-7_20

tool are accessible from the FO library ROMULUS at http://www.thezfiles.co.za/ROMULUS/ontologyInterchange.html. The remainder of this paper outlines the design of SUGOI, provides an example and implementation and demo details.

2   Design of SUGOI

SUGOI interchanges domain ontologies between DOLCE, BFO, and GFO, which are all stored as OWL files. This requires mappings between the selected FOs, for which we use the results obtained by [3,5]: its equivalence and subsumption mappings between entities in the three different ontologies have been investigated in detail, are logically consistent, and are available as machine-processable OWL files from the ontology repository ROMULUS [4].

Several ontology files are being used in the interchangeability being:
- The *Source Ontology* ($^s\mathcal{O}$) to be interchanged, comprising the *Source Domain Ontology* ($^s\mathcal{O}_d$) and the *Source Foundational Ontology* ($^s\mathcal{O}_f$), and any equivalence or subsumption mappings between entities in $^s\mathcal{O}_d$ and $^s\mathcal{O}_f$.
- The *Target Ontology* ($^t\mathcal{O}$) that has been interchanged, comprising the *Target Domain Ontology* ($^t\mathcal{O}_d$), the chosen *Target Foundational Ontology* ($^t\mathcal{O}_f$), and any equivalence or subsumption mappings between entities in $^t\mathcal{O}_d$ and $^t\mathcal{O}_f$.
- *Mapping ontology*: the mapping ontology between the $^s\mathcal{O}_f$ and the $^t\mathcal{O}_f$.
- *Domain entity*: an entity (class or property) from $^s\mathcal{O}_d$ or $^t\mathcal{O}_d$.

The SUGOI algorithm accepts a $^s\mathcal{O}$ consisting of a $^s\mathcal{O}_d$ linked to a $^s\mathcal{O}_f$ and interchanges it to a $^t\mathcal{O}$ with a different $^t\mathcal{O}_f$. SUGOI has twenty consistent mapping files [3] pre-loaded to interchange between DOLCE, BFO and GFO modules, and accesses the remainder of the ontology files either by loading the ontology from the online URI, or from an offline file, depending on the version in use (see below). After the interchange process, all the domain entities from the $^s\mathcal{O}_d$ are present in the $^t\mathcal{O}_d$. SUGOI links domain entities from the $^s\mathcal{O}_d$ to the $^t\mathcal{O}_f$ by mapping a domain entity's superentity in the $^s\mathcal{O}_f$ to its corresponding superentity in the $^t\mathcal{O}_f$ using the mapping ontology. If the domain entity's superentity does not have a mapping entity, SUGOI then looks for a corresponding mapping entity at a higher level up in the taxonomy. Thus, eventually, the domain entity from the $^s\mathcal{O}_d$ is mapped with on-the-fly subsumption.

The source and two output ontologies are shown for sao:Membrane Surface from the SAO ontology in Fig 1, interchanged to DOLCE and GFO. The next example illustrates the process in sequence for the DMOP ontology [2].

Example 1. The basic steps of the algorithm for interchanging between DOLCE to GFO are as follows, using the data mining DMOP ontology [2] as an example:
1. Create a new ontology file, a $^t\mathcal{O}$: dmop-gfo.owl.
2. Copy the entire $^t\mathcal{O}_f$ to the $^t\mathcal{O}$: copy the GFO ontology into dmop-gfo.owl.
3. Copy the axioms from the $^s\mathcal{O}_d$ to the $^t\mathcal{O}$: e.g., consider the axioms, axiom1: dmop:DecisionBoundary $\sqsubseteq$ dolce:abstract and axiom2: dmop:Strategy $\sqsubseteq$ dolce:Non PhysicalEndurant which exist in the $^s\mathcal{O}$ DMOP. We add these axioms to the dmop-gfo.owl $^t\mathcal{O}$ and they are referred to as 'new' axioms.

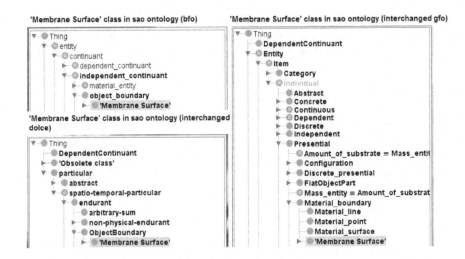

Fig. 1. The position of the sao:Membrane Surface class in source and target ontologies

4. Change the 'new' axioms to reference ${}^t\mathcal{O}_f$ entities, if mappings exist: for axiom1, there is an equivalence mapping between gfo:Abstract and dolce:abstract, hence we change axiom1 dmop:DecisionBoundary ⊑ dolce:abstract to dmop:DecisionBoundary ⊑ gfo:Abstract. For axiom2, there is no equivalence mapping between dolce:NonPhysicalEndurant and GFO entities; we skip this step.

5. If a mapping does not exist, perform on-the-fly subsumption: For axiom2, dolce:NonPhysicalEndurant has a superclass dolce:Endurant and the mapping ontology has dolce:endurant ≡ gfo:Presential, so dolce:NonPhysicalEndurant ⊑ gfo:Presential is added to dmop-gfo.owl.

6. Delete entities that exist in the ${}^t\mathcal{O}$ that are from the ${}^s\mathcal{O}_f$ but do not appear in an axiom with entities from the ${}^t\mathcal{O}_d$, resulting in the final ${}^t\mathcal{O}$, dmop-gfo.owl. Delete the dolce:abstract entity from dmop-gfo.owl.

There are currently three platform-independent versions of SUGOI:

1. Applet: an online web version integrated into the ROMULUS repository [4].
2. Desktop online version: a platform independent jar file to be executed on a local machine, but requires internet connectivity.
3. Desktop offline version: a platform independent jar file to be executed on a local machine, and is bundled with foundational and mapping ontology files.

SUGOI was developed in Java using the OWLAPI v3.5.0 in Netbeans IDE 8.0. The Applet of SUGOI is deployed online within any browser that has the Java TM Platform plugin installed and activated. The desktop versions of SUGOI are platform independent jar files with dependencies (all bundled together) that require minimal disk space, and Java runtime components installed. For future work, we consider creating a SUGOI Protégé plugin.

SUGOI generates not only a target ontology annotated with its provenance (that it automatically linked to a FO by SUGIO), but also a log file with the changes that have been made and a *raw interchangeability* measure. This measure factors in the so-called 'good target linking' and 'bad target linking', where the former counts direct alignments to a $^{t}\mathcal{O}_f$ and the latter that some entity of the $^{s}\mathcal{O}_f$ was needed as intermediary, indicating how successful the interchange was. For instance, the raw interchangeability for the afore-mentioned SAO to DOLCE is 50% and to GFO was 55% and for DMOP to GFO it was 12% (rounded) [6]. We conducted an evaluation with 16 ontologies that were aligned to a FO, which are described in [6].

3 Demonstration of SUGOI

In the demo session, we will show the easy use of the tool and elaborate on analysis of the output data. Attendees also can bring their own ontology, or some other that they are interested in, that is aligned to either DOLCE, BFO or GFO, and use SUGOI to change its FO. The resulting ontology will be inspected and analysed to see what has changed for this particular instance, which can be augmented on the spot with the deeper analysis involving the mappings among the FOs that are used by the algorithm.

References

1. Herre, H.: General formal ontology (GFO): a foundational ontology for conceptual modelling. In: Poli, R., Healy, M., Kameas, A. (eds.) Theory and Applications of Ontology: Computer Applications, pp. 297–345. Springer, Heidelberg (2010). chap. 14
2. Keet, C.M., Lawrynowicz, A., d'Amato, C., Hilario, M.: Modeling Issues, Choices in the Data Mining OPtimization Ontology. In: Proc. of OWLED 2013. CEUR Workshop Proceedings, vol. 1080. CEUR-WS.org, Montpellier, France, 26–27 May 2013
3. Khan, Z., Keet, C.M.: Addressing issues in foundational ontology mediation. In: Proc. of KEOD 2013, pp. 5–16. SCITEPRESS - Science and Technology Publications, Vilamoura, 19–22 September 2013
4. Khan, Z.C., Keet, C.M.: The foundational ontology library ROMULUS. In: Cuzzocrea, A., Maabout, S. (eds.) MEDI 2013. LNCS, vol. 8216, pp. 200–211. Springer, Heidelberg (2013)
5. Khan, Z., Keet, C.M.: Toward semantic interoperability with aligned foundational ontologies in ROMULUS. In: Proc. of K-CAP 2013. ACM proceedings, Banff, Canada. (poster/demo), 23–26 June 2013
6. Khan, Z.C., Keet, C.M.: Feasibility of automated foundational ontology interchangeability. In: Janowicz, K., Schlobach, S., Lambrix, P., Hyvönen, E. (eds.) EKAW 2014. LNCS, vol. 8876, pp. 225–237. Springer, Heidelberg (2014)
7. Masolo, C., Borgo, S., Gangemi, A., Guarino, N., Oltramari, A.: Ontology library. WonderWeb Deliverable D18 (ver. 1.0, 31–12–2003). http://wonderweb. semanticweb.org (2003)
8. Mizoguchi, R.: YAMATO: Yet Another More Advanced Top-level Ontology. In: Proceedings of the Sixth Australasian Ontology Workshop. Conferences in Research and Practice in Information, pp. 1–16, Sydney: ACS (2010)
9. Niles, I., Pease, A.: Towards a standard upper ontology. In: Welty, C., Smith, B. (eds.) Proc. of FOIS 2001, Ogunquit, Maine, 17–19 October 2001

WebVOWL: Web-Based Visualization of Ontologies

Steffen Lohmann[1]([✉]), Vincent Link[1], Eduard Marbach[1], and Stefan Negru[2]

[1] Institute for Visualization and Interactive Systems (VIS),
University of Stuttgart, Universitätsstr. 38, 70569 Stuttgart, Germany
steffen.lohmann@vis.uni-stuttgart.de
[2] Faculty of Computer Science, Alexandru Ioan Cuza University,
Strada General Henri Mathias Berthelot 16, 700483 Iasi, Romania
stefan.negru@info.uaic.ro

Abstract. We present WebVOWL, a responsive web application for the visualization of ontologies. It implements the Visual Notation for OWL Ontologies (VOWL) and is entirely based on open web standards. The visualizations are automatically generated from JSON files, into which the ontologies need to be converted. An exemplary OWL2VOWL converter implemented in Java and based on the OWL API is currently used for this purpose. The ontologies are rendered in a force-directed graph layout according to the VOWL specification. Interaction techniques allow to explore the ontologies and customize their visualizations.

1 Introduction

Ontology visualizations are important to knowledge engineering, as they can assist in the exploration, verification, and sensemaking of ontologies [8,11]. They are particularly useful for people less familiar with ontologies, but can also give expert users a new perspective on ontologies. The Visual Notation for OWL Ontologies (VOWL) provides a visual language for the user-oriented representation of ontologies [11]. In contrast to related work, VOWL aims for an intuitive visualization that is also understandable to casual ontology users.

As a first implementation of VOWL, a plugin for the ontology editor Protégé has been developed [10]. In this paper, we present WebVOWL, an alternative and more advanced implementation of VOWL entirely based on open web standards. WebVOWL is easy to use and understand and therefore also appropriate for casual ontology users, as confirmed by an evaluation [11]. It features several interaction techniques that allow to explore the ontology and customize its visualization. It is released under the MIT license and available at http://vowl.visualdataweb.org.

WebVOWL is the first ontology visualization tool of its kind to the best of our knowledge. Like ProtégéVOWL, most other ontology visualizations are implemented in Java and are provided as plugins for ontology editors [5,8,11]. WebVOWL is independent of any ontology editor. It works with all modern web browsers that implement SVG, CSS, and JavaScript to a sufficient degree.

© Springer International Publishing Switzerland 2015
P. Lambrix et al. (Eds.): EKAW 2014 Satellite Events, LNAI 8982, pp. 154–158, 2015.
DOI: 10.1007/978-3-319-17966-7_21

Related tools running in web browsers, such as FlexViz [6], are based on technologies like Adobe Flex that require proprietary browser plugins. LodLive [3] is technically comparable to WebVOWL but focuses on the visual exploration of Linked Data and not on the visualization of ontologies.

In the following, we describe the technical realization and the interactive features of WebVOWL. The interested reader is referred to the related EKAW paper [11] and VOWL specification [12] for more information on VOWL. The EKAW paper also reports on a user study where VOWL and its implementation in WebVOWL have been evaluated. In the demo at EKAW, we will visualize several ontologies with WebVOWL, showcase the interactive features of the tool, and give conference attendees the opportunity to visualize and explore ontologies of interest by their own.

2 Ontology Preprocessing

Instead of being tied to a particular OWL parser, we defined a JSON schema for WebVOWL that ontologies need to be converted into. The JSON schema is optimized with regard to VOWL, i.e., its format differs from typical OWL serializations in order to enable an efficient generation of the interactive graph visualization. For that reason, it is also different from other JSON schemas that emerged in the context of the Semantic Web, such as RDF/JSON [4] and JSON-LD [13]. The VOWL-JSON file contains the TBox of the ontology, i.e., the classes, properties, and datatypes along with type information (*owl:ObjectProperty*, *xsd:dateTime*, etc.). ABox information (individuals and data values) is not considered for the time being but planned to be integrated in the future. Additional characteristics of the elements (inverse, functional, deprecated, etc.) as well as header information (ontology title, version, etc.) and optional ontology statistics (number of classes, properties, etc.) are separately listed. If no ontology statistics are provided in the JSON file, they are computed in WebVOWL at runtime.

Even though WebVOWL is based on JavaScript, the transformation of the OWL ontology into JSON does not need to be performed with JavaScript but can also be done with other programming languages. We implemented a Java-based OWL2VOWL converter, using the well-tested OWL API of the University of Manchester [7]. The converter accesses the ontology representation provided by the OWL API and transforms it into the JSON format required by WebVOWL.

3 VOWL Visualization

The VOWL visualization is generated from the JSON file at runtime. WebVOWL renders the graphical elements according to the VOWL specification, i.e., it takes the SVG code and CSS styling information provided by the specification. The force-directed graph layout is created with the JavaScript library D3 [2]. It uses a physics simulation where the forces are iteratively applied, resulting in an animation that dynamically positions the nodes of the graph. The energy of the forces cools down in each iteration and the layout animation stops automatically after some time to provide a stable graph visualization and remove load from the processor.

An example of the resulting graph visualization is given in Figure 1. It shows a screenshot of WebVOWL (version 0.2.13) used to visualize revision 1.35 of the SIOC Core Ontology [1]. Metadata about the ontology, such as its title, namespace, author(s), and version, is shown in the sidebar, along with the ontology description and aforementioned statistics. An accordion widget helps to save screen space in the sidebar.

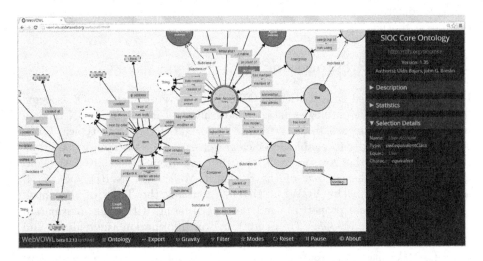

Fig. 1. SIOC Core Ontology visualized with WebVOWL. The class *User Account* has been selected and the class *Site* has been pinned.

4   Interaction and Exploration

Users can optimize the graph visualization and adapt it to their needs by rearranging nodes via drag and drop. The graph layout can also be adjusted by modifying the forces between nodes through the *gravity* settings. Datatypes have a separate force so that they can be placed in close proximity to the classes they are linked with.

Whenever a node is dragged, the force-directed algorithm is triggered and the rest of the nodes are repositioned with animated transitions. To prevent this behavior, users can *pause* the automatic layout in favor of a manual positioning of the nodes. In addition, WebVOWL implements a "pick and pin" *mode* inspired by the RelFinder [9]: It allows to decouple selected nodes from the automatic layout and pin them at custom positions on the canvas. Pinned nodes are indicated by a needle symbol (cf. class *Site* in Figure 1) that can be removed to recouple the nodes with the force-directed layout.

Users can zoom in and out, pan the background, and select elements in the graph visualization. Details about selected elements are displayed in the accordion widget of the sidebar, such as for the selected class *User Account* in Figure 1. IRIs are provided as hyperlinks that can be opened in another tab of the web browser for further exploration. Related elements (e.g., subproperties) are interactively highlighted according to the VOWL specification.

Another group of interactive features are *filters* that help to reduce the size of the VOWL graph and increase its visual scalability. Two filters are currently implemented, one for datatypes and another for "solitary subclasses", which are subclasses only connected to their superclass but not to other classes.

Finally, WebVOWL allows to export the ontology visualization as SVG image that can be opened in other applications, scaled without loss of quality, edited, shared, and printed.

5   Conclusion and Future Work

The current WebVOWL implementation already considers a large portion of the OWL 2 language constructs. We aim to further extend the VOWL specification, OWL2VOWL converter, and WebVOWL to cover as many OWL constructs as possible. Furthermore, we plan to develop features that allow to hide selected subgraphs for a more compact visualization of large ontologies. Future work will also need to address features that help to keep a "mental map", for example, by allowing users to save a VOWL visualization with all its settings as an annotated JSON file. Other open issues are multi-language support, improved search functionality, and the inclusion of ABox data in the JSON schema, converter, and WebVOWL user interface.

WebVOWL can be used in different interaction contexts, including settings with touch interfaces. For instance, zooming can either be performed with the mouse wheel, a double click/tap, or a two fingers zooming gesture (on multi-touch devices). A desirable application of WebVOWL would be a web service where users could upload arbitrary ontologies to get them visualized. Apart from that, we hope that WebVOWL will be useful to others and in related projects, such as ontology editing, ontology alignment, or Linked Data exploration.

References

1. Bojārs, U., Breslin, J.: SIOC Core Ontology Specification. http://rdfs.org/sioc/spec/ (2010)
2. Bostock, M., Ogievetsky, V., Heer, J.: D3: Data-driven documents. IEEE Transactions on Visualization and Computer Graphics **17**(12), 2301–2309 (2011)
3. Camarda, D.V., Mazzini, S., Antonuccio, A.: LodLive, exploring the web of data. In: I-SEMANTICS 2012, pp. 197–200. ACM (2012)
4. Davis, I., Steiner, T., Hors, A.L.: RDF 1.1 JSON Alternate Serialization (RDF/JSON). http://www.w3.org/TR/rdf-json/ (2013)

5. Dudáš, M., Zamazal, O., Svátek, V.: Roadmapping and navigating in the ontology visualization landscape. In: Janowicz, K., Schlobach, S., Lambrix, P., Hyvönen, E. (eds.) EKAW 2014. LNCS, vol. 8876, pp. 137–152. Springer, Heidelberg (2014)
6. Falconer, S.M., Callendar, C., Storey, M.-A.: A visualization service for the semantic web. In: Cimiano, P., Pinto, H.S. (eds.) EKAW 2010. LNCS, vol. 6317, pp. 554–564. Springer, Heidelberg (2010)
7. Horridge, M., Bechhofer, S.: The OWL API: A java API for OWL ontologies. Semantic Web **2**(1), 11–21 (2011)
8. Lanzenberger, M., Sampson, J., Rester, M.: Visualization in ontology tools. In: CISIS 2009, pp. 705–711. IEEE (2009)
9. Lohmann, S., Heim, P., Stegemann, T., Ziegler, J.: The RelFinder user interface: interactive exploration of relationships between objects of interest. In: IUI 2010, pp. 421–422. ACM (2010)
10. Lohmann, S., Negru, S., Bold, D.: The protégéVOWL plugin: ontology visualization for everyone. In: Presutti, V., Blomqvist, E., Troncy, R., Sack, H., Papadakis, I., Tordai, A. (eds.) ESWC 2014 Satellite Events. LNCS, vol. 8798, pp. 394–399. Springer, Heidelberg (2014)
11. Lohmann, S., Negru, S., Haag, F., Ertl, T.: VOWL 2: user-oriented visualization of ontologies. In: Janowicz, K., Schlobach, S., Lambrix, P., Hyvönen, E. (eds.) EKAW 2014. LNCS, vol. 8876, pp. 266–281. Springer, Heidelberg (2014)
12. Negru, S., Lohmann, S., Haag, F.: VOWL: Visual notation for OWL ontologies. http://purl.org/vowl/spec/ (2014)
13. Sporny, M., Kellogg, G., Lanthaler, M.: JSON-LD 1.0 - A JSON-based Serialization for Linked Data. http://www.w3.org/TR/json-ld/ (2014)

LSD Dimensions: Use and Reuse of Linked Statistical Data

Albert Meroño-Peñuela[1,2(✉)]

[1] Department of Computer Science, VU University Amsterdam, Amsterdam, NL
albert.merono@vu.nl
[2] Data Archiving and Networked Services, KNAW, Amsterdam, NL

Abstract. RDF Data Cube (QB) has boosted the publication of Linked Statistical Data (LSD) on the Web, making them linkable to other related datasets and concepts following the Linked Data paradigm. In this demo we present **LSD Dimensions**, a web based application that monitors the usage of *dimensions* and *codes* (variables and values in QB jargon) in Data Structure Definitions over six hundred public SPARQL endpoints. We plan to extend the system to retrieve more in-use QB metadata, serve the dimension and code data through SPARQL and an API, and provide analytics on the (re)use of statistical properties in LSD over time.

Keywords: Semantic web · Statistics · Linked statistical data

1 Motivation

RDF Data Cube (QB) has boosted the publication of Linked Statistical Data (LSD) as Linked Open Data (LOD) by providing a means "to publish multi-dimensional data, such as statistics, on the web in such a way that they can be linked to related data sets and concepts" [4]. QB defines *cubes* as sets of *observations* consisting of *dimensions*, *measures* and *attributes*. For example, the observation "the measured life expectancy of males in Newport in the period 2004-2006 is 76.7 years" has three dimensions (*time period*, with value *2004-2006*; *region*, with value *Newport*; and *sex*, with value *male*), one measure (*population life expectancy*) and two attributes (the units of measure, *years*; and the metadata status, *measured[1]*). In some cases, it is useful to also define *codes*, a closed set of values that a dimension can get (e.g. sensible codes for the dimension *sex* could be *male* and *female*). All dimension, measure and attribute properties used by a cube are specified in its *Data Structure Definition*.

There is a vast diversity of domains to publish LSD about, and lots of dimensions and codes can be heterogeneous, domain specific and hardly comparable [2,3,5,6]. To this end, QB allows users to mint their own URIs to create arbitrary

---

Web application at http://lsd-dimensions.org
Source code at https://github.com/albertmeronyo/LSD-Dimensions/
[1] Other metadata statuses could be e.g. *estimated* or *provisional*

© Springer International Publishing Switzerland 2015
P. Lambrix et al. (Eds.): EKAW 2014 Satellite Events, LNAI 8982, pp. 159–163, 2015.
DOI: 10.1007/978-3-319-17966-7_22

```
1   PREFIX qb: <http://purl.org/linked–data/cube#>
2   PREFIX skos: <http://www.w3.org/2004/02/skos/core#>
3   PREFIX rdfs: <http://www.w3.org/2000/01/rdf–schema#>
4   SELECT DISTINCT ?dimensionu ?dimension ?codeu ?code
5   WHERE {
6   ?dimensionu a qb:DimensionProperty ;
7   rdfs:label ?dimension .
8   OPTIONAL {?dimensionu qb:codeList ?codelist .
9   ?codelist skos:hasTopConcept ?codeu .
10  ?codeu skos:prefLabel ?code . }
11  } GROUP BY ?dimensionu ?dimension ?codeu ?code ORDER BY ?dimension
```

Listing 1.1. SPARQL sent to all endpoints to retrieve LSD dimensions and codes

dimensions and associated codes. Conversely, some other dimensions and codes are quite common in statistics, and could be easily reused. However, publishers of LSD have no means to monitor the dimensions and codes currently used in other datasets published in QB as LOD, and consequently they cannot (a) link to them; nor (b) reuse them.

This is the motivation behind our demoed tool. LSD Dimensions monitors the usage of existing dimensions and codes in LSD. It allows users to browse, search and gain insight into these dimensions and codes, and to explore the Data Structure Definitions they belong to. We depict the diversity of statistical variables in LOD, and we improve their reusability.

In Section 2 we describe the current LSD Dimensions system, available online at http://lsd-dimensions.org/. Source code is available at https://github.com/albertmeronyo/LSD-Dimensions/. In Section 3 we discuss extensions that will be added to LSD Dimensions in the future.

2   LSD Dimensions

Retrieving LSD dimensions. The system queries automatically the CKAN API of Datahub.io and retrieves the most up-to-date list of publicly available SPARQL endpoints (637 at the moment of writing this paper) in the LOD cloud. Once every day, these endpoints are sent the SPARQL query shown in listing 1.1. The query retrieves all defined qb:DimensionProperty (dimensions) in each endpoint, and optionally all resources belonging to a qb:CodeList (codes) and associated to each qb:DimensionProperty, together with their labels (if available). We also retrieve Data Structure Definitions (DSD) in these endpoints. The system stores all data in a NoSQL (MongoDB) database.

User interface. LSD Dimensions provides two different views to allow users browse dimensions (3098 at the moment of writing this paper).

The main view is shown in Figure 1. It shows the full list of retrieved dimensions, listing their URIs, labels (if available) and *references* (a count of how many times that dimension is referred by the endpoints). By default, the list is sorted in descending order of references, but it can be sorted by any other field. To enhance the browsing experience, the main view provides two functionalities: (a) pagination customization (page browsing and number of results per page);

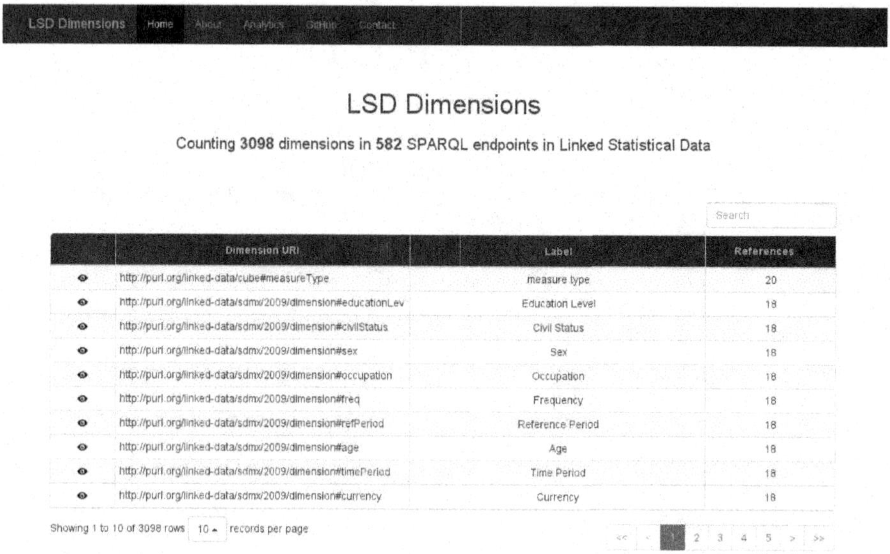

Fig. 1. Screenshot of the main view of the LSD Dimensions user interface, listing retrieved dimensions from the LOD cloud in the last day. Users can browse and search through the results.

and (b) a search feature that looks up the given string in the dimension labels and URIs, filtering the list accordingly.

Users can get insight into a chosen dimension by clicking on the corresponding eye icon, leading to the dimension details view, shown in Figure 2. This view shows the list of SPARQL endpoints that use the selected dimension, together with a list of assigned codes to that dimension (if any). All URIs are clickable and users can browse through their dereferenced representations.

By clicking on the *Analytics* tab, users can get an overview of the current usage of dimensions and codes in LSD: (1) a line chart shows the *logarithmic law* followed by the usage of dimensions; (2) a pie chart shows the ratio of SPARQL endpoints defining at least one QB dimension (48, 8.2% over all endpoints); and (3) another pie chart shows the ratio of dimensions defining at least one code (26, 0.8% over all dimensions). Defined codes are thus very scarce.

3   Future Extensions

The current implementation of LSD Dimensions monitors the daily usage of dimensions and codes in Linked Statistical Data. We wish to further extend LSD Dimensions in several ways. First, we will retrieve dimensions and values directly from qb:Observation, in addition to the current definitions. Second, we will share the collected data by (a) making it available via a SPARQL endpoint; and (b) offering an API so that client applications can get suggested dimensions

Fig. 2. Screenshot of the dimension details for a chosen dimension, including endpoints using the dimension and popular codes assigned to it

to link to, improving reusability of dimensions in LSD. Third, we will monitor additional QB metadata. Fourth, we will leverage `owl:sameAs` links to match identical dimensions. Fifth, we will run further analyses on the retrieved data (e.g. distribution on the evolution of dimension usage) to better understand practice in the LSD community. Finally, we plan to make use of [1] to study how much LSD is left out of the SPARQL endpoints in Datahub.io.

Acknowledgments. This work was supported by the Computational Humanities Programme of the KNAW (see http://ehumanities.nl) and the Dutch national program COMMIT.

References

1. Beek, W., Rietveld, L., Bazoobandi, H.R., Wielemaker, J., Schlobach, S.: LOD laundromat: a uniform way of publishing other people's dirty data. In: Mika, P., Tudorache, T., Bernstein, A., Welty, C., Knoblock, C., Vrandečić, D., Groth, P., Noy, N., Janowicz, K., Goble, C. (eds.) ISWC 2014, Part I. LNCS, vol. 8796, pp. 213–228. Springer, Heidelberg (2014)
2. Capadisli, S., Auer, S., Riedl, R.: Linked statistical data analysis. In: Proceedings of the 1st International Workshop on Semantic Statistics (SemStats 2013), ISWC. CEUR (2013)
3. Capadisli, S., Meroño-Peñuela, A., Auer, S., Riedl, R.: Semantic similarity and correlation of linked statistical data analysis. In: Proceedings of the 2nd International Workshop on Semantic Statistics (SemStats 2014), ISWC. CEUR (2014)

4. Cyganiak, R., Reynolds, D., Tennison, J.: The RDF Data Cube Vocabulary. Tech. rep., World Wide Web Consortium (2013). http://www.w3.org/TR/vocab-data-cube/

5. Meroño-Peñuela, A.: Semantic web for the humanities. In: Cimiano, P., Corcho, O., Presutti, V., Hollink, L., Rudolph, S. (eds.) ESWC 2013. LNCS, vol. 7882, pp. 645–649. Springer, Heidelberg (2013)

6. Meroño-Peñuela, A., Guéret, C., Hoekstra, R., Schlobach, S.: Detecting and reporting extensional concept drift in statistical linked data. In: 1st International Workshop on Semantic Statistics (SemStats 2013), ISWC. CEUR (2013)

Storyscope: Using Setting and Theme to Assist the Interpretation and Development of Museum Stories

Paul Mulholland[1](✉), Annika Wolff[1], Eoin Kilfeather[2], and Evin McCarthy[2]

[1] Knowledge Media Institute, The Open University, Walton Hall, Milton Keynes, UK
{p.mulholland,a.l.wolff}@open.ac.uk
[2] Digital Media Centre, Dublin Institute of Technology, Aungier Street, Dublin, Ireland
{eoin.kilfeather,evin.mccarthy}@dit.ie

Abstract. Stories are used to provide a context for museum objects, for example linking those objects to what they depict or the historical context in which they were created. Many explicit and implicit relationships exist between the people, places and things mentioned in a story and the museum objects with which they are associated. Storyscope is an environment for authoring museum stories comprising text, media elements and semantic annotations. A recommender component provides additional context as to how the story annotations are related directly or via other concepts not mentioned in the story. The approach involves generating a concept space for different types of story annotation such as artists and museum objects. The concept space of an annotation is predominantly made up of a set of events, forming an event space. The story context is aggregated from the concept spaces of its associated annotations. Narrative notions of setting and theme are used to reason over the concept space, identifying key concepts and time-location pairs, and their relationship to the rest of the story. The author or reader can use setting and theme to navigate the context of the story.

Keywords: Storytelling · Museums · Concept space · Event space · Theme · Setting

1 Introduction

Stories are often used in the presentation of museum objects. The story describes a context for the object, describing for example, how the object was created, or how the artwork can be seen as a response to conditions of the time. A story may relate multiple museum objects, describing how the creation of one was in reaction to, or in some way influenced, by another. Stories therefore provide a valuable mechanism for interpreting museum objects and understanding them within a wider context.

Storyscope embodies the narrative concepts of setting and theme to provide a focus and abstraction for how the potentially large knowledge space around the story is explored, in which themes are key concepts of the story and settings are times and places at which events in the story occurred [1].

© Springer International Publishing Switzerland 2015
P. Lambrix et al. (Eds.): EKAW 2014 Satellite Events, LNAI 8982, pp. 164–167, 2015.
DOI: 10.1007/978-3-319-17966-7_23

2   Story Authoring

Storyscope provides a lightweight authoring environment (see figure 1), in which story text can be associated with media elements (images, videos). The annotations of the story are associated with Freebase topics, using a variant of Freebase Suggest widget. The story is themed for presentation according to a pre-defined template. The authoring component is paired with a recommender component that provides access to the surrounding context of the story. The link between the two components is the set of story annotations. By selecting one of the Story Tags the reader or author can access the concept space for the whole story or one of its constituent annotations. The authoring and recommender components are implemented as modules in the Drupal Content Management System.

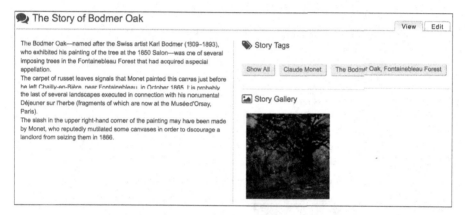

Fig. 1. The authoring environment for writing stories and adding media and annotations

3   Concept Space of a Story Annotation

The recommender component produces a concept space from the Freebase annotations associated with the story (figure 2). The recommender component can be used both by the author to assist in story development and by the reader to explore beyond the story. Annotations are used to generate a concept space comprising associated attributes (e.g. name and description of an artwork) and events (e.g. creation, ownership and exhibition events of an artwork) of the annotation. Events are modeled using a simple schema focused around agents, times, locations and other associated concepts (termed Tags). Narrative notions of setting and theme are then used to extract elements from the concept space of potential greater relevance to the author or reader. Settings are calculated from time and location event attributes (i.e. start time, end time, location) and themes from other event attributes (e.g. agent, tags) and direct attributes of the annotation (e.g. associated movement of the artist).

Themes can be generated for any single or multi-annotation concept space. The concepts contained in the concept space are scored in terms of: (i) *Coverage* - How many story annotations they are associated with either as direct attributes of the annotation (e.g. art movement or an artist) or through co-occurring in an event with the annotation (e.g. tag of an event in which the artist is an agent); and (ii) *Frequency* - How many times the concept appears in the concept space as either an attribute of a story annotation or attribute of an event. The candidate themes of the event space are then ordered primarily in terms of coverage and secondarily in terms of frequency.

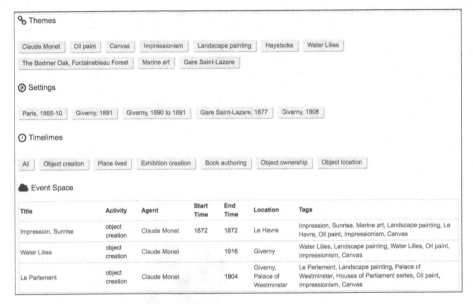

Fig. 2. Part of the concept space for the Bodmer Oak annotation

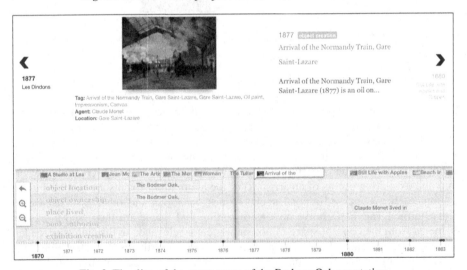

Fig. 3. Timeline of the event space of the Bodmer Oak annotation

Settings indicate both when and where something happened in a story. Setting is important as it identifies a point in time and space where characters or other objects in the story intersected. The candidate settings of an event space are all the times and locations associated in an event. A setting may include a time point (for events that have only a start or end time) or a time span (for events that have both a start and end time). Candidate settings are ranked using a similar approach to theme ordering. Settings are primarily ordered according to coverage, defined as the number of annotations associated with events featuring that particular setting. Frequency is again used as the secondary ordering principle, defined as the number of times the setting features in the event space.

The entire event space or events of one activity (e.g. object creation) can be visualized on a timeline (excluding events for which there is no time information) (see figure 3).

4   Themes of a Story Setting

A setting can be used to generate a further space of events related to that setting (figure 4). Events are retrieved that match as well as contain the setting in terms of location and time. This gives the user a view of larger scale events that may, but not necessarily, have had an influence on the events directly associated with the setting. So for example, if a setting was derived from the creation of an artwork and that setting fell during a national or global event then details of that event are included in the event space of the setting.

Fig. 4. Settings derived from the event space of three story annotations

Reference

1. Mulholland, P., Wolff, A., Kilfeather, E., McCarthy, E.: Using event spaces, setting and theme to assist the interpretation and development of museum stories. In: Janowicz, K., Schlobach, S., Lambrix, P., Hyvönen, E. (eds.) EKAW 2014. LNCS, vol. 8876, pp. 320–332. Springer, Heidelberg (2014)

A Linked Data Approach to Know-How

Paolo Pareti[1,2]([✉]), Benoit Testu[1], Ryutaro Ichise[1],
Ewan Klein[2], and Adam Barker[3]

[1] National Institute of Informatics, Tokyo, Japan
p.pareti@sms.ed.ac.uk, benoit.testu@u-psud.fr, ichise@nii.ac.jp
[2] University of Edinburgh, Edinburgh, UK
ewan@inf.ed.ac.uk
[3] University of St. Andrews, St. Andrews, UK
adam.barker@st-andrews.ac.uk

Abstract. The Web is one of the major repositories of human generated know-how, such as step-by-step videos and instructions. This knowledge can be potentially reused in a wide variety of applications, but it currently suffers from a lack of structure and isolation from related knowledge. To overcome these challenges we have developed a Linked Data framework which can automate the extraction of know-how from existing Web resources and generate links to related knowledge on the Linked Data Cloud. We have implemented our framework and used it to extract a Linked Data representation of two of the largest know-how repositories on the Web. We demonstrate two possible uses of the resulting dataset of real-world know-how. Firstly, we use this dataset within a Web application to offer an integrated visualization of distributed know-how resources. Lastly, we show the potential of this dataset for inferring common sense knowledge about tasks.

1 Introduction

Cooking recipes, software tutorials and standard operating procedures are some examples of the procedural knowledge currently available on the Web. We call this particular type of knowledge *human know-how*. Unlike other well-known types of procedural knowledge, such as program code, human know-how describes procedures which are primarily meant to be executed by humans.

Human know-how on the Web could be used in a wide variety of applications, such as for Information Retrieval and Service Recommendation [2]. Intelligent systems accessing this knowledge can also directly benefit Web users by discovering relevant procedures and resources. These potential applications, however, are currently hindered by the limitations of the available know-how. The most severe limitations are the lack of structure and the isolation from other knowledge sources. To overcome these limitations, we have developed a Linked Data framework which can represent human know-how [4]. This framework can automatically acquire the Linked Data representation of procedures from existing Web articles and then integrate it with related resources.

© Springer International Publishing Switzerland 2015
P. Lambrix et al. (Eds.): EKAW 2014 Satellite Events, LNAI 8982, pp. 168–171, 2015.
DOI: 10.1007/978-3-319-17966-7_24

Existing methods for representing procedural knowledge are usually concerned with a moderate number of well defined procedures. Human know-how on the Web, on the contrary, is inherently noisy, in constant evolution, large in size, distributed across multiple repositories and covers many different domains. The proposed Linked Data representation is robust to these challenges and, where needed, can act like a bridge to more sophisticated representations.

Our knowledge extraction and integration experiments resulted in the creation of a large amount of Linked Data representing real-world human know-how. We present two possible uses of this dataset. Firstly, an integrated visualization of distributed resources through a Web application. Lastly, examples of semantically rich queries that can extract common sense knowledge from this dataset.

1.1 Methodology

Our framework for the representation of human know-how is divided into two components. The first component automates the extraction of know-how from existing Web articles. The extracted knowledge is represented using a simple and light-weight Linked Data vocabulary [3]. Similarly to the DBpedia project [1], we focus our extraction on semi-structured resources. Semi-structured know-how resources, such as the articles available on WikiHow,[1] can be analyzed reliably, as they are explicitly divided into a number of steps, methods and requirements.

The second component of our framework automates the integration of the extracted know-how with other related knowledge. One possible integration involves the inputs and the outputs of a procedure, which can be linked to the related DBpedia types. For example, the ingredient of a procedure labelled "30 grams of sugar" can be linked to the DBpedia entity representing the concept of sugar. Links can also directly connect different procedures. For example, the step "prepare a short resume" could be linked to the relevant procedure "how to prepare a resume". The generation of those links is based on a Machine Learning classifier which utilizes, among others, textual features extracted using Natural Language Processing.

1.2 Experimental Results

We have implemented our framework and we have validated it in a real world setting [4]. Our experiment resulted in the extraction of over 200,000 procedures from two different know-how websites, namely WikiHow and Snapguide.[2] These procedures were represented as Linked Data and integrated with (1) other know-how resources and (2) other existing Linked Data, such as DBpedia. We have evaluated the quality of our automatic integration against existing integration efforts and showed its superiority across all the dimensions considered, such as the quantity and the precision of the links.

---

[1] http://www.wikihow.com/
[2] http://snapguide.com/

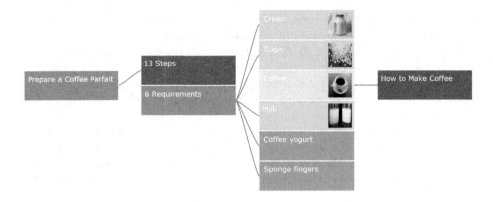

Fig. 1. Screenshot of the Web application

2   Case Studies

To better understand the challenges and the opportunities of a Linked Data representation of human know-how we present two different uses of a real-world dataset. Firstly, we describe a Web application which offers an integrated visualization of distributed know-how resources. Secondly, we show the potential of this dataset for inferring common sense knowledge. The dataset used in these case studies is the one extracted by our system from the WikiHow and Snapguide websites [4]. This dataset includes the links generated by our automatic integration system, such as the links between related WikiHow and Snapguide instructions.

2.1   Web Application

The results of our knowledge extraction and integration experiment are available online through a Web application.[3] This application allows users to visualize procedures in a tree-like structure. After finding a procedure using keyword search, the title of this procedure is displayed as the root node of the tree. By clicking on the children of this node, the user can expand the representation and obtain more information about the steps, the requirements and the outputs of this procedure. The links generated by our integration experiment allow the original tree to be expanded with additional information on the related procedures and DBpedia types. For example, Figure 1 shows a screenshot of this application visualizing the requirement "Coffee" of the procedure "Prepare a Coffee Parfait". The description of this requirement originally consisted only of a short textual label. Thanks to the links generated by our integration system, this description is now expanded with a picture of its type retrieved from DBpedia, and the link to a procedure that can create such requirement. This application

---

[3] http://w3id.org/prohow/main/

demonstrates how Linked Data can be used to have an integrated visualization of both procedural and declarative knowledge retrieved from different sources.

2.2 Semantic Queries

Human know-how can be analysed to infer common sense knowledge. This can be demonstrated by running semantically rich queries on the dataset generated by our experiment. For example, it is possible to calculate the number of times a task is used as a sub-step of other tasks. This can be used to distinguish very specific tasks, such as "how to install Android OS 4.3 on Windows 8", from basic and highly reusable tasks, such as instructions on "how to preheat an oven". Basic tasks can help identifying useful basic skills, and are ideal candidates for optimization and automation. Another example of a semantically rich query can evaluate the correlation between entities. For example, it is possible to discover the common sense fact that the entity "pen" and the entity "paper" are typically used together.

3 Conclusion

In this document we have introduced our Linked Data framework to represent human know-how on the Web. This framework has been tested in a knowledge extraction and integration experiment which generated a large dataset of real-world know-how. We have described two possible applications of this dataset. The first is a Web application for the visualization of distributed know-how resources. The second is the direct acquisition of common sense knowledge from the dataset using semantically rich queries.

References

1. Auer, S., Bizer, C., Kobilarov, G., Lehmann, J., Cyganiak, R., Ives, Z.G.: DBpedia: a nucleus for a web of open data. In: Aberer, K., Choi, K.-S., Noy, N., Allemang, D., Lee, K.-I., Nixon, L.J.B., Golbeck, J., Mika, P., Maynard, D., Mizoguchi, R., Schreiber, G., Cudré-Mauroux, P. (eds.) ASWC 2007 and ISWC 2007. LNCS, vol. 4825, pp. 722–735. Springer, Heidelberg (2007)
2. Myaeng, S.-H., Jeong, Y., Jung, Y.: Experiential Knowledge Mining. Foundations and Trends in Web Science **4**(1), 71–82 (2013)
3. Pareti, P., Klein, E., Barker, A.: A semantic web of know-how: linked data for community-centric tasks. In: Proceedings of the 23rd International Conference on World Wide Web Companion, pp. 1011–1016 (2014)
4. Pareti, P., Testu, B., Ichise, R., Klein, E., Barker, A.: Integrating know-how into the linked data cloud. In: Janowicz, K., Schlobach, S., Lambrix, P., Hyvönen, E. (eds.) EKAW 2014. LNCS, vol. 8876, pp. 385–396. Springer, Heidelberg (2014)

OntoEnrich: A Platform for the Lexical Analysis of Ontologies

Manuel Quesada-Martínez[1]([✉]), Jesualdo Tomás Fernández-Breis[1],
Robert Stevens[2], and Nathalie Aussenac-Gilles[3]

[1] Facultad de Informática, Universidad de Murcia, IMIB-Arrixaca,
CP 30100 Murcia, Spain
{manuel.quesada,jfernand}@um.es

[2] University of Manchester, Oxford Road, Manchester M13 9PL, UK
stevens@cs.manchester.ac.uk

[3] Université Paul Sabatier, IRIT, 118 Route de Narbonne, F-31062 Toulouse, France
aussenac@irit.fr

Abstract. The content of the labels in ontologies is usually considered hidden semantics, because the domain knowledge of such labels is not available as logical axioms in the ontology. The use of systematic naming conventions as best practice for the design of the content of the labels generates labels with structural regularities, namely, lexical regularities. The structure and content of such regularities can help ontology engineers to increase the amount of machine-friendly content in ontologies, that is, to increase the number of logical axioms.

In this paper we present a web platform based on the OntoEnrich framework, which detects and analyzes lexical regularities, providing a series of useful insights about the structure and content of the labels, which can be helpful for the study of the engineering of the ontologies and their axiomatic enrichment. Here, we describe its software architecture, and how it can be used for analyzing the labels of ontologies, which will be illustrated with some examples from our research studies.

1 Introduction

Many ontologies have been developed in recent years. For instance, BioPortal (http://bioportal.bioontology.org/) contains 388 biomedical ontologies at the time of this writing. Ontology authors include strings of characters as labels that describe ontology classes. These labels can embed hidden semantics that is not represented as logical axioms in the ontology. The Open Biomedical Ontologies (OBO) Foundry defines criteria to be followed by biomedical ontology authors such as the use of a systematic naming in ontology labels. Then, the analysis of regularities in ontology labels might help to detect hidden semantics. For example, in the Gene Ontology Molecular Function ontology (GO-MF) [2], regularities like "binding" can be converted into patterns like "X binding" that enrich the ontology with axioms like *"subClassOf enables some (binds some ?x)"*; and these axioms can be re-used in other more specific patterns like "X receptor binding" and "X domain binding".

© Springer International Publishing Switzerland 2015
P. Lambrix et al. (Eds.): EKAW 2014 Satellite Events, LNAI 8982, pp. 172–176, 2015.
DOI: 10.1007/978-3-319-17966-7_25

Our hypothesis is that supporting ontology authors in the analysis of the lexical regularities (LRs) from ontology labels can result in axiomatically enriched ontologies, which should be more useful for their application in real projects. Tools like OntoCheck and OntoCure (http://protegewiki.stanford.edu/wiki/OntoCheck) foster lexical harmonization in ontology labels. Besides, Caméléon [1] uses a supervised process of candidate patterns for relation acquisition from texts, and they use and refine patterns from a catalog. In this paper, we present the OntoEnrich platform, which implements our method for lexical analysis (LAs) and characterization of ontologies [3]. The main advantage of our method is providing tools for the interactive analysis of LRs, which could elucidate patterns like the Caméléon candidate patterns but without starting from a catalog.

2   OntoEnrich

OntoEnrich supports ontologists to analyze ontologies from the lexical perspective. Fig. 1 shows the components of the OntoEnrich platform. Each user has a profile with personal execution and storage constraints. The LA of an ontology starts by the lexical analysis, which produces a set of LRs. This is done once for each ontology and it is automatically performed. Its execution time depends on the ontology size. The results are stored in a reusable XML file. The algorithms and methods are encapsulated in the Onto-Enrich Java API, which uses external libraries like the OWL API (http://owlapi.sourceforge.net/) for manipulating ontologies, and the Stanford CoreNLP (http://nlp.stanford.edu/software/corenlp.shtml) for tokenization, part-of-speech tagging and lemmatization of labels, which is used for building a graph of tokens used for detecting the LRs. Further details about how the LRs are detected can be found in [3].

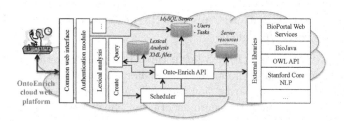

Fig. 1. General component architecture of the OntoEnrich platform

Each LR has some *general descriptors* like: its text, if it is a class of the ontology, the labels that exhibit it and the type of word/s that it is. For example, "binding" appears in 1222 labels of the GO-MF, it is a class and it is a noun or the nominal form of the verb "to bind" in the labels that exhibit it. If an LR has different forms (e.g., noun vs. verb) it can be split in two according to the role played. Other *advanced features* associated with each LR are:

- **Sub/super-regularities:** a sub-regularity is a sub-sequence of an LR, while a super-regularity is obtained by extending the LR in any direction. Their analysis helps to refine LRs. For example, "receptor binding" (339 repetitions) is more specific than "binding".

- **Generalization of regularities:** the alignment of the labels that exhibit an LR helps in the automatic identification of patterns like "translation X factor activity" several LRs. For this, we have adapted bioinformatics multiple sequence alignment algorithms.

- The **cross-product extension metric** informs about the degree of enrichment of an LR using matches obtained from other ontology selected by the user, and the **localization and modularization metrics** inform about the distribution in the asserted hierarchy of classes that exhibit an LR. For example, if an LR is a class in the ontology: (1) this class should be the common ancestor of the classes that exhibit such an LR, or (2) these classes should be linked with other type of relationship.

3   Example of the Inspection of Lexical Regularities

We illustrate the OntoEnrich platform with the GO-MF, and how the inspection of LRs might help to identify deviations or lexico-syntactic patterns like those manually detected in [2] (see Fig. 2). We omit the LA step. For further details, please check the tutorials in our website (see Fig. 2-1).

Fig. 2 shows the screenshots for the "binding" and "forming" LRs. Fig. 2-3 shows the information of the LR under inspection. We can navigate through the LRs (see Fig. 2-8). In Fig. 2-4 the *general descriptors* of the active LR are shown, and the labels that exhibit the LR can be explored in Fig 2-5. *More complex features* of the LR are analyzed independently and they are chosen using Fig. 2-6. Panel 5 shows the labels in which the LR appears. Panel 7 contains information about the super-patterns, sub-patterns, or alignment of labels, depending on the option selected in Panel 6.

Use Case 1 - "binding" (Fig. 2 left): this LR is quite general, so the inspection of the super-regularities can be useful. For example, there are 23 classes that exhibit the super-regularity "ion binding", which is a class in the ontology; however, the least common sub-summer of these 23 classes is "binding" instead of "ion binding", which suggests the inspection of the labels that exhibit "ion binding" for discarding that there are irregularitites in the naming of the labels. Hence, this analysis could serve to inspect the correlation between the lexical regularities and relationships between the corresponding classes.

Use Case 2 - "forming" (Fig. 2 right): this LR is recognized as a verb by the NLP modules and, according to [1], verbs usually codify semantic relationships. If we align and analyze the labels that exhibit this LR, the first 6 labels could be generalized as: 'ligase activity, forming ?x'. Then, if ?y represents classes that follow such a pattern, these classes can be enriched with the axioms *'?y subClassOf "ligase activity"* and *'?y subClassOf enables some (forming some ?x)',*

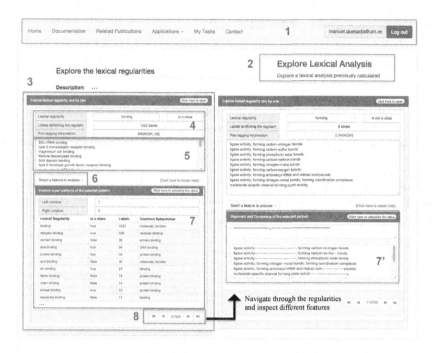

Fig. 2. Example of the online inspection of lexical regularities
(http://sele.inf.um.es/ontoenrich/files/ekaw2014ontoenrichImg.pdf)

where the LR is created as an object property. However, the alignment of labels that exhibit the LR does not obtain consensus as "nucleoside-specific channel forming porin activity" does not follow the pattern "Y, forming X". In the other two labels several elements are formed, so two axioms with an AND clause might be created.

In general, this information might be used to debug the ontology in case abnormalities are found and to automatically generate Ontology Design Patterns (http://ontologydesignpatterns.org/), which can be implemented in OPPL scripts (http://oppl2.sourceforge.net/) to refine the class hierarchy.

4 Availability and Future Work

OntoEnrich is available at http://sele.inf.um.es/ontoenrich. We hope to extend it with algorithms that help in the automatic detection of lexico-syntactic patterns and its codification as OPPL scripts that create the ontology axioms.

Acknowledgments. This project has been possible thanks to the Spanish Ministry of Science and Innovation and the FEDER Programme through grant TIN2010-21388-C02-02 and fellowships BES-2011-046192 (MQM) and EEBB-I-14-08700 (MQM), and by the Fundación Séneca (15295/PI/10).

References

1. Aussenac-Gilles, N., Jacques, M.-P.: Designing and evaluating patterns for relation acquisition from texts with Caméléon. Terminology **14**(1), 45–73 (2008)
2. Fernandez-Breis, J.T., Iannone, L., Palmisano, I., Rector, A.L., Stevens, R.: Enriching the gene ontology via the dissection of labels using the ontology pre-processor language. In: Cimiano, P., Pinto, H.S. (eds.) EKAW 2010. LNCS, vol. 6317, pp. 59–73. Springer, Heidelberg (2010)
3. Quesada-Martínez, M., Fernández-Breis, J.T., Stevens, R.: Lexical characterization and analysis of the BioPortal ontologies. In: Peek, N., Marín Morales, R., Peleg, M. (eds.) AIME 2013. LNCS, vol. 7885, pp. 206–215. Springer, Heidelberg (2013)

Integrating Unstructured and Structured Knowledge with the KnowledgeStore

Marco Rospocher$^{(\boxtimes)}$, Francesco Corcoglioniti, Roldano Cattoni,
Bernardo Magnini, and Luciano Serafini

Fondazione Bruno Kessler—IRST, Via Sommarive 18, Trento I-38123, Italy
{rospocher,corcoglio,cattoni,magnini,serafini}@fbk.eu

Abstract. We showcase the KnowledgeStore, a scalable, fault-tolerant, and Semantic Web grounded framework for interlinking unstructured (e.g., textual documents, web pages) and structured (e.g., RDF, LOD) contents, enabling to jointly store, manage, retrieve, and query, both typologies of contents.

1 Introduction

Nowadays, a preponderant amount of information on the Web and within organizations remain available only in unstructured form, despite the increasing availability of structured data sources and initiatives such as the Linked Open Data (LOD). Structured and unstructured contents differ in forms but are often related in content, as they speak about the very same entities of the world (e.g., persons, organizations, locations, events), their properties and relations. Despite the last decades achievements in Natural Language Processing (NLP), now supporting large scale extraction of knowledge from unstructured text, frameworks enabling the seamless integration and linking of knowledge coming both from structured and unstructured contents are still lacking.[1]

In this demo we showcase the **KnowledgeStore (KS)**, a scalable, fault-tolerant, and Semantic Web grounded storage system to jointly store, manage, retrieve, and query, both structured and unstructured data. Fig. 1a shows schematically how the **KS** manages unstructured and structured contents in its three *representation layers*. On the one hand (and similarly to a file system) the *resource layer* stores unstructured content in the form of resources (e.g., news articles), each having a textual representation and some descriptive metadata. On the other hand, the *entity layer* is the home of structured content, that, based on Knowledge Representation and Semantic Web best practices, consists of *axioms* (a set of ⟨subject, predicate, object⟩ triples), which describe the *entities* of the world (e.g., persons, locations, events), and for which additional metadata are kept to track their provenance and to denote the formal *contexts* where they hold (e.g., point of view, attribution). Between the aforementioned two layers there is the *mention layer*, which indexes *mentions*, i.e., snippets of resources (e.g.,

---

[1] See [1] for an overview of works related to the contribution presented in this demo.

© Springer International Publishing Switzerland 2015
P. Lambrix et al. (Eds.): EKAW 2014 Satellite Events, LNAI 8982, pp. 177–181, 2015.
DOI: 10.1007/978-3-319-17966-7_26

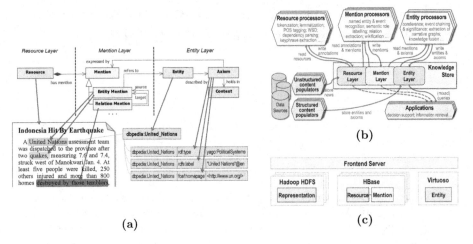

Fig. 1. (a) The three **KS** layers; (b) Interactions with external modules; (c) Components

some characters in a text document) that denote something of interest, such as an entity or an axiom of the entity layer. Mentions can be automatically extracted by NLP tools, that can enrich them with additional attributes about how they denote their referent (e.g., with which name, qualifiers, "sentiment"). Far from being simple pointers, mentions present both unstructured and structured facets (respectively snippet and attributes) not available in the resource and entity layers alone, and are thus a valuable source of information on their own.

Thanks to the explicit representation and alignment of information at different levels, from unstructured to structured knowledge, the **KS** supports a number of usage scenarios. It enables the development of enhanced applications, such as effective *decision support systems* that exploit the possibility to semantically query the content of the **KS** with requests combining structured and unstructured content, such as "retrieve all the documents mentioning that person Barack Obama participated to a sport event". Then, it favours the design and empirical investigation of information processing tasks otherwise difficult to experiment with, such as cross-document *coreference resolution* (i.e., identifying that two mentions refer to the same entity of the world) exploiting the availability of interlinked structured knowledge. Finally, the joint storage of (i) extracted knowledge, (ii) the resources it derives from, and (iii) extracted metadata provides an ideal scenario for developing, training, and evaluating ontology population techniques.

2   System Overview

In this section we briefly outline the main characteristics of the **KS**. For a more exhaustive presentation of the **KS** design, we point the reader to [1].

More documentation, as well as binaries and source code,[2] are all available on the **KS** web site [2].

Data Model. The data model defines what information can be stored in the **KS**. It is organized in three layers (resource, mention and entity), with properties that relate objects across them. To favour the exposure of the **KS** content according to LOD principles, the data model is defined as an OWL 2 ontology (available on [2]). It contains the TBox definitions and restrictions for each model element and can be extended on a per-deployment basis, e.g., with domain-specific resource and linguistic metadata.

API. The **KS** offers a number of interfaces through which external clients may access and manipulate stored data. These interfaces are offered through two HTTP ReST endpoints. The *CRUD endpoint* provides the basic operations to access and manipulate (CRUD: create, retrieve, update, and delete) any object stored in any of the layers of the **KS**. Operations of the CRUD endpoint are all defined in terms of sets of objects, in order to enable bulk operations as well as operations on single objects. The *SPARQL endpoint* allows to query axioms in the entity layer using SPARQL. It provides a flexible and Semantic Web-compliant way to query for entity data, and leverages the grounding of the **KS** data model in Knowledge Representation and Semantic Web best practices. A Java client is also offered to ease the development of (Java) client applications.

Architecture. The **KS** is a storage server whose services are utilized by external clients to store and retrieve the contents they process. From a functional point of view, we identify three main typologies of clients (see Fig. 1b): (i) *populators*, that feed the **KS** with basic contents needed by other applications (e.g., documents, background knowledge from LOD sources); (ii) *linguistic processors*, that read input data from the **KS** and write back their results; and, (iii) *applications*, that mainly read data from the **KS** (e.g., decision support systems). In particular, linguistic processors are responsible for the extraction of mentions from textual resources and their linking to (existing or new) entities, thus effectively realizing the interlinking of unstructured and structured contents according to the **KS** data model; off-the-shelf NLP tools realizing named entity recognition, entity linking and coreference resolution can be used for this purpose. Internally, the **KS** consists of a number of software components (see Fig. 1c) distributed on a cluster of machines: (i) the *Hadoop HDFS* filesystem provides a reliable and scalable storage for the physical files holding the representations of resources (e.g., texts and linguistic annotations of news articles); (ii) the *HBase* column-oriented store builds on Hadoop to provide database services for storing and retrieving semi-structured information about resources and mentions; (iii) the *Virtuoso* triple-store stores axioms and provides services supporting reasoning and online SPARQL query answering; and, (iv) the *Frontend Server* has been

---

[2] Released under the terms of the Apache License, Version 2.0.

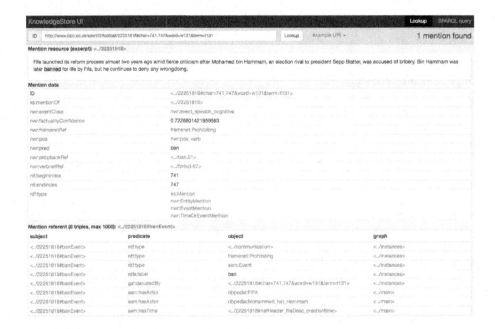

Fig. 2. KS UI. Lookup of a mention. Note the three boxes (Mention resource, Mention Data, Mention Referent) corresponding to the three representation layers of the KS.

specifically developed to implement the operations of the CRUD and SPARQL endpoints on top of the components listed above, handling global issues such as access control, data validation and operation transactionality.

User Interface (UI). The KS UI (see Fig. 2) enables human users to access and inspect the content of the KS via two core operations: (i) the *SPARQL query* operation, with which arbitrary SPARQL queries can be run against the KS SPARQL endpoint, obtaining the results directly in the browser or as a downloadable file; and, (ii) the *lookup* operation, which given the URI of an object (i.e., resource, mention, entity), retrieves all the KS content about that object. These two operations are seamlessly integrated in the UI to offer a smooth browsing experience to users, which can navigate from one object to any related object by following the relations in the data model.

3   System Demonstration and Concluding Remarks

During the Posters and Demos session, we will demonstrate live how to access the KS content via the UI (similarly to the detailed demo preview available at [3]), highlighting the possibilities offered by the KS to navigate back and forth from unstructured to structured content. For instance, we will show how to run arbitrary SPARQL queries, retrieving the mentions of entities and triples in the query result set, and the documents where they occur. Similarly, starting from a document URI, we will show how to access the mentions identified in the document, up to the entities and triples they refer to.

In the last months, several running instances of the **KS** were set-up (on a cluster of 5 average specs servers) and populated using the NewsReader Processing Pipeline [4] with contents coming from various domains: to name a few, one on the global automotive industry [5] (64K resources, 9M mentions, 316M entity triples), and one related to the FIFA World Cup (212K resources, 75M mentions, 240M entity triples), both augmented with entities and RDF background knowledge extracted from DBpedia and used as the target of mention linking. The FIFA World Cup instance was also exploited in a Hackathon event [6], where 38 developers accessed the **KS** to build their applications (over 30K SPARQL queries were submitted – 1 query/s avg. with peaks of 25 queries/s).

Acknowledgments. The research leading to this paper was supported by the European Union's 7th Framework Programme via the NewsReader Project (ICT-316404).

References

1. Corcoglioniti, F., Rospocher, M., Cattoni, R., Magnini, B., Serafini, L.: Interlinking unstructured and structured knowledge in an integrated framework. In: 7th IEEE International Conference on Semantic Computing (ICSC), Irvine, CA, USA (2013)
2. http://knowledgestore.fbk.eu
3. http://youtu.be/if1PRwSll5c
4. https://github.com/newsreader/
5. http://datahub.io/dataset/global-automotive-industry-news
6. http://www.newsreader-project.eu/come-hack-with-newsreader/

Doctoral Consortium

Assessing the Spatio-Temporal Fitness of Information Supply and Demand on an Adaptive Ship Bridge

Christian Denker[(✉)]

R&D Division Transportation, OFFIS - Institute for Information Technology,
Oldenburg, Germany
denker@offis.de

Abstract. The *information supply* to crew on nautical ship bridges has a significant impact on the probability of accident occurrences. A reason is, too much or too less information is supplied, not satisfying the *information demand*. A solution to this problem is the Adaptive Ship Bridge - a system that closes this *information gap* between supply and demand by adaptation. However, to create an effective Adaptive Ship Bridge it is necessary to assess the information gap during design time. The thesis introduced in this paper proposes a novel method for assessment in spatio-temporal and information quality dimensions. The method will allow designing Adaptive Ship Bridges that will help to reduce accident risk.

Keywords: Information supply and demand · Information gap · Adaptive ship bridge · Situation awareness · Systems engineering

1   Problem

"Around 90% of world trading is carried out by the shipping industry" [4] and shipbuilders are constantly enlarging their new builds' capacities for cargo and passengers. While ship sizes increase, the potential risk to human life and the fatality of impacts on the environment through accidents increase as well. Besides environmental influences or technical faults, human error is in up to 85% the main contributing factor to accidents in shipping. Thereof 71% are affected by degraded situation awareness (SA) [9].

This means on the one hand, that the crew has problems to satisfy their information demand during navigation. On the other hand nowadays ship bridges provide a static working environment, which does not sufficiently supply demanded information The reason is that information are distributed across different locations on the ship bridge and are often not well presented. In comparison to other means of transport such as airplanes, trains and cars, the bridge of merchant ships are having huge cockpits. Positioning of equipment and workstations influence walking distances and thus can highly contribute to delays in access to these. Adverse weather conditions, such as heavy swell and strong winds, can further contribute to that delay. Adjustments of the crew's work organization, such as adding additional personnel or altering work shifts,

© Springer International Publishing Switzerland
P. Lambrix et al. (Eds.): EKAW 2014 Satellite Events, LNAI 8982, pp. 185–192, 2015.
DOI: 10.1007/978-3-319-17966-7_27

ought to be a solution, but cause additional cost, require additional communication between the crew and/or may reduce periods of rest. The latter two may introduce further risks, e.g. failures in communication and reduction of work force. On ships equipment from various manufactures are often ad-hoc integrated during the build and installed on consoles providing fixed information content, mostly displayed in analog or digital values continuously in every shipping situation. This does not fit the seafarers' situation-dependent and task-based information demand. E.g. information about the anchor winch status may only be needed when willing to anchor the ship. During bridge work the crew has to find, sort, process and integrate information [6] before they can derive knowledge about the current situation. Knowledge derivation is done by seafarers interpreting and predicting the perceived information. Barely workstations and equipment give supportive advice, reducing the crews work in finding, sorting, processing and integrating information.

To close the information gap (IG) between supply and demand, the crew, the bridge or both have to adapt. A system, in which both crew and bridge try to minimize the gap via adaption to each other, is what we call an Adaptive Ship Bridge (ASB). However, for adaptiveness it is necessary to detect and assess the IG.

In this thesis the challenge is to create a method, which allows assessing the IG at design time, taking the spatio-temporal and information qualitative resolution for crew members and the bridge into account. Therefore, a model-based approach is proposed.

2   State of the Art

Three main research areas are relevant for the definition of a method for assessing IG in ASB, namely Situation awareness (SA), Distributed Situation Awareness (DSA) and Information Quality Management (IQM). State of the art work in these areas is briefly recalled in this section.

Situation awareness (SA) can be seen as a state in the human decision-making process. According to Endsley, SA is composed of three successive levels including the perception (level 1), comprehension (level 2) and projection (level 3) of information [6]. SA fosters a view on one individual. Matheus et al. [12] have built core ontology for situation awareness, which aims to support descriptions of various scenarios of SA. The ontology has been applied in the BeAware software framework for control centers and extended with spatio-temporal reasoning concepts [2]. Its purpose is to support building of SA applications for single operators in control tasks and not to evaluate the collaborative work with such an application in the control center or on a ship bridge respectively. The quality of information presentations to the operators is not in BeAware's focus.

In complex collaborative human machine systems, such as the ship bridge, several seafarers work together in a spatial distributed team, to reach a common goal. According to Salmon et al. [14] these systems cannot be understood by analyzing its components separately, but by considering the system as a whole. This understanding led to the theory of DSA. DSA builds up on the idea of Distributed Cognition Theory

[10] that focuses on overall system analysis, comprising all agents (human and machine) and artefacts (f.i. user interfaces). Cognition is herein seen as a function of the overall system and can be studied by analyzing interactions between agents and between agents and artefacts. DSA is following this idea, by defining SA as an attribute of the overall system, which goes beyond individual humans and is distributed amongst all agents and artefacts. Deficiencies of one agent can be compensated by another, in a way that the overall system has sufficient SA. In DSA, agents can have a so-called Compatible SA. Since SA is influenced by individual factors (e.g. experience, skills, and training) and depends on the agent's task, it's unlikely that two agents have identical awareness about a situation [15]. Although all agents might have similar information available, they are using them in different fashion, but the multiple individual SA have to be compatible to enable team work. Another DSA concept is SA Transactions. In complex cooperative human machine systems SA relevant information is often distributed and has to be communicated within the system. The exchange of SA relevant information is done via SA Transactions, which can be executed via various communication channels between agents and artefacts [14]. SA Transactions cause an update on the recipient's SA. The DSA theory allows describing information as quantities of information elements (IE), but is in need of qualitative aspects of IE for an assessment.

In the field of Information Quality Management (IQM) information quality (IQ) for Management Information Systems is well defined [7]. Wang and Strong define IQ from the viewpoint of an information consumer as the information that is "fit for use by data consumers" [17]. The field has originated several dimension concepts of IQ attributes. E.g. Wang and Strong [17] categorize in the dimensions intrinsic, contextual, representational and accessibility data quality. Bovee et al. [3] propose the dimensions of accessibility, interpretability, relevance and integrity. Lee et al. [11] proposed a generalized methodology to assess IQ in organizations called AIMQ. AIMQ consists of an IQ model, a questionnaire to measure IQ and an analysis technique for measurement interpretation. The method can be used to identify gaps between an organization and best practices.

3   Proposed Approach

In this thesis a model-based method for Information Gap Analysis (IGA) is proposed, which generally consists of four iterative steps: (1) Specification of Analysis Scope, which includes the identification of the user interfaces of the ASB, the crew's tasks and of the navigational situation influencing the former two; (2) Modelling of crew's tasks and ASB, which includes specification of spatio-temporal and IQ dimensions of information supply and demand in navigational situations; (3) Detection of Information Gaps, which includes analyzing whether a misfit between information supply and demand exists; and (4) Assessment of Information Gaps, which includes calculating a metric which can be used to compare different ASB-crew configurations. More details on a first version of the method and its application are described in [5].

To develop such a method properly it is necessary to answer the following scientific question and sub-questions:

How to assess ASBs for crew's information demand in navigational situations?

I.   Which methods/techniques are needed to…
    a.   represent information supply and demand of ASB and crew?
        i.   represent the spatial and temporal aspects?
        ii.   represent the IQ aspects of information supply and demand?
    b.   represent navigational situations and their influence on ASB and crew?
II.   Which metrics are appropriate to assess the Information Gap between information supply and demand for spatio-temporal and IQ dimensions?

The following subsections elaborate on how to answer these questions.

3.1   Representing Information Supply and Demand

For the purpose of assessing IGs, a descriptive model is needed which represents the spatio-temporal information supply and demand. The model further needs to foster concrete instances of IQ dimensions of the bridge and crew and to integrate the description of the nautical situation. Concerning the nautical situations, it is necessary that causal relations, such as manual or automatic adaption of the ASB to e.g. crew or environment, can be modelled. In terms of DSA this means, that the ASB, the crew and the navigational situation under assessment are specified in detail as agents and artefacts in their environment. Therefore, it is necessary to define task, system, team and individual factors. This allows using the concepts of compatible SA and SA transactions.

An initial model solely fulfilling the spatio-temporal and (part wise) adaptation requirements was created. It is based on the BPMN [1] and facilitates its temporal and multi-user modelling paradigms. Further the model implies a systems perspective, in which both the ASB and the crew play are a role. Each role can supply and demand information in the spatio-temporal dimensions. To model the existence and the order of the roles' information supply and demand BPMN's sequential flows are used. The model additionally introduces information flows and command flows. An exemplary model instance is shown in Fig. 1.

Information flows are defining at which information supply an information demand is tried to be satisfied. Command flows are changes of the information supply induced by an information demand, e.g. changing a user interface's state. Since information flows and command flows can both be inter-role connected to a common information supply and information demand, additional temporal order is assigned to the flows, to distinct timing between them. In Fig. 1 the relative temporal order of flow execution is indicated by the ordinal number annotating a flow arrow. Further the spatial dimension is describable with discrete locations that can be assigned to every information supply and demand. This allows expressing where information is supplied and where it is demanded.

Besides the spatio-temporal dimensions, IQ dimensions have to be considered. This is done by extending the BPMN model with annotations about the IQ properties. An example of an IQ property is for instance the importance of information in an information demand or an integrity property in the supply, which can influence the satisfaction of the demand or hinder the supply.

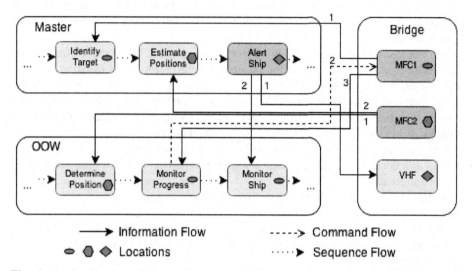

Fig. 1. A visualization of the spatio-temporal information supply (blue) and information demand (green) model, depicting a Master and an Officer of the watch (OOW) during navigation on a ship bridge, consisting of two multifunctional consoles (MFC) and a VHF radio

3.2   Assessing Information Gaps

Corresponding to the representation, metrics need to be created to assess IGs. Basically the metrics measure how good the following four tasks are fulfilled by the ASB:

a. Determining task and situation dependent information demand and supply,
b. Categorization and prioritization of information,
c. Support in finding, sorting, integrating and processing information and
d. Presentation of information, interpretations and predictions.

The metrics indicate the fitness of information supply and demand in these tasks on the spatial, temporal and IQ dimensions. In the ideal case the ASB supplies and demands information at the right place, at the right time and in the right quality for the crew. Misfits between information supply and demand are negatively reflected in the metrics.

A candidate assessment metric for the initial model, described in section 3.1, is currently under development. The metric is used to measure the determination of task and situation dependent information demand and supply. Therefore, life and motion configurations are automatically created from the initial model, described in section 3.1. Life and motion configurations allow describing the states of existence and presence of an object, and spatio-temporal relations between two objects [8]. The corresponding information supply and demand from the model are used as objects with spatio-temporal relations. The metric measures the spatial misfits, temporal misfits and how these relate to each other during "birth", "life" and "death" of the information supply and demand.

Since the model does not cater for the situational aspects, this method does neither. The same applies to the IQ dimensions. A challenge in this thesis will be to align the assessment of IGs to a more concrete model and its interrelations between ASB, crew and situation.

Further assessments shall provide answers to the question "How much effort would be needed by a role, to eliminate the information gap?". From this question, specific sub-questions can be derived for every dimension. Sub-questions are e.g.: "How many interactions are needed to make an information present?"; "How long does it take to receive an information?"; "How many spaces would agents need move through, to get an information?"; "What is the mismatch of IQ?"; and combinations of these questions can be answered as well. The assessment explains the IG's size and results in a normalized metric, which allows a comparison between different bridge-crew configurations.

In previous work [5] a basic normalized metric was created to measure the fitness of information supply and demand. The metric is based on the Tversky ratio model similarity [16] and integrates a property of importance to the information demand. A challenge to the thesis is to find a metric that is appropriate to assess the IG in the described dimensions.

4 Methodology

The research will be performed by following the design science research process [13] for producing and presenting information systems research. The process adopts five steps:

1. Problem identification and motivation - Accident reports are used to identify maritime accident causes. A literature review reveals how system engineers reduce the causes during design time nowadays.
2. Objectives of a solution - Shortcomings of nowadays methods are identified and used to derive requirements to improve the systems engineering of a ship.
3. Design and development - A method is developed that tackles the objective. A software prototype is implemented, which supports the method.
4. Demonstration - The method and prototype are demonstrated in multiple use cases to provide a proof-of-concept for different aspects of the method.
5. Evaluation - The results from the demonstration are used to identify potential for improvement. The method and prototype are further evaluated with system engineers and human factor experts to assess the applicability, benefits and shortcomings of the method, with practical examples. Suggestions for improvements and identified shortcomings are fed back into steps 2 and 3.

5   Evaluation Protocol

The tool-supported method for IG assessment, as a product of the research process, will be evaluated with domain experts. They will be asked to estimate benefits and shortcomings of the proposed method in comparison to nowadays methods. Further different ASBs will be modelled and assessed based on scenarios from detailed accident reports and crew tasks gathered from field observations and nautical literature. The models and results of the assessment will be used to evaluate, whether representation and assessment is capable of detecting IGs. Again systems engineers, human factor and maritime domain experts will be integrated into evaluation. Experts' feedback will be used to advance the state of the method and tool.

A first evaluation [5] showed that future work needs to advance methods, techniques and metrics to make the IG measurable, in terms of spatio-temporal and IQ dimensions.

6   Results

Currently the thesis is in an early stage. The problem identification and motivation was carried out by literature research and interviews with seafarers, system engineers and human factor experts. Further, existing related work was identified in the areas of human factors, information quality management, business sciences, systems engineering, formal verification and geographical information systems. At the moment, the method and a prototype of a supporting software tool are under development, which includes concepts for representing spatio-temporal ASB and crew configurations. An initial evaluation of the method with maritime system engineers and a human factors ergonomist has been performed, to estimate the applicability, benefits and shortcomings of the method. The importance of spatio-temporal dimensions and the relevance of modelling multi-user interfaces was emphasizes by the experts.

Acknowledgement. This research has been performed with support from the EU FP7 project CASCADe, GA No.: 314352. Any contents herein are from the author and do not necessarily reflect the views of the European Commission. The author would like to thank his supervisor Prof. Dr.-Ing. Axel Hahn, all members of the OFFIS groups HCD and CMS, especially Florian Fortmann, Dr.-Ing. Sebastian Feuerstack, Dr. Cilli Sobiech and Dr. Andreas Lüdtke, for the intense discussions and shared insights, and of course the partners in CASCADe and the participating domain experts who supported this work.

References

1. Allweyer, T.: BPMN 2.0 - Business Process Model and Notation: Einführung in den Standard für die Geschäftsprozessmodellierung, 2 edn, p. 168. Books on Demand (2009)
2. Baumgartner, N., Mitsch, S., Müller, A., Retschitzegger, W., Salfinger, A., Schwinger, W.: A tour of BeAware–A situation awareness framework for control centers. Information Fusion **20**, 155–173 (2014)
3. Bovee, M., Srivastava, R.P., Mak, B.: A conceptual framework and belief-function approach to assessing overall information quality. International journal of intelligent systems **18**(1), 51–74 (2003)
4. Chauvin, C., Lardjane, S., Morel, G., Clostermann, J.-P., Langard, B.: Human and organisational factors in maritime accidents: analysis of collisions at sea using the HFACS. Accident; Analysis and Prevention **59**, 26–37 (2013). doi:10.1016/j.aap.2013.05.006
5. Denker, C., Fortmann, F., Ostendorp, M.C., Hahn, A.: Assessing the fitness of information supply and demand during user interface design. In: Proceedings of the 5th International Conference on Applied Human Factors and Ergonomics AHFE 2014 (2014)
6. Endsley, M.R.: Designing for situation awareness: An approach to user-centered design. CRC Press (2012)
7. Ge, M., Helfert, M.: A review of information quality research – develop a research agenda. In: Proceedings of the 12th International Conference on Information Quality, MIT (2007)
8. Hallot, P., Billen, R.: Life and motion configurations: a basis for spatio-temporal generalized reasoning model. In: Song, I.-Y., Piattini, M., Chen, Y.-P.P., Hartmann, S., Grandi, F., Trujillo, J., Opdahl, Andreas L., Ferri, F., Grifoni, P., Caschera, M.C., Rolland, C., Woo, C., Salinesi, C., Zimányi, E., Claramunt, C., Frasincar, F., Houben, G.-J., Thiran, P. (eds.) Advances in Conceptual Modeling–Challenges and Opportunities. LNCS, vol. 5232, pp. 323–333. Springer, Heidelberg (2008)
9. Hetherington, C., Flin, R., Mearns, K.: Safety in shipping: The human element. Journal of Safety Research **37**(4), 401–411 (2006). doi:10.1016/j.jsr.2006.04.007
10. Hutchins, E.: Cognition in the wild. Bradford Books. MIT Press (1995)
11. Lee, Y.W., Strong, D.M., Kahn, B.K., Wang, R.Y.: AIMQ: a methodology for information quality assessment. Information & management **40**(2), 133–146 (2002)
12. Matheus, C.J., Kokar, M.M., Baclawski, K.: A core ontology for situation awareness. In: Proceedings of the Sixth International Conference on Information Fusion, vol. 1, pp. 545–552 (2003)
13. Peffers, K., Tuunanen, T., Gengler, C., Rossi, M., Hui, W., Virtanen, V., Bragge, J.: The design science research process: a model for producing and presenting information systems research. In: Proceedings of the 1st International Conference on Design Science in Information Systems and Technology, pp. 83–106 (2006)
14. Salmon, P.M., Stanton, N.A., Walker, G.H., Jenkins, D.P.: Distributed Situation Awareness: Theory, Measurement and Application to Teamwork. Human Factors in Defence. Ashgate Publishing (2009)
15. Stanton, N.A., Stewart, R., Harris, D., Houghton, R.J., Baber, C., McMaster, R., Green, D.: Distributed situation awareness in dynamic systems: theoretical development and application of an ergonomics methodology. Ergonomics **49**(12-13), 1288–1311 (2006)
16. Tversky, A.: Features of Similarity. Psychological Review **84**(4), 327–352 (1977)
17. Wang, R.J., Strong, D.M.: Beyond Accuracy: What Data Quality Means to Data Consumers. Journal of Management Information Systems **12**(4), 5–33 (1996)

Versatile Visualization, Authoring and Reuse of Ontological Schemas Leveraging on Dataset Summaries

Marek Dudáš[(✉)]

Department of Information and Knowledge Engineering, University of Economics,
Prague Nám. W. Churchilla 4, 130 67 Praha 3, Czech Republic
marek.dudas@vse.cz

Abstract. Ontologies and vocabularies written in the OWL language are a crucial part of the semantic web. OWL allows to model the same part of reality using different combinations of constructs, constituting 'modeling styles'. We draft a novel approach to supporting ontology reuse and development with respect to this heterogeneity. The central notion of this approach is to use ontological background models to describe reality in a way that is OWL-independent and yet can be mapped to OWL. Using such models should enable easy comparison of ontologies from the same domain when they are designed using different modeling styles, automated generation of OWL style variants from existing ontologies or even generating completely new OWL ontologies in the desired style. The PhD thesis focuses on development and implementation of methods for design of ontological background models and their transformation to OWL. The methods include summarization of the actual ontology usage in an existing dataset, which can serve as a starting point for design of ontological background models and might also help to learn how to use the ontology for data annotation properly.

1   Problem Definition

OWL [13] allows to model the same situation using different language constructs, which might lead to difficulties when an ontology is reused (Section 1.1). Finding a proper way to reuse an ontology without sufficient documentation might be problematic as well (Section 1.2). As explained throughout the paper, a part of the solution of the former might also help with the latter.

1.1   OWL Modeling Style Heterogeneity

Different use cases of OWL ontologies on the semantic web fit different ontology modeling styles – using different combination of OWL constructs. For example, simple semantic web vocabularies like Schema.org tend to model attributes of

---

2nd-year PhD candidate supervised by Dr. Vojtěch Svátek.

© Springer International Publishing Switzerland 2015
P. Lambrix et al. (Eds.): EKAW 2014 Satellite Events, LNAI 8982, pp. 193–200, 2015.
DOI: 10.1007/978-3-319-17966-7_28

some entity as datatype properties, where any string can be used as their value. More formal ontologies, like FRBR,[1] often model the same kind of attribute as an object property or through class membership. The former approach might be followed to develop an easy-to-use vocabulary while the latter can be motivated by emphasis on accurate modeling of reality and/or reasoning capabilities. There are (at least) two issues related to this.

(a) Reusing an existing ontology might be difficult or even impossible if its modeling style does not fit the intended usage.
(b) Current ontology visualization tools (as surveyed in [11]) either display the OWL language constructs directly or only offer very lightweight generalization, as in [8]. When the user wants to compare the coverage of several ontologies from a similar domain in a visual manner, s/he has to first translate the OWL language constructs into a mental model to abstract from the modeling differences.

1.2 Separation of the Definition of an Ontology and the Description of its Usage

Ontology/vocabulary source code in OWL does not contain the specification of its usage and such specification has to be either added as free-text comments or written as a separate free-text guide. The ontology defines what combinations of concepts *can* be used to annotate data in general but not what particular combinations of these concepts *should* be used to annotate particular situations. For example, when looking at the source code of the GoodRelations [10] ontology, we can find that the relevant concepts for describing that "someone wants to buy something" are BusinessEntity and Offering. But the information that the proper way of annotation is to link instances of BusinessEntity and Offering with the seeks property and to connect the instance of Offering to a predefined instance Sell of the BusinessFunction class with the property hasBusinessFunction is not explicitly defined in OWL. Some of it can be inferred from the domain/range axioms, but the rest has to be learned from the comments and/or the GoodRelations user guide. If it is insufficient, a possible option is to learn directly from the dataset where the ontology is used (i.e. learning from examples). However, manually browsing a large dataset might be virtually impossible.

2   State of the Art

The problem of heterogeneity of ontologies is targeted by a whole research area of ontology mapping [12]. It aims at enabling usage of a combination of different ontologies, however, it is not concerned with the modeling style heterogeneity.

---

[1] http://purl.org/vocab/frbr/core#

Meta-modeling approaches might allow to abstract from the OWL modeling differences. *PURO ontological background models* (OBM) [16] allows to model a part of reality in a representation that relaxes some of the constraints imposed to OWL by its description logic grounding and can be mapped to different OWL modeling styles. PURO OBMs are based on two main distinctions: between particulars and universals and between relationships and objects (hence the PURO acronym). The *term types* in the PURO OBM language are to some extent analogous to OWL meta-model types. For example, *B-relations* are analogous to object properties with the difference that the arity of *B-relations* is not limited to 2. *B-relations* are thus often modeled in OWL as classes whose instances represent the relationships ('relation reification'). *B-types* are analogous to OWL classes, but in some cases they are modeled as instances in OWL; types of types (higher-order types) are also allowed in PURO. An OBM consists of named instances of these terms and relationships between them. OBMs have been so far used for ontology coherence testing [17]. A similar meta-modeling approach for coherence testing offers *OntoClean* [7], which however only focuses on *classes* in a *taxonomy*. *OntoUML* [1] is a version of UML for conceptual modeling where the modeling primitives are grounded in concepts of a foundational ontology. That allows validation of the models against syntactical errors and application of ontological design patterns. An existing tool, OLED [1], even allows to transform OntoUML models into OWL fragments. However, the purpose of OntoUML is conceptual modeling and is not intended for ontology engineering.

Knowledge pattern extraction and ontology learning from datasets is presented in [15], though not in association with the problem discussed in Section 1.2. There is on the other hand a number of *dataset visualization* methods [4], but they focus on visualizing the data itself rather than its structure. Similar situation is in *ontology visualization* [11]: there are many methods focusing on visualization of OWL constructs, but none of them try to visualize an OWL-independent background model such as OBM.

3   Proposed Approach: Tools and Use Cases

We propose an architecture consisting of three tools: PURO Modeler, LOD-Sight and OBOWLMorph. PURO Modeler will enable graphical design of OBMs. Using OBMs to abstract from modeling differences might make ontology comparison easier (see Section 3.1). LODSight will serve for dataset summarization in a way that supports learning ontology usage (Section 3.2). The combination of all three tools will allow easy transformation of existing ontologies into more fitting modeling style or automatic generation of new ontologies in a desired modeling style (Section 3.3).

3.1   Use Case 1: Local Coverage Comparison with PURO Modeler

OBMs should allow to easily compare, in a visual manner, the capability of different ontologies to express a certain cluster of relationships (which we denote as *local coverage*[2]). When the user is choosing an ontology for data annotation, instead of just looking at the source code or visualizations of possibly suitable ontologies and their documentation, s/he can first design an OBM of the situation s/he needs to describe and then highlight the parts of it that are 'locally covered' by each of the ontologies. This way the user gets an explicit visualization of the comparison in a single diagram. This is possible thanks to the fact that OBM is OWL-independent (it looks the same regardless that a part of it might be implemented as a data property in one ontology and an object property in another) but can still be mapped to OWL (i.e. we can tell which part of it is implemented by which OWL fragment of an ontology).

3.2   Use Case 2: Learning the Ontology Usage with LODSight

LODSight will offer a dataset summarization visualized as a type-property graph showing which types of instances (displayed as nodes) are used in combination with which properties (displayed as edges connecting the nodes). It will allow to select a part of the displayed graph and display examples of instances of selected types connected by given properties, i.e. instantiations of the selected graph pattern that are actually present in the dataset. The user will choose, on each 'type' node, whether the displayed instances/literals are to be (1) mutually identical, (2) different, but as similar as possible, or, (3) as dissimilar as possible, using adequate metrics.[3] This will enable switching between 'local browsing' (1 and 2) of 'jumping over' (3) the dataset.

3.3   Use Case 3: Getting the Desired OWL Modeling Style via Synergy of Tools

We propose an approach analogical to best practices in relational database design: in CASE tools such as PowerDesigner,[4] a conceptual, implementation-independent model of the data can be created, from which the codes for specific database systems can be generated automatically. OBMs might be used in this way, as a (loose) analogy of conceptual models in relational database modeling. Our proposed approach is as follows. Let there be an ontology that is already in use and can be reused elsewhere but this other use case requires a different modeling style, i.e. using different OWL features. By analyzing the usage of the ontology in a *particular dataset* using LODSight,[5] an OBM of the state of affairs could be designed in PURO Modeler. Such OBM would then serve as the main

---

[2] We discuss the ability of an ontology to describe a specific state of affairs where typically only a few entities and relationships are involved (e.g. a book, its author and its subject). To differentiate from the coverage of the whole domain (e.g. bibliography), we use the term 'local coverage.'

[3] The metrics are yet to be developed.

[4] http://www.sybase.com/products/modelingdevelopment/powerdesigner

[5] OBMs are created as models based not on the ontology itself but rather on the real world situation as described by the ontology, at the *instance* (dataset) level.

input of a transformation framework based on [20] with graphical UI (OBOWL-Morph), which would produce several alternatives of the original ontology using different modeling styles. The user would then choose the most suitable one. In case that a completely new ontology is developed, the OBM can be designed from scratch, omitting the existing ontology analysis in LODSight.

4   Implementation and Evaluation Proposals

The preliminary version of **PURO Modeler** implements a standard *node-link* visualization method, common in the ontology visualization domain, where instances of OBM language terms are visualized as nodes. The first version of PURO Modeler will allow graphical creation of OBMs and their import into OBOWLMorph. Future versions might also visualize occurrences of OBMs in a dataset, i.e. visualize OBMs in the context or linked to their 'implementation' in OWL, and allow semi-automated generation of OBMs based on input from LODSight.

LODSight implementation that is currently being experimentally developed is based on finding type-property paths [15,17] and characteristic sets [14] and combining the results, selecting the paths with high occurrence counts and adding characteristic sets to them. SPARQL is used to access the datasets, but we are considering using HDT [9] instead, to make the summarization faster.

The interface of **OBOWLMorph** will use an extended version of the *pattern-based ontology transformation framework*[6] (PatOMat) [20] currently used in the OWL-to-OWL transformation tool GUIPOT [21]. GUIPOT takes an ontology and a transformation pattern as input and can transform an ontology fragment described by the transformation pattern into a different OWL ontology fragment. The input of OBOWLMorph will be an OBM created in PURO Modeler and, optionally, an ontology that is to be transformed. Analogically to the current (OWL-to-OWL) PatOMat framework, OBOWLMorph will be based on (OBM-to-OWL) transformation patterns. Each pattern will describe a fragment of OBM and a corresponding OWL ontology fragment (both in an abstracted form, with placeholders). An example of such pattern is in Figure 1.

OBM-to-OWL Transformation Example The example is based on analysis of several recipe ontologies.[7] Figure 1a represents an OBM pattern of a situation where there is a B-object that is a B-instanceOf some B-type (e.g., "Czech Recipe"), which is a B-subtypeOf of some other 'parent' type (e.g., "Recipe"). The names of the B-types are formed from placeholders (marked with question marks): e.g., the name of the instantiation of the B-subtype must have the name of the parent B-type as suffix. Example instantiation of the pattern is shown as labels in quotation marks above the nodes. Possible corresponding OWL ontology fragments (parts b,c,d in the Figure 1) are shown analogically. Fragment (b) follows the modeling style where the subtype of the instance (e.g., the origin

---

[6] http://patomat.vse.cz
[7] Available at http://tomhanzal.github.io/owl-modeling-styles/#part2

198   M. Dudáš

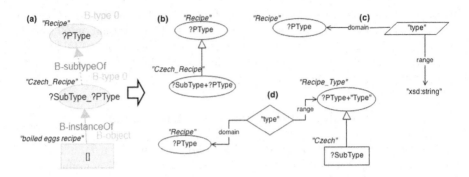

Fig. 1. An OBM-to-OWL transformation pattern example. (a) is the OBM pattern. (b), (c) and (d) are patterns of OWL fragments which the OBM can be transformed into.

of a recipe) is represented by class membership (in our example, there has to be a subclass of Recipe for each possible origin). In fragment (c), the type of the instance is modeled as a datatype property. In (d), it is an object property, whose possible values might be included in the ontology.

The tool will be provided with a large database of such patterns designed on the basis of empirical analysis of existing ontologies/vocabularies currently in use on the semantic web (implementation of ontology design patterns [6] will be considered), and will automatically select appropriate patterns for each OBM. Linguistic methods will be involved for naming the resulting OWL constructs based on the names used for OBM entities.

Evaluation If the development of OBOWLMorph is successful, evaluation will focus on the ontologies produced from OBMs, e.g., using comparison against existing 'gold standard' ontologies or evaluation by usage. The evaluation of LODSight and PUROModeler will be focused mainly on testing their GUIs with groups of selected users. The users will be asked to perform predefined tasks with the GUI (such as comparison of local coverage or preparation for ontology generation in PURO Modeler or learning of proper usage of a selected part of an ontology in LODSight, designing an OBM based on LODSight output etc.) and the time needed will be measured for variants of the GUI. The users will be also asked to fill a questionnaire afterwards.

Preliminary Results We have tested a preliminary implementation of PURO Modeler[8] in an analysis of local coverage of several bibliography and food/recipe ontologies [5]. A prototypical implementation of LODSight along with several other examples of dataset summarizations is available as a web application.[9] The results suggest the summarization works, but not all current SPARQL endpoints

---

[8] Available at http://lod2-dev.vse.cz/puromodeler/

[9] The application along with further details: http://lod2-dev.vse.cz/lodsight

support demanding queries that are needed to obtain the summary. Summarization of a dataset containing several millions of triples takes about an hour. We plan to gradually "crawl" large number of datasets and store the summarizations for offline viewing.

5 Conclusions and Future Work

We proposed an architecture consisting of three tools: LODSight for dataset analysis regarding the typical ways an ontology is used in it, PURO Modeler for graphical design of PURO OBMs, and OBOWLMorph: a tool for pattern-based transformation of OBMs into OWL ontologies. The architecture addresses the issue that OWL allows to model the same state of affairs using different constructs and that ontologies on the same topics indeed use different modeling styles, either to fit the demands of applications and users or even quite randomly. The proposed set of tools has two main possible usage scenarios. First, if an ontology covering the desired domain already exists but does not fulfill the requirements on its modeling style regarding its intended usage, *variants of the ontology* could be automatically generated and a more appropriate one could be chosen once the ontology background model has been designed in PURO Modeler with the help of LODSight. Second, an ontology background model could be designed from scratch and several variants (using different OWL modeling styles) of a *completely new ontology* could be generated. The most appropriate variant regarding the intended usage of the ontology could then be chosen. LODSight could be also applied alone for *ontology usage analysis*, leveraging on existing datasets as an alternative or supplement to guides and manuals. OBM visualized in PURO Modeler could, in turn, serve as an aid for analysis of *local coverage* of ontologies. PURO Modeler and LODSight have been preliminary implemented and tested. The future work will include development of guidelines for OBM design, extension of the *PURO OBM language* required for the OBM-to-OWL transformation and the development of *transformation patterns and algorithm*.

The research is supported by VŠE IGA grant F4/34/2014. I would like to thank to Vojtěch Svátek, my advisor, and Tomáš Hanzal, who did a survey of ontologies where PURO Modeler was tested.

References

1. Albuquerque, A., Guizzardi, G.: An ontological foundation for conceptual modeling datatypes based on semantic reference spaces. In: 2013 IEEE Seventh International Conference on Research Challenges in Information Science (RCIS), pp. 1–12
2. Brunetti, J.M., Garcia, R., Auer, S.: From overview to facets and pivoting for interactive exploration of semantic web data. Int. J. Semantic Web Inf. Syst. **9**, 120 (2013)
3. Campinas, S., et al.: Introducing RDF graph summary with application to assisted SPARQL formulation. In: International Workshop on Web Semantics (WebS) at DEXA (2012)

4. Dadzie, A.S., Rowe, M.: Approaches to visualising linked data: A survey. Semantic Web **2**(2), 89–124 (2011)
5. Dudáš, M., Hanzal, T., Svátek, V.: What Can the Ontology Describe? Visualizing Local Coverage in PURO Modeler. In: VISUAL at EKAW 2014, Linkoping (2014)
6. Gangemi, A., Presutti, V.: Ontology design patterns. In: Staab, S., Studer, R. (eds.) Handbook on Ontologies. International Handbooks on Information Systems, pp. 221–243. Springer, Heidelberg (2009)
7. Guarino, N., Welty, C.: An Overview of OntoClean. In: Staab, S., Studer, R. (eds.) Handbook on Ontologies. International Handbooks on Information Systems, pp. 201–220. Springer, Heidelberg (2009)
8. Hayes, P., et al.: Collaborative knowledge capture in ontologies. In: Proceedings of the 3rd International Conference on Knowledge Capture - K-CAP 2005. ACM (2005)
9. Fernandez, J., et al.: Binary RDF representation for publication and exchange (HDT). In: Web Semantics: Science, Services and Agents on the World Wide Web, 19 (2013)
10. Hepp, M.: GoodRelations: an ontology for describing products and services offers on the web. In: Gangemi, A., Euzenat, J. (eds.) EKAW 2008. LNCS (LNAI), vol. 5268, pp. 329–346. Springer, Heidelberg (2008)
11. Katifori, A., et al.: Ontology Visualization Methods - A Survey. ACM Comput. Surv. **39**, 1043 (2007)
12. Shvaiko, P., Euzenat, J.: Ontology matching: state of the art and future challenges. IEEE Transactions on Knowledge and Data Engineering **25**(1), 158–176 (2013)
13. OWL 2 Web Ontology Language Document Overview. W3C Recommendation (2009)
14. Neumann, T., Moerkotte, G.: Characteristic sets: Accurate cardinality estimation for RDF queries with multiple joins. In: 2011 IEEE 27th International Conference on Data Engineering (ICDE), pp. 984–994. IEEE (2011)
15. Presutti, V., et al.: Extracting core knowledge from Linked Data. In: Proceedings of the Second Workshop on Consuming Linked Data, COLD (2011)
16. Svátek, V., et al.: Mapping structural design patterns in OWL to ontological background models. In: K-CAP 2013. ACM (2013)
17. Svátek, V., et al.: B-Annot: supplying background model annotations for ontology coherence testing. In: 3rd Workshop on Debugging Ontologies and Ontology Mappings at ESWC 2014, Heraklion, Crete (2014)
18. Svátek, V., et al.: Metamodeling-Based Coherence Checking of OWL Vocabulary Background Models. In: OWLED (2013)
19. Svátek, V., et al.: LOD2 deliverable 9a.3.1: Application of data analytics methods of linked data in the domain of PSC, 8 June 2014. [cit. 2014-08-25]. http://svn. aksw.org/lod2/D9a.3.1/public.pdf
20. Šváb-Zamazal, O., Svátek, V., Iannone, L.: Pattern-based ontology transformation service exploiting OPPL and OWL-API. In: Cimiano, P., Pinto, H.S. (eds.) EKAW 2010. LNCS, vol. 6317, pp. 105–119. Springer, Heidelberg (2010)
21. Šváb-Zamazal, O., Dudáš, M., Svátek, V.: User-friendly pattern-based transformation of OWL ontologies. In: ten Teije, A., Völker, J., Handschuh, S., Stuckenschmidt, H., d'Acquin, M., Nikolov, A., Aussenac-Gilles, N., Hernandez, N. (eds.) EKAW 2012. LNCS, vol. 7603, pp. 426–429. Springer, Heidelberg (2012)

Linked Data Cleansing and Change Management

Magnus Knuth[✉]

Hasso Plattner Institute, University of Potsdam, Potsdam, Germany
magnus.knuth@hpi.uni-potsdam.de

Abstract. The Web of Data is constantly growing in terms of covered domains, applied vocabularies, and number of triples. A high level of data quality is in the best interest of any data consumer.

Linked Data publishers can use various data quality evaluation tools prior to publication of their datasets. But nevertheless, most inconsistencies only become obvious when the data is processed in applications and presented to the end users. Therefore, it is not only the responsibility of the original data publishers to keep their data tidy, but progresses to become a mission for all distributors and consumers of Linked Data, too.

My main research topic is the inspection of feedback mechanisms for Linked Data cleansing in open knowledge bases. This work includes a change request vocabulary, the aggregation of change requests produced by various agents, versioning data resources, and consumer notification about changes. The individual components form the basis of a Linked Data Change Management framework.

Keywords: Linked data · Data cleansing · Error correction · RDF · Patchr · Dataset

1 Problem Statement

More and more Linked Data datasets are published to the Web of Data, but often they show insufficient quality. Low quality can have various reasons, e. g. the nature of their upspring (automatic extraction, conversion and integration of legacy data), outdated values and incomplete facts since the world is constantly changing. For the data publisher it is often difficult to recognize these errors, while data consumers need to deal with it or simply disagree with the presented data. Therefore, data consumers should be enabled to give feedback on what should be changed in the dataset.

But let's first clarify what *data quality* actually means. Data quality has been defined by Orr being "a measure of [...] agreement between data views presented by an information system and the same data in the real-world" [12]. It is unlikely that an information system will ever achieve a data quality of 100 %, the real challenge is not to get a perfect agreement, but that the data quality is satisfactory to the users' needs or it is "fit for use" in it's intended role [7], e. g. the data needs to be free of defects (accuracy, currency, completeness, consistency, etc.) and to possess the desired features (relevancy, comprehensiveness, etc.).

© Springer International Publishing Switzerland 2015
P. Lambrix et al. (Eds.): EKAW 2014 Satellite Events, LNAI 8982, pp. 201–208, 2015.
DOI: 10.1007/978-3-319-17966-7_29

The needs of data consumers might differ depending on the use case. The problems of low data quality mainly affects data consumers – they will experience difficulties in using low grade datasets.

A well-suited use case is the DBpedia dataset [4]. DBpedia is a generic RDF database that includes concepts from a broad range of domains and therefore is of high interest for knowledge workers and application developers. Unfortunately, DBpedia data suffers from low quality. Such low data quality even prevents users from adopting data from this dataset and Linked Open Data in general within own applications, e. g. users regularly report about incorrect or missing data in DBpedia on the DBpedia-Discussion mailing list[1] and ask for correction. Linked Open Data datasets of convincing quality are one key factor for adoption of Linked Data and Semantic Web technologies [2]. Moreover, technologies to handle changing Linked Data and to improve it's qualities is also crucial for the adoption of Semantic Web technolgies in closed environments, such as companies.

2   State of the Art

The problem of data quality has been addressed since data has been raised and collected. Especially in the field of data warehouse management, data cleansing has been a topic for a long time [1]. Errors commonly addressed in this field are deduplication, linking, and data value correction [14].

My research targets Linked Data in particular[2]. In order to raise quality in Linked Data applications various work has concentrated on syntactical and logical data consistency by providing validators for the Semantic Web languages RDF and OWL, e. g., W3C's RDF Validator[3], Vapour[4], and OWL Validator[5]. The problem of syntactical incorrectness has been widely solved, due to the application of standardized and well-tested RDF libraries syntactical errors in RDF occur only rarely. Data quality in Linked Data has been criticized, as e. g., by the Pedantic Web group[6], Hogan et al. analyzed typical errors and set up the RDF:Alerts Service[7] that detects syntax and datatype errors to support publishers of Linked Data [6]. Nevertheless, recent analyses provided by LODStats[8] show that there is still a vast amount of erroneous Linked Datasets available [3]. Most of the listed errors orginate from missing files or unavailable SPARQL endpoints.

Multiple approaches aim to identify incorrect or missing statements in Linked Data datasets: Amoung other approaches currently emerging, *WhoKnows?* [15],

---

[1] http://sourceforge.net/p/dbpedia/mailman/dbpedia-discussion/
[2] It does not matter whether it is Linked Open Data, Linked Data published under a restrictive license, or even accessible in closed environments.
[3] http://www.w3.org/RDF/Validator/
[4] http://validator.linkeddata.org/vapour
[5] http://owl.cs.manchester.ac.uk/validator/
[6] http://pedantic-web.org/
[7] http://swse.deri.org/RDFAlerts/
[8] http://stats.lod2.eu/rdfdoc/?errors=1

RDFUnit [10], *SDType* [13], and *TripleCheckMate* [11] have been applied to the DBpedia dataset. *WhoKnows?* is a quiz game that generates questions from DBpedia RDF triples. It allows the player to report incorrect or missing triples in case the quiz question, answering options, or the correct answers do not make sense to the player. *TripleCheckMate* was a crowdsourcing effort that analyzed the results of the DBpedia extraction process. Manually detected errors have been classified and commented, a subset of these can be used as deletion requests. *RDFUnit* allows to check for correct application of vocabularies to a dataset in the form of unit tests, automatically generated from the vocabularies according to defined patterns. Originally, it simply reports errors in the dataset. With an extension, I generate patch requests within the framework that solve these errors[9]. *SDType* aims to find resource type information in noisy RDF data. This dataset has already been contributed to the DBpedia, but only for untyped resources and suggestions with a particular threshold. The main problem with such efforts is that they mostly target systematic errors in particular datasets and are not generalizable for all error types on any dataset.

A solution to modify RDF resource directly has been proposed by the Read-Write-Web community. Besides *HTTP POST* and *PUT*, the Linked Data Platform (LDP) working group is currently working on the standardization of *HTTP PATCH*[10] for RDF, which aims to update resources directly within the publishers' repository. The standard assumes a direct update, without consideration of the publisher. In productive use, it will demand access control to prevent updates from unknown or less reliable parties.

3   Methodology

I apply the design-science research method for my thesis. Sec. 1 describes the problem of low data quality and Sec. 2 the state-of-the-art aproaches and lack of change management standards in the Web of Data. We currently collect change-sets for a number of Linked Data datasets in order to generate statistics that allow to draw valuable conclusions about typical changes. Based on these findings requirements are derived for a change management framework. According to the requirements the following artifacts are developed: the patch request vocabulary, a policy language for change application to a dataset, and best-practices on change management for data publishers. The novelty of these artifacts is shown by comparison to related approaches. The verification of usefulness is provided by a proof-of-concept implementation in form of the PatchR framework and by applying the framework in varying scenarios.

4   Proposed Approach

The base idea of my approach is that change requests are sent from the data consumer to the publisher, where they are collected within a patch repository

---

[9] There are usually multiple possibilties to solve such errors, therefore all solutions are suggested as alternatives.

[10] Similarity in naming is absolutely coincidential.

and combined. The data publisher than decides which changes to apply to his dataset.

To describe Linked Data change requests I created the Patch Request Ontology[11], a vocabulary that can be used to communicate change requests to the dataset publisher. The vocabulary has been presented in [8]. The vocabulary has evolved over time including suggestions from the community and support for further requirements. It reuses PROV-O[12] to describe provenance and the Graph Update Ontology[13] to describe changes.

Listing 1.1. A sample patch request from agent :SDtype asking for insertion of the triple dbp:Maria_Callas a dbo:Artist with a rather low confidence.

```
1  :patch-1 a pat:Patch ;
2      pat:appliesTo <http://dbpedia.org/void/Dataset> ;
3      pat:status pat:ACTIVE ;
4      pat:update [
5          guo:target_subject dbp:Maria_Callas ;
6          guo:insert [
7              a dbo:Artist
8          ] ]
9      prov:wasGeneratedBy [
10         prov:wasAssociatedWith :SDtype ;
11         pat:confidence "0.17729138"^^xsd:double ;
12         prov:atTime "2014-07-16T13:43:18.245+02:00"^^xsd:dateTime
13     ] .
```

A sample patch request is given in Listing 1.1. It includes the affected dataset, the initial status, the requested update, and provenance information. The dataset should be described as a void:Dataset. The initial state is *active* and may change to *resolved* when the requested triple has been inserted or deleted on the target dataset. The update describes the changes to perform, it consists of a target subject and a subgraph that is requested to be *inserted* or *deleted*. The provenance information contains the performing agent and a confidence expressed as a numerical value in the range of $(0, 1]$, whereas a high value means higher confidence and a value of 1 signifies absolute certainty. This confidence needs to be determined by the submitting agent. In case multiple agents propose the same patch, only the provenance is added to an existing patch. Consequently, the confidence grows that this change is valid and should be applied to the dataset. The publisher or any service acting on its behalf collects these change requests within a patch repository. A viable alternative to a central repository would be the publication of patch requests on the clients' side, whereas the data publisher needs to be informed about newly published patch requests pertaining its dataset.

The Patchr API[14] enables simple creation of patch requests, as well as repository management including access, aggregation of equivalent change requests, calculation of combined confidences and allows arbitrary filtering.

---

[11] http://purl.org/hpi/patchr
[12] http://www.w3.org/ns/prov
[13] http://webr3.org/owl/guo
[14] https://github.com/mgns/patchr

Finally, the data publishers decide about which change requests will be applied to their datasets. This decision may be made automatically according to defined rules, or according to a filtering or manual selection. Furthermore, change requests may give valuable hints towards programmatic root causes of future errors. This particularly holds for DBpedia, since it is extracted from Wikipedia articles using the *DBpedia extraction framework*[15] and configurations from the *DBpedia Mappings Wiki*[16]. Fixing errors in Wikipedia or in the extraction pipeline prevents future errors which complies with second-generation quality systems described by Juran [7].

The architecture of a Linked Data change management system also includes a versioning and a change notification component: Versioning is necessary to keep track of changes and change requests, that actually refer to outdated versions of a resource. This is even more relevant for constantly updated datasets, such as DBpedia Live where changes to Wikipedia articles are extracted in almost real-time. Change requests become obsolete as soon as the resource changed respectively. The particular resource can be determined by requesting a Memento service [5] with the time information given in the provenance for the patch.

Since Linked Data consists of distributed datasets it is necessary to hold local copies (or caches) of external resources for better availability and performance. In case external resources change it is necessary to invalidate and update these copies. In order to not frequently retrieve external datasets (pull strategy), notification about updated resources would be desirable (push strategy). There is currently no mechanism in the Web of Data for doing such. Furthermore, notification allows patch submitters to get informed about the acceptance of their change requests.

5   Evaluation

The architecture developed in this work can hardly be evaluated. It can be applied on multiple datasets and integrated into Linked Data publishing systems to show its feasability. By doing so, I am going to develop guidelines and best practices for its application.

To evaluate the effectiveness of patch requests various evaluation settings are conceivable. A straightforward evaluation would be to let domain experts validate the change requests. According to the experts' votes, the precisioncan be determined. The recall can only be compared to the overall proposed changes. Since it might be unfeasible to validate all change requests by domain experts, the total numbers might be extrapolated or the task can be performed as a crowdsourcing task.

An unsupervised approach would be to introduce random errors into a curated test dataset and check whether these errors can be found. While this kind of evaluation on examplary data should work well for automatic error spotters, approaches employing human voting might be irritating for the turkers. Due to the lack of

---

[15] https://github.com/dbpedia/extraction-framework
[16] http://mappings.dbpedia.org/

curated datasets of high interest to a sufficiently large crowd, a faulty dataset could be used if the results can be normalized. To normalize the results such experiments should be performed in form of an A/B test, where resources are presented either in their original form (A) or with arbitrary errors (B). I plan to extend DBpedia Widgets, embeddable snippet presentations of DBpedia resources[17], for these experiments. Though, further interfaces are always welcome.

6   Preliminary Results

The idea to consolidate the patch requests of multiple agents has been presented at the 11th ESWC Conference in 2014 [9]. The approach in general received very good feedback from the community, who often asked for a possibility to submit change requests to DBpedia or other datasets. I also received feedback to consider further approaches and datasets that I was not aware of before.

A consolidated dataset of collected change requests from multiple data cleansing approaches for DBpedia is currently work in progress. As to now, results from the *WhoKnows?* game, *TripleCheckMate*, and *SDType* have been collected. An extension of *RDFUnit* has been created, which produces solutions in form of patch requests from the identified errors. Results for a subset of tests have been produced with this extension, that already allowed to recognize an overlap of requested changes. It could have been shown, that actual useful change request with low confidence, had have been boosted by combination.

I identified a feasible operation to combine the confidences of multiple submitters a and b ($c_{p|a}$ and $c_{p|b}$) for the same patch p. The following associative, commutative, uniformly continuous operation $\oplus$ can be applied:

$$
\begin{aligned}
c_{p|a,b} = c_{p|a} \oplus c_{p|b} &= 1 - ((1 - c_{p|a}) * (1 - c_{p|b})) \\
&= c_{p|a} + c_{p|b} - (c_{p|a} * c_{p|b})
\end{aligned}
\tag{1}
$$

To achieve the reliability of a patch, the confidence can be multiplied with the trust in the respective agent. Multiple reliabilities are combined again by the operation $\oplus$.

We have implemented a change tracking and versioning extension for DBpedia Live, using the Memento approach [5] to access the evolution steps of single resources.

7   Conclusions and Future Work

There is an obvious drift of data curation responsibilities from data publishers to data consumers. Data distributors and end users actually see how the data is applied and presented, that is why they experience problems in the data. On the one hand automatic approaches can not provide an entire solution for data curation and on the other hand manual data curation is very expensive. That is

---

[17] https://github.com/dbpedia/dbpedia-widgets

why it should be distributed over the shoulder of many. PatchR allows this distribution on many shoulders and can integrate and process multiple contributions.

The next steps include setting up the PatchR pipeline for DBpedia using DBpedia Widgets and collect patch requests there. Afterwards I will perform the evaluation by modifying the presented facts in the Widgets. The versioning and notification components will be applied to the German DBpedia Live dataset at first.

Acknowledgments. I would like to express my grateful thanks to my supervisors Dr. Harald Sack and Prof. Dr. Christoph Meinel (both Hasso Plattner Institute) for their ongoing support in writing this thesis.

References

1. Arnold, S.E.: Information manufacturing: The road to database quality. Database **15**(5), 32–39 (1992)
2. Auer, S., Bühmann, L., Dirschl, C., Erling, O., Hausenblas, M., Isele, R., Lehmann, J., Martin, M., Mendes, P.N., van Nuffelen, B., Stadler, C., Tramp, S., Williams, H.: Managing the life-cycle of linked data with the LOD2 stack. In: Cudré-Mauroux, P., Heflin, J., Sirin, E., Tudorache, T., Euzenat, J., Hauswirth, M., Parreira, J.X., Hendler, J., Schreiber, G., Bernstein, A., Blomqvist, E. (eds.) ISWC 2012, Part II. LNCS, vol. 7650, pp. 1–16. Springer, Heidelberg (2012)
3. Auer, S., Demter, J., Martin, M., Lehmann, J.: LODStats – an extensible framework for high-performance dataset analytics. In: ten Teije, A., Völker, J., Handschuh, S., Stuckenschmidt, H., d'Acquin, M., Nikolov, A., Aussenac-Gilles, N., Hernandez, N. (eds.) EKAW 2012. LNCS, vol. 7603, pp. 353–362. Springer, Heidelberg (2012)
4. Bizer, C., Lehmann, J., Kobilarov, G., Auer, S., Becker, C., Cyganiak, R., Hellmann, S.: DBpedia - a crystallization point for the web of data. Web Semantics: Science, Services and Agents on the World Wide Web **7**(3), 154–165 (2009)
5. de Sompel, H.V., Sanderson, R., Nelson, M.L., Balakireva, L., Shankar, H., Ainsworth, S.: An HTTP-based versioning mechanism for linked data. In: LDOW2010, Raleigh, USA, April 2010
6. Hogan, A., Harth, A., Passant, A., Decker, S., Polleres, A.: Weaving the pedantic web. In: LDOW 2010. CEUR Workshop Proceedings. vol. 628 (2010)
7. Juran, J., Godfrey, A.: Juran's quality handbook. Juran's quality handbook, 5e. McGraw Hill (1999)
8. Knuth, M., Hercher, J., Sack, H.: Collaboratively patching linked data. In: USEWOD 2012, Lyon, France, April 2012
9. Knuth, M., Sack, H.: Data cleansing consolidation with PatchR. In: ESWC2014, Best Poster Award, May 2014
10. Kontokostas, D., Westphal, P., Auer, S., Hellmann, S., Lehmann, J., Cornelissen, R., Zaveri, A.: Test-driven evaluation of linked data quality. In: WWW2014 (2014)
11. Kontokostas, D., Zaveri, A., Auer, S., Lehmann, J.: TripleCheckMate: a tool for crowdsourcing the quality assessment of linked data. In: Klinov, P., Mouromtsev, D. (eds.) KESW 2013. CCIS, vol. 394, pp. 265–272. Springer, Heidelberg (2013)
12. Orr, K.: Data quality and systems theory. Communications of the ACM **41**(2), 66–71 (1998)

13. Paulheim, H., Bizer, C.: Type inference on noisy RDF data. In: Alani, H., Kagal, L., Fokoue, A., Groth, P., Biemann, C., Parreira, J.X., Aroyo, L., Noy, N., Welty, C., Janowicz, K. (eds.) ISWC 2013, Part I. LNCS, vol. 8218, pp. 510–525. Springer, Heidelberg (2013)
14. Singh, R., Singh, K.: A descriptive classification of causes of data quality problems in data warehousing. International Journal of Computer Science Issues 7(3), 41–50 (2010)
15. Waitelonis, J., Ludwig, N., Knuth, M., Sack, H.: WhoKnows? - evaluating linked data heuristics with a quiz that cleans up DBpedia. International Journal of Interactive Technology and Smart Education (ITSE) 8(3), 236–248 (2011)

Culture-Aware Approaches to Modeling and Description of Intonation Using Multimodal Data

Gopala Krishna Koduri[✉]

Music Technology Group, Universitat Pompeu Fabra, Barcelona, Spain
gopala.koduri@upf.edu

Abstract. Computational approaches that conform to the cultural context are of paramount importance in music information research. The current state-of-the-art has a limited view of such context, which manifests in our ontologies, data-, cognition- and interaction-models that are biased to the market-driven popular music. In a step towards addressing this, the thesis draws upon multimodal data sources concerning art music traditions, extracting culturally relevant and musically meaningful information about melodic intervals from each of them and structuring it with formal knowledge representations. As part of this, we propose novel approaches to describe intonation in audio music recordings and to use and adapt the semantic web infrastructure to complement this with the knowledge extracted from text data. Due to the complementary nature of the data sources, structuring and linking the extracted information results in a symbiosis mutually enriching their information. Over this multimodal knowledge base, we propose similarity measures for the discovery of musical entities, yielding a culturally-sound navigation space.

1 Problem

Music traditions from around the world share a few common characteristics. Yet, they differ substantially when viewed within their geographical and cultural context [1]. Consider the fundamental melodic unit. In Indian art music, the definition of this unit, called svara, constitutes a frequency with an allowed space around it owing to its shared context with the neighboring svaras. This space is further constrained by certain motifs as allowed/disallowed by the melodic framework it belongs to, called rāga [2]. This formulation differs to a great extent compared to the definitions of analogous concepts in other music traditions like notes in Makam music of Turkey or Western classical music. Indeed, the similarity/relation[1] between rāgas is dictated by terms different to those concerning makams or scales.

The current state of the music information research (MIR) and most commercial music platforms are largely agnostic to such differences, which inhibit them from adapting their information models to meet the cultural diversity.

---

[1] The terms similarity and relation are used synonymously henceforth.

© Springer International Publishing Switzerland 2015
P. Lambrix et al. (Eds.): EKAW 2014 Satellite Events, LNAI 8982, pp. 209–217, 2015.
DOI: 10.1007/978-3-319-17966-7_30

The need for integrating and using cultural context in MIR has been emphasized time and again [1,3]. In part, this is to address an increasing bias towards the market-driven popular music in the information models developed and used by the research and the development communities. This is reflected even in the tasks as basic as music browsing: most of the popular music library services[2] structure the content using the severely limited artist-album-track schema. For music information research and technologies to evolve beyond their current limitations in this regard, it is imperative to rely on the cultural context of the music which broadens their purview and further opens up new avenues for research [1].

Within this context, the progress in semantic web technologies over the last decade assumes a significant relevance for MIR. The linked open data movement has resulted in an increasing number of structured data sources for music including Freebase, DBpedia and LinkedBrainz. This has spawned the research and development of music applications built around such resources, some of which are reviewed in sec. 2. On the other hand, development of expressive description logics [4] has resulted in ontology languages that can be used to represent complex musical concepts such as the melodic sequences/patterns [5]. In summary, the current state of the semantic web technologies turns the problem into a tenable one. Addressing it further helps in expanding the scope of linked open data resources in the music domain by combining the information extracted from different modalities of data, and testing the limitations of the ontology languages in structuring the music domain knowledge.

In a step to address the problem described, we propose: a) developing/adapting methodologies to extract musically meaningful information about the melodic units from different modalities of data (audio music recordings and text), b) structuring this information to create an integrated multimodal knowledge base, and c) developing similarity/relatedness measures over this resource to relate the entities to facilitate exploration and navigation that conforms to the cultural context of the music.

2   State of the Art

Within the context-based[3] MIR, there are broadly two classes of approaches to music similarity and recommendation: those which use the knowledge inherent in the contextual data in an implicit manner, and those which take advantage of the semantic web technologies. The former draws upon data sources such as tags, lyrics and unstructured text for applications ranging from playlist generation and auto tagging, to music recommendation, search engines and interfaces (see [6] for a recent review of the related work).

The latter class of approaches is a relatively recent direction in MIR, which can broadly be understood to address information management, music similarity and recommendation. Raimond developed the Music Ontology, which builds on

---

[2] such as iTunes, Amarok, Windows media player etc.

[3] *Context* in MIR refers to non-audio data about music such as lyrics, community-generated data etc.

top of several existing ontologies, defining generic music-specific vocabulary [7]. It allows describing music creation workflows, temporal events and editorial metadata. Recently, Oramas proposed a methodology to structure the social media content using the community-generated data such as tags, with formal knowledge representations [8].

Foafing-the-music [9] uses multiple data sources such as contextual-data from RSS feeds, content-based features and user profiles, and links them by describing the data using a common ontology. This information is further used for music recommendation. Jacobson *et al* [10] show that the network structure of artists on Myspace correspond to the genres. This data was published using music ontology [7] to be used by other music applications. DBrec system [11] uses a linked-data based semantic distance to relate musical entities, based on the link structure of the music-related resources on DBpedia, resulting in explanatory recommendations.

In the content-based[4] MIR, there is a steadily growing interest in incorporating the musicological knowledge in the information retrieval methodologies. Srinivasamurthy *et al* [12] review several state-of-the-art approaches to rhythm description and evaluate them on Indian art music traditions and Makam music of Turkey. Gulati *et al* [13] evaluate various tonic identification approaches over Indian art music traditions using diverse datasets under different conditions of the data (E.g., duration of the input audio clip, presence/absence of metadata etc). Rao *et al* [14] propose methods to classify melodic patterns in Indian art music and evaluate them using retrieval experiments.

In summary, the context- and content-based approaches are advancing to incorporate culture-specific information. However, to fully realize the potential benefits in this direction, we believe that a) the information extracted from different modalities must be used to complement and enrich each other and b) the approaches themselves must have an integrated access to the information extracted from one another.

3   Proposed Approach

3.1   Methodology

Creating a multimodal knowledge base for a music involves content-based analyses: melodic (tonic identification, motif detection, intonation description and so on) and rhythmic (downbeat estimation, cycle tracking and so on), and context-based analyses. We choose two of these tasks, one from each, to be addressed in this thesis: intonation description, and using the linked data clound and adapting open information extraction (Open IE) for knowledge base population of a given music. Fig. 1 shows an overview of our approach, which is detailed in the rest of this section.

Intonation: It is a fundamental music concept that is relevant to most melodic music traditions. It is characteristic of the melodic framework and key to the

---

[4] *Content* in MIR is analogous to audio data.

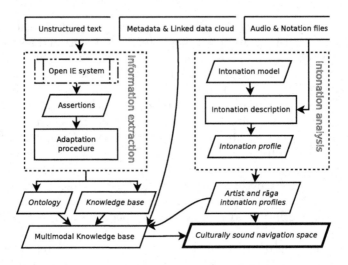

Fig. 1. An overview of the proposed approach

musical expression of the artist. Describing intonation is of importance to several music information retrieval tasks. The research questions that we address are: *How can we computationally model the concept of intonation? How concisely can we describe the intonation of notes/svaras in a given music recording? In what ways is this description useful to relate the musical entities? How do we adapt the method to a given music tradition?*

Open IE for Knowledge Base population: In the past decade, domain-independent approaches to information extraction have paved way for its web-scale applications. Open IE is one such paradigm that has been used to extract assertions from unstructured data at web-scale with a considerable success [15]. Until recently, domain-specific approaches to information extraction from text required manual knowledge engineering as a prerequisite [16]. The Open IE approaches, however, do not require a pre-specified vocabulary and/or relation-specific input. Therefore, adapting them to information extraction from thematic domains would alleviate the need for manual knowledge engineering.

The process of channeling the assertions extracted from these approaches into a coherent knowledge base poses certain challenges. There has been little work so far to identify and address such issues. The advances in Open IE, including the recent systems such as NELL[5], are largely directed towards taking advantage of the volume of web data. In doing so, the recall of the systems is often traded off for a good precision. The adaptation of such systems to acquire knowledge from a given domain is an exciting prospective direction. The research questions addressed in this direction are: *How do we process the assertions from an open information extraction system to be used for knowledge base population? Given a thematic domain, how do we adapt open IE systems?*

---

[5] http://rtw.ml.cmu.edu/rtw/

Multimodal Knowledge Base: Let us consider an example to understand the potential benefits of structuring and combining information obtained from content- and context-based analyses. Consider two artists who are said to be similar. For a listener to appreciate/understand the similarity, it is necessary to quantify this relation (how similar are they?) and provide a meaningful description (why are they similar?).

Structuring the information using ontologies and combining the different sources using the linked data framework reveals non-trivial, deeper relations between entities. The content-based analyses give us an objective view of such relations between entities (E.g., Are the two artists singing a particular phrase in a similar way? Is there a lot of variation in how they intone svaras?). Let us say that the two artists in our example are similar by this analyses. The context-based analyses reveal information that is not part of the audio content: biographical details, social connections, popularity etc. This information gives us the possible reasons for their similarity (E.g., They received training from the same teacher, or they belong to same lineage, etc.). The research questions that we address towards achieving this are: *How do we represent the complex musical concepts related to intonation in an ontology? What are the ways to combine the information extracted from content- and context-based approaches? How do we model culturally-relevant similarity measures over the multimodal knowledge base?*

3.2   Data Repertoires

The two art music traditions of the Indian subcontinent - Carnatic and Hindustani - are among the oldest yet actively practiced. With a thriving community of scholars, there are thorough musicological and cultural studies about them. The terminology and the structuring of the knowledge in these music traditions differ substantially from the information models in vogue in the MIR community [2]. Therefore, they make a suitable and challenging test-ground for developing culture-aware information models. The data for our work include audio, metadata and community-generated text data. The audio collection is carefully curated with experts' inputs and the corresponding metadata is stored on MusicBrainz, whose schema is accordingly extended to incorporate the new concepts and relation-types. Table. 3.2 shows statistics of the current snapshots of Carnatic and Hindustani music collections[6]. The community-generated data includes Wikipedia pages, online discussion forums and web pages concerning these music traditions.

Table 1. Statistics of the Carnatic and Hindustani music collections

	Releases	Recordings	Hours	Artists	Rāgas
Carnatic	248	1650	346	233	246
Hindustani	233	1096	300	360	176

---

[6] For further information, see http://compmusic.upf.edu/corpora

4   Evaluation

We quantitatively evaluate the different parts of the thesis. As intonation is a characteristic of the rāga, we use rāga classification task for a comparative evaluation with the state-of-the-art. We assess the changes we effect to an Open IE system by comparing the results to that of the original system over a text corpus labeled with the desired concepts and the relation-types. Further we also perform an extrinsic evaluation on the tasks of knowledge base population, using a gold standard consisting of manually engineered ontologies[7] [5].

On the other hand, the similarity measures developed on the multimodal knowledge base will be implemented and tested within a music discovery platform, Dunya[8] [17]. It is an online culture-aware navigation and discovery system being developed as part of the CompMusic project [1] to which this thesis will contribute. The similarity computed between the musical entities will be used for generating recommendations to a query entity which the user is interested in. Users of this system will have access to both the baseline (state-of-the-art) music similarity algorithms and the ones we develop. We use the logged activity of the users to analyze their subjective preferences and evaluate the similarity measures.

5   Results

Intonation: The information model commonly used in MIR for melodic notes and intervals identifies notes as a set of discrete points on frequency spectrum separated by certain intervals. One important limitation of this model is that it cannot account for the variability in a given note/svara. Therefore, we proposed a statistical model of notes, that defines the notes as probabilistic phenomenon on frequency spectrum. We have so far proposed three different approaches based on this model which are discussed in detail in [18]. In the first method, we compute the characteristics (such as mean, standard deviation, skewness etc.) of distribution of pitch values around each interval in the pitch-histogram. The improvement over the state-of-the-art which uses just the interval locations and their frequency of occurrence, is not significant. However, using feature selection task, we discovered that they do carry useful information to distinguish rāgas. This aggregate approach discards the contextual information of pitches: mainly the melodic & temporal contexts. Our second approach addresses this by obtaining this contextual information to a limited extent using a moving window as detailed in [18]. This resulted in an intonation description that distinguished rāgas better. Table. 5 shows the results for rāga classification task using the two methods.

To further improve it qualitatively, we have semi-automatically annotated few songs that are sung to notation without much improvisation, with svara

---

[7] Available at https://github.com/gopalkoduri/ontologies

[8] Available at http://dunya.compmusic.upf.edu/

Table 2. Accuracies obtained using different classifiers in the rāga classification experiment using the Histogram and Contextual-information based approaches for intonation description

	Naive Bayes	3-Nearest Neighbours	SVM	Random forest	Logistic regression	Multilayer Perceptron
Histogram	78.26	78.46	71.79	81.16	78.61	78.78
Cont. info	82.63	82.83	79.90	82.69	81.11	82.17

labels[9]. The distribution for each svara is obtained by constructing a histogram of pitch values from its contours. These are verified by domain experts to be representative and meaningful of their respective rāgas. Therefore, our current direction of work involves using the notation alongside the audio to automate the labeling of melodic contours with svaras. We then use the svara contours and the aggregate distribution of all the corresponding pitch values in obtaining a more accurate intonation description (see fig. 1).

OpenIE for Knowledge Base population: In order to validate our hypothesis of diversity in music quantitatively, we have developed an approach that rank-orders the characteristics of a given music based on their salience using a text corpus. The approach uses cross references between the musical entities (E.g., individual instances of *Composers*) in their respective text descriptions to compute their relevance in the music. Then, the different characteristics of the music (E.g., Composers) are assigned a rank based on the importance of the constituent entities. We employed this approach on the Indian art music traditions, Baroque, Flamenco and Jazz. The results support our hypothesis showing the distinct features of each music differentiating it from the rest, such as the prominence of religion in Carnatic music, dance in Flamenco, and gharanas/schools in Hindustani music, and so on. We have further developed a rudimentary distance measure using this knowledge to compute the similarity between various musical entities within a given music. The work in progress involves structuring this knowledge using our ontologies and improving the distance measure.

On the other hand, as a first step in the direction of adapting Open IE systems to knowledge base population, we devised a comprehensive framework for a comparative evaluation. The first part of the framework compares the volume of extracted assertions along different aspects: sentences, entities, relation-types and concepts/classes, with an aim to understand the coverage of the domain quantitatively. In the second part of the framework, the assertions are used in three fundamental tasks of knowledge base population: entity identification, concept identification, and semantic relation extraction. The framework is demonstrated using Indian art music domain, and the results from each task are validated against structured content in Wikipedia and/or using manually engineered ontologies. The results from the two parts of the framework, when juxtaposed against each other, gave us concrete insights into the differences between the

---

[9] This dataset is openly available at http://compmusic.upf.edu/carnatic-varnam-dataset

performances and the nature of the approaches. The results indicate that the approach based on deep semantic parsing [19,20] performs better compared to the ones based on shallow semantic parsing (or semantic role labeling)[10] [21] and dependency parsing [22]. Our current line of work in this direction involves adapting the deep semantic parsing based approach to music domain, specifically Indian art music.

6 Conclusions and Future work

We have discussed the need for culture-aware approaches in music information research. Towards addressing this, we have identified the specific issues that will be dealt with in the thesis: intonation description and knowledge base population of music domain using Open IE. We presented the methodology and the results from our work so far. Both the branches (information extraction and intonation analysis) shown in the flowchart in Fig. 1 are far into development, and the results are reaffirming of our hypothesis that using cultural-context can lead to better music similarity measures. Our future work involves:

- Using the ontologies to structure and combine the information obtained from audio and text sources. Two major challenges involved are: disambiguation of concepts and relation-types, and linking the information obtained from different modalities.
- Developing similarity measures that conform to the cultural context of the music.

Acknowledgments. This thesis is supervised by Dr. Xavier Serra, and was partly funded by the European Research Council under the European Union's Seventh Framework Program, as part of the CompMusic project (ERC grant agreement 267583).

References

1. Serra, X.: A multicultural approach in music information research. In: ISMIR, pp. 151–156 (2011)
2. Krishna, T.M., Ishwar, V.: Karik Music : Svara, Gamaka, Phraseology And Rga Identity. In: 2nd CompMusic Workshop, pp. 12–18 (2012)
3. Serra, X., Magas, M., Benetos, E., Chudy, M., Dixon, S., Flexer, A., Gómez, E., Gouyon, F., Herrera, P., Jordà, S., Paytuvi, O., Peeters, G., Schlüter, J., Vinet, H., Widmer, G.: Roadmap for Music Information Research (2013)
4. Baader, F., Calvanese, D., McGuinness, D.L., Nardi, D., Patel-Schneider, P.F. (eds.): The Description Logic Handbook. Cambridge University Press, Cambridge (2007)
5. Koduri, G.K., Serra, X.: A knowledge-based approach to computational analysis of melody in Indian art music. In: International Workshop on Semantic Music and Media colocated with International Semantic Web Conference, pp. 1–10 (2013)

---

[10] We used the implementation available at https://github.com/knowitall/openie

6. Knees, P., Schedl, M.: A Survey of Music Similarity and Recommendation from Music Context Data. ACM Trans. Multimedia Comput. Commun. Appl. **10**(1), 2:1–2:21 (2013)

7. Raimond, Y.: A Distributed Music Information System. PhD thesis, University of London (2008)

8. Oramas, S.: Harvesting and structuring social data in music information retrieval. In: Presutti, V., d'Amato, C., Gandon, F., d'Aquin, M., Staab, S., Tordai, A. (eds.) ESWC 2014. LNCS, vol. 8465, pp. 817–826. Springer, Heidelberg (2014)

9. Celma, Ò.: Foafing the music: bridging the semantic gap in music recommendation. In: Cruz, I., Decker, S., Allemang, D., Preist, C., Schwabe, D., Mika, P., Uschold, M., Aroyo, L.M. (eds.) ISWC 2006. LNCS, vol. 4273, pp. 927–934. Springer, Heidelberg (2006)

10. Jacobson, K., Sandler, M., Fields, B.: Using Audio Analysis and Network Structure to Identify Communities in On-Line Social Networks of Artists. In: ISMIR, pp. 269–274 (2008)

11. Passant, A., Decker, S.: Hey! ho! let's go! explanatory music recommendations with dbrec. The Semantic Web: Research and Applications **1380**(2), 411–415 (2010)

12. Srinivasamurthy, A., Holzapfel, A., Serra, X.: In Search of Automatic Rhythm Analysis Methods for Turkish and Indian Art Music. Journal of New Music Research **43**(1), 94–114 (2014)

13. Gulati, S., Bellur, A., Salamon, J., Ranjani, H.G., Ishwar, V., Murthy, H.A., Serra, X.: Automatic Tonic Identification in Indian Art Music: Approaches and Evaluation. Journal of New Music Research **43**(01), 55–71 (2014)

14. Rao, P., Ross, J.C., Ganguli, K.K., Pandit, V., Ishwar, V., Bellur, A., Murthy, H.A.: Classification of Melodic Motifs in Raga Music with Time-series Matching. Journal of New Music Research **43**(1), 115–131 (2014)

15. Etzioni, O., Banko, M.: Open Information Extraction from the Web. Communications of the ACM **51**(12), 68–74 (2008)

16. Sarawagi, S.: Information Extraction. Foundations and Trends in Databases **1**(3), 261–377 (2008)

17. Porter, A., Sordo, M., Serra, X.: Dunya: A System for Browsing Audio Music Collections Exploiting Cultural Context. In: ISMIR, Curitiba, Brazil, pp. 101–106 (2013)

18. Koduri, G.K., Ishwar, V., Serrà, J., Serra, X.: Intonation Analysis of Rgas in Carnatic Music. Journal of New Music Research **43**(01), 72–93 (2014)

19. Harrington, B., Clark, S.: Asknet: Automated semantic knowledge network. In: AAAI, pp. 889–894 (2007)

20. Steedman, M.: The Syntactic Process. MIT Press, Cambridge (2000)

21. Mausam, Schmitz, M., Bart, R., Soderland, S., Etzioni, O.: Open language learning for information extraction. In: Conference on Empirical Methods in Natural Language Processing and Computational Natural Language Learning (2012)

22. Fader, A., Soderland, S., Etzioni, O.: Identifying Relations for Open Information Extraction. In: Empirical Methods in Natural Language Processing (2011)

RDF Based Management, Syndication and Aggregation of Web Content

Niels Ockeloen[✉]

The Network Institute, VU University Amsterdam,
De Boelelaan 1081, 1081, HV Amsterdam, The Netherlands
niels.ockeloen@vu.nl
http://wm.cs.vu.nl

Abstract. Significant parts of the web exist of documents that are automatically generated, or an aggregation of content from different sources. These practises rely on three major tasks: Management, Syndication and Aggregation of web content. For these a heterogeneous set of imperative tools, scripts and systems is available, which are either not compatible or only along very thin lines, e.g. using RSS. In this document, we will propose a novel architecture for dealing with management, syndication and aggregation of web content based on web standards, in particular RDF and Linked Data principles. A declarative, compatible and more efficient way of performing these tasks that effectively merges them, while narrowing the gap between the web of documents and the web of data.

Keywords: RDF · Linked data · CMS · Web of data · Web of documents · Content management · Syndication · Aggregation · PROV

1 Introduction

Traditionally, the web consisted mainly of independent web documents which link to other web documents and as such form a world wide web. However, web documents more and more become an aggregation of content that originates from different sources. These sources can be spread among different domains, content owners, physical servers and organisations. Contributing factors are:

- The increased use of web services (e.g. Geo-location and feed aggregators)
- The increase of users' ability to edit web content (e.g. Web CMS, Blogs)
- The increase of sharable content (e.g. YouTube, Flickr)
- The rise of social media (e.g. Facebook, Twitter)

Several solutions exist to include content originating from other sources into web documents, such as code inclusions, the use of Iframe elements, content feeds such as RSS and thousands of plug-ins for various Web Content Management Systems. However, despite these solutions, creating web documents that integrate aggregated content from multiple sources is not as trivial as it seems.

© Springer International Publishing Switzerland 2015
P. Lambrix et al. (Eds.): EKAW 2014 Satellite Events, LNAI 8982, pp. 218–224, 2015.
DOI: 10.1007/978-3-319-17966-7_31

2   Problem Statement

Management, syndication and aggregation of web content is hard to *organise*, because the various solutions, tools and plug-ins that are available have different formats for which conversion or interpretation is needed. Modules and plug-ins can break down or have incorrect settings. Web services can go down or cease to exist, and source code needs to be altered to facilitate code inclusions. Furthermore, current syndication solutions lack the ability to define more specific semantics for the provided content.

Current systems for management of web content are complicated. To give two examples of popular systems, WordPress[1] offers 28.284 plug-ins and 2.140 templates, plus thousands more from third parties. Drupal[2] is available in 720 different distributions for which 24.699 modules are available. The questions are: Which one to choose? How to create a working setup containing the right elements? For special needs, one either has to consult an expert, or become one.

No Web CMS Standards. Web Content Management Systems have become important tools in creating and maintaining web sites. Around 40% of all web sites uses a known CMS.[3] These systems aim to facilitate non-technical users in authoring, administrating and collaborating. Both proprietary and open source systems exist, but all of them are built as imperative software solutions that have their own specific implementation details and data models. This makes it hard or even impossible for these systems to exchange content between them without relying on intermediate data formats and serialisations such as RSS. As such, migrating from one system to another is hard, leading to customer lock-in. There is no reference standard or data model to perform Web Content Management, which developers could use to implement a 'standard compliant' Web CMS.

Research Questions. Based upon the issues as laid out in this section, we formulate the following research questions:

1. What are good metrics to determine the baseline of current practices in management, syndication and aggregation of web content?
2. Which combination of web standards can be used to create a novel architecture for dealing with management, syndication and aggregation of web content that is declarative in nature, allowing for multiple implementations to adhere to formulated standards and co-operate?
3. What methodology is needed to support such an architecture, i.e. to use it?

---

[1] http://www.wordpress.com, retrieved 28 june 2014.
[2] http://www.drupal.org/, retrieved 28 june 2014.
[3] http://w3techs.com/technologies/overview/content_management/all,
     retrieved 27 may 2014.

3 State of the Art

Our approach overlaps the traditionally viewed as distinct subjects of web content management, syndication and aggregation. There is great amount of related work in these areas which we cannot comprehensively handle in this paper. We will give notable examples divided in five categories.

General Web Technology. HTML5 introduces new elements for better document structure,[4] such as 'Section', 'Article', 'Header' and 'Footer'. E.g. an 'article' represents a piece of content "intended to be independently distributable or reusable, e.g. in syndication".[5] However, the syndication itself is outside of the HTML5 scope. The HTML Iframe element and code inclusions are very often used to include or embed content. These techniques are very basic, and limited in various ways including semantic operability.

Content Management. According to the site W3Techs,[3] WordPress is by far the most used Content Management System (22.5% of all websites), followed by Joomla[6] (3.1%) and Drupal (1.9%). Worth discussing separately is Drupal, which has RDF support [4]. Making it possible for Drupal users to expose information as Linked Data in RDFa through mappings made to the internal data structure. Internally, Drupal stores content using its own custom database schema.

Web Syndication. The Meta Content Framework (MCF) was one of the first attempts to structure and manage *meta content* [6]. MCF never saw widespread adoption, but can be considered as one of the ancestors of the Resource Description Framework (RDF), which in turn inspired the development of RSS,[7,8] which started out as "RDF Site Summary". Together with Atom[9] these are the main web feed formats. They have become popular because their simple structure allowed for easy adoption in software tools, however this also provides limitations. Extensions can be made for both formats, but support is mostly absent.

Web Aggregation. Syndicated web feeds can be aggregated to form (part of) a new web document using scripts or web services. Examples of scripts are MagpieRSS[10] and Simple Pie.[11] Examples of web services include ChimpFeedr[12]

---

[4] http://www.w3.org/TR/html5-diff/#new-elements, retrieved 20 June 2014.

[5] http://www.w3.org/TR/html5/semantics.html#the-article-element, retrieved 27 may 2014.

[6] http://www.joomla.org/, retrieved 28 june 2014.

[7] http://web.resource.org/rss/1.0/, retrieved 27 june 2014.

[8] http://www.rssboard.org/rss-specification, retrieved 27 june 2014.

[9] http://tools.ietf.org/html/rfc4287, retrieved 27 june 2014.

[10] http://magpierss.sourceforge.net/, retrieved 28 june 2014.

[11] http://simplepie.org/, retrieved 28 june 2014.

[12] http://www.chimpfeedr.com, retrieved 28 june 2014.

and RSS Mix.[13] Aggregation of web content in a broader sense can be achieved using 'pipe' solutions such as Yahoo pipes[14] and DERI Pipes.[15] DERI Pipes also supports RDF. Extensive knowledge is required to use these platforms.

Linked Data/RDF Solutions. Displaying machine readable data for human consumption is not trivial. Fresnel [10] is an OWL-based vocabulary dealing with this subject, that allows to define *lenses* to select data and *formats* to define the display of that data.

The Callimachus project [2] aims to make the management of Linked Data easier, as well as its use in web applications. The system uses 'view templates' that consist of classes associated with the data to be displayed.

OntoWiki-CMS [7] provides a valuable way of integrating semantically enriched content into web documents, using a template system. It also features a dynamic syndication system.

4   Proposed Approach

Our main hypothesis is that Semantic Web technology can be used to define a novel architecture for management, syndication and aggregation of web content, that effectively merges these tasks, while allowing a wider variety of content to be syndicated and aggregated with better semantic operability.

To test our hypotheses and answer our research questions, we propose to investigate the creation of an ontology called 'Data 2 Documents' (D2D), a methodology for working with this ontology and a reference implementation. In the following sections we will discuss the main principles behind our approach.

4.1   Capture the Hierarchical Build-Up of Web Documents

By breaking down web documents into small, more or less self contained pieces of content, we can individually describe, classify and reference them. For this, we need to describe the hierarchical structure of web documents, their parts and their internal dependencies. This can be done using an ontology, which should describe concepts such as page, section and article. These relate to similar concepts in the W3C HTML5 specification, mentioned in section 3. By breaking down web documents into smaller pieces of content, they become parts of the 'web of data', while documents as such become a composition of these parts. Hence, we can compose 'documents' out of 'data' using the formulated ontology.

4.2   Use Linked Data Principles

By using Linked Data principles and defining each individual content element, e.g. article, section or page, as a *resource* in the web of data, we can specify and

---

[13] http://www.rssmix.com, retrieved 28 june 2014.

[14] http://pipes.yahoo.com/pipes/, retrieved 28 june 2014.

[15] http://pipes.deri.org, retrieved 28 june 2014.

perform the syndication of content while at the same time describing the internal structure of a document; effectively merging the tasks of content management, syndication and aggregation. Each article can be referenced by its own IRI. Hence, to *syndicate* an article on third party web document, the article can be retrieved by dereferencing its IRI. This will provide an RDF description of its contents such as the 'fields' that make up the article. If multiple articles need to be syndicated, i.e. a news feed, a section grouping together these articles can be dereferenced. Using the intrinsic properties of RDF and Linked Data, a form of 'content management' can be achieved that transcends individual web documents, domains, servers and implementations. To *manage* the placement of an article on a page, we simply add a triple: 'HOME-PAGE' *hasArticle* 'INTRO'.

Aggregation of web content is also simplified. While e.g. XML data is serialised, RDF data is not. Hence, aggregation of content is as simply as appending the results from multiple queries and/or dereferences. The results will get aggregated automatically, e.g. articles sorted on publication date, during the standard procedure of parsing the data to produce the resulting document.

4.3   Separate 'Composition' and 'Serialisation'

Pages, Sections and Articles need to be specified by two separate kinds of definitions, to allow for more specialised forms of content management and syndycation; a 'composition' definition that defines the 'fields', i.e. data elements, of which an article is composed, and a second definition that determines how these fields should be serialised. By doing so, multiple different serialisation definitions can be specified for a single composition definition. This allows for easy re-use of content within the originating web site, as well as across third party websites. Third parties can choose to use the serialisation definition indicated by the content provider, or specify their own serialisation definition while only using the actual content. Compared to current practises, the first scenario comes closest to using an Iframe or code inclusion construction, while the latter can be compared to using an RSS feed to syndicate content only.

The composition definitions should also allow to specify what types of articles are allowed to be placed on a specific page or section, etc. This is another aspect in which RDF proves to be well equipped for the task; RDFS and OWL already facilitate this through the 'domain' and 'range' constructs.

4.4   Additional Benefits

The proposed architecture can provide a number of additional benefits, which arise from the ability to easily use various existing semantic web technology. For example, having small pieces of content as identifiable resource in the web of data allows for detailed provenance information to be attached. Hence, our architecture helps to address this "vitally important area for the future of the Web" [5]. The needed PROV [8] data can be generated by the reference implementation. Our architecture also facilitates the use of existing linked data in web documents. Other examples include access control and load balancing.

5   Methodology

The research proposed in this document will be carried out using the Design Science Research methodology [1]. In order to address the issues as laid out in section 2 and answer the research questions stated in 2, the following main steps will be undertaken:

- Establish a baseline for current practices
- Gather requirements for the D2D ontology
- Create a first version of the ontology
- Devise a methodology for working with the ontology
- Implement a reference implementation
- Evaluation

In addition to these steps, we plan the development of a product based upon the reference implementation, which can be used as a vehicle to carry out the research. A path successfully taken by the Open PHACTS project.[16]

Evaluation Strategy.   In order to evaluate our architecture for dealing with content management, syndication and aggregation of content on the web, we plan to conduct a user study. In this experiment, two groups of users will be given a set of tasks, i.e. to create a web document using specific content from different sources. One group will be instructed to use our novel architecture, i.e. the reference implementation. The other group will be able to use whatever other tool they want to use. The groups do not now of each others existence; they both think they are the (only) primary group in a study to investigate the easiness of e.g. aggregating web content. Result from both groups are compared in two ways; quantitatively, e.g. the time it took to perform the minimal letter of the assignments; and qualitatively, e.g. by rating the produced documents by a third group. Apart from rating the resulting documents, the architecture itself can be evaluated using Think Aloud Protocol [11] and System Usability Scale [3]. The evaluation will be carried out in multiple stages. First a pilot is run with a few participants to verify the experimental setup, i.e. to see if the assignments can be carried out, the data is available and the rating metric is accurate and understandable. Thereafter, the actual experiment is run. Repeated session can be done with different types groups.

6   Preliminary Results

Within the context of the BiographyNet project,[17] we have examined the requirements for of a data schema that allows for multiple publications regarding the same subject to co-exist, while storing detailed provenance information in cases

---

[16] http://www.openphacts.org, retrieved 10 juli 2014.
[17] http://www.biographynet.nl, retrieved 25 july 2014.

where one such publication was derived from another. This provenance information is stored on two levels; an aggregated level intended for the end user, and a detailed level targeted at a system engineer. Results were published at the Linked Science (LISC) workshop 2013 [9]. These results are part of the requirements gathering process for the D2D ontology.

Acknowledgments. The author would like to thank Guus Schreiber and Victor de Boer for their guidance and support in writing this paper. This work was supported by the BiographyNet project[17] (Nr. 660.011.308), funded by the Netherlands eScience Center (http://esciencecenter.nl/). Partners in this project are the Netherlands eScience Center, the Huygens/ING Institute of the Royal Dutch Academy of Sciences and VU University Amsterdam.

References

1. von Alan, R.H., March, S.T., Park, J., Ram, S.: Design science in information systems research. MIS quarterly **28**(1), 75–105 (2004)
2. Battle, S., Wood, D., Leigh, J., Ruth, L.: The callimachus project: Rdfa as a web template language. In: COLD (2012)
3. Brooke, J.: Sus-a quick and dirty usability scale. Usability evaluation in industry **189**, 194 (1996)
4. Corlosquet, S., Delbru, R., Clark, T., Polleres, A., Decker, S.: Produce and consume linked data with drupal!. In: Bernstein, A., Karger, D.R., Heath, T., Feigenbaum, L., Maynard, D., Motta, E., Thirunarayan, K. (eds.) ISWC 2009. LNCS, vol. 5823, pp. 763–778. Springer, Heidelberg (2009)
5. Groth, P., Gil, Y., Cheney, J., Miles, S.: Requirements for provenance on the web. International Journal of Digital Curation **7**(1) (2012)
6. Guha, R.: Meta content framework. Research report Apple Computer, Englewoods, NJ (1997). http://www.guha.com/mcf/wp.html
7. Heino, N., Tramp, S., Auer, S.: Managing web content using linked data principles-combining semantic structure with dynamic content syndication. In: Computer Software and Applications Conference (COMPSAC), 2011 IEEE 35th Annual, pp. 245–250. IEEE (2011)
8. Moreau, L., Missier, P., Belhajjame, K., B'Far, R., Cheney, J., Coppens, S., Cresswell, S., Gil, Y., Groth, P., Klyne, G., Lebo, T., McCusker, J., Miles, S., Myers, J., Sahoo, S., Tilmes, C.: PROV-DM: The PROV Data Model. Tech. rep., W3C (2012). http://www.w3.org/TR/prov-dm/
9. Ockeloen, N., Fokkens, A., ter Braake, S., Vossen, P., de Boer, V., Schreiber, G., Legêne, S.: Biographynet: managing provenance at multiple levels and from different perspectives. In: Proceedings of the Workshop on Linked Science (LISC2013) at ISWC (2013)
10. Pietriga, E., Bizer, C., Karger, D.R., Lee, R.: Fresnel: a browser-independent presentation vocabulary for RDF. In: Cruz, I., Decker, S., Allemang, D., Preist, C., Schwabe, D., Mika, P., Uschold, M., Aroyo, L.M. (eds.) ISWC 2006. LNCS, vol. 4273, pp. 158–171. Springer, Heidelberg (2006)
11. Van Someren, M.W., Barnard, Y.F., Sandberg, J.A., et al.: The think aloud method: A practical guide to modelling cognitive processes, vol. 2. Academic Press London (1994)

Towards Ontology Refinement by Combination of Machine Learning and Attribute Exploration

Jedrzej Potoniec[✉]

Institute of Computing Science, Poznan University of Technology,
ul. Piotrowo 2, 60-965 Poznan, Poland
Jedrzej.Potoniec@cs.put.poznan.pl

Abstract. We propose a new method for knowledge acquisition and ontology refinement for the Semantic Web. The method is based on a combination of the attribute exploration algorithm from the formal concept analysis and active learning approach to machine learning classification task. It enables utilization of Linked Data during the process of an ontology refinement in a manner that it is possible to use remote SPARQL endpoints. We also report on a preliminary experimental evaluation and argue that our method is reasonable and useful.

1 Problem Statement

Knowledge acquisition is a process of gathering knowledge from a human expert and thus it concerns all environments and systems grounded in that kind of knowledge. Because it is a difficult and time-consuming process, it is said to be a major bottleneck in a development of an intelligent systems [10]. Problems come for example from the open world assumption or disjointness axioms [5,14].

Typically, an ontology engineer starts by gathering vocabulary and requirements for an ontology, build some structure on top of the vocabulary and later add complex dependencies [16]. Our aim is to propose a method to support knowledge acquisition for an ontology construction. Especially we address the last part of the process, where some basic knowledge is already gathered and more complex dependencies are to be included.

Ideally, the user should be able to extend only a part of an ontology (e.g. one branch) but in relationship to the whole ontology. For example, the user extends an ontology about means of transport and she is interested in trains. She would like to know that a railbus is a kind of a train, but also that a locomotive requires a human driver, even though humans are not in her current area of interest. Yet, she does not want to consider if a car requires a driver. To give the user further support, it should be possible to use Linked Data [2], where many interesting relations are already gathered, but usually distributed and loosely structured.

2 State of the Art

Many approaches addressing a task of knowledge acquisition for an ontology development have been proposed so far. The simplest are general-purpose ontology

© Springer International Publishing Switzerland 2015
P. Lambrix et al. (Eds.): EKAW 2014 Satellite Events, LNAI 8982, pp. 225–232, 2015.
DOI: 10.1007/978-3-319-17966-7_32

editors, such as *Protégé*[1]. In addition to that, there are methodologies helpful in ontologies development, such as *NeOn* [16]. These solutions are very general and applicable to virtually any case, but they do not overcome the issue of the user workload. More specialized approaches are described below.

In [20] proposed is an algorithm for assessing the relevance of new facts added to the ontology, based on similar facts that can be found in various ontologies in the Web. Outcome of this algorithm could be further refined with application of the algorithm described in Section 4, to find additional relations between preexisting and new vocabulary. Further information as well as references for tools and algorithms can be found in a survey about ontology evolution [19].

2.1   Attribute Exploration

One of the most prominent approach is the attribute exploration algorithm based on Formal Concept Analysis [1]. Assume that there is a finite set of attributes M. A *partial object description* is a tuple (A, S) such that $A \cup S \subseteq M$ and $A \cap S = \emptyset$. An object described by a given tuple has all attributes from A and none from S. Set of partial object descriptions is called *partial context*.

The aim of the algorithm is to discover all valid implications of form $L \to R$, where $L, R \subseteq M$. An input of the algorithm is a partial context, which serves as an indicator what is possible and what is already not. For every implication $L \to R$, the implication is said to be *refuted by a partial context* if there is a tuple (A, S) within this context, such that $L \subseteq A \wedge S \cap R \neq \emptyset$. Every non-refuted implication is presented to the user, who decides if the implication is valid. If it is not, the user is supposed to provide a counterexample.

In [1] and [15] an application of the attribute exploration algorithm to ontological knowledge bases has been proposed. Attributes are Description Logics expressions and a partial context is derived from the ontology. Implications are equivalent to subsumptions: $L \to R$ is equivalent to $\sqcap L \sqsubseteq \sqcap R$. For every implication it is first checked if the decision can be made based on the ontology and if it can, the implication is not presented to user.

After application of the algorithm, the ontology is complete w.r.t. all valid subsumptions considering the given set of attributes. Unfortunately, the algorithm can not handle noise in the partial context, and thus can not be applied to Linked Data directly.

2.2   Induction of Ontologies from Linked Data

In [18] a Linked Data repository is transformed to a set of database tables, which are used to mine association rules, corresponding to axioms in an ontology. Unfortunately, this approach does not consider an existing ontology at all and thus it is unclear how to integrate it into an ontology refinement workflow.

In the work [6] proposed is a methodology to create an ontology along with a set of mappings to various Linked Data sources and use them to populated

---

[1] http://protege.stanford.edu/

the ontology. Although very promising, this work does not support an ontology construction, only its population with individuals and optionally linking with Linked Data.

[3] proposes a method for inducing an expressive class description based on a set of instances in SPARQL endpoints. While this work seems scalable and useful, it is data-driven and lacks an interaction with the user, who could guide the process of learning.

2.3   Active Learning

The idea behind the machine learning is to build a computer program able to learn from examples [11]. One of the considered tasks is a classification task, where the program (called *classifier*) is to predict for a given example a label from a finite set of classes. Usually, every example is represented as a vector of numerical features.

In the following work, we expect a classifier to generate probabilities of assignments of an example to classes. It is important to note that some classifiers can not generate useful probabilities, e.g. rule or tree induction systems. Generating probabilities can be also represented as a regression problem. This approach is used e.g. in [8], where output of multiple simple classifiers is combined to obtain an accurate probability estimation.

Typically, to solve these tasks, a set of labelled examples (i.e. the examples with assignments to correct classes) is required. Sometimes it is expensive to obtain, so an active learning approach is applied [4]. During the learning phase, the algorithm is presented unlabelled data and asks an oracle (e.g. a human expert) to label chosen examples. The number of questions that can be posed to the oracle is limited, so the algorithm has to decide which examples are to be labelled.

3   Proposed Approach

Our main research question is *how to extend an ontology with meaningful, valid and non-trivial axioms taking into consideration available data and the user workload?* Our hypothesis is that a process based on attribute selection and the use of linked data as a source of candidate knowledge for ontology refinement could contribute in answering this question. We therefore refine our general research question into the following more specific ones:

1. How to focus the attribute exploration algorithm on a particular subset of attributes?
2. How to limit interaction with the user only to axioms that are of interest?
3. How to incorporate Linked Data into a workflow of knowledge acquisition?
4. How to limit the user workload compared to a normal application of the attribute exploration algorithm?

We expect that the user can select a set of attributes, for which she has a particular interest. As our main concern is a practical usability to the knowledge engineers and to address the description of the ideal system presented in the Section 1, the following hypotheses will have to be verified:

1. More implications considered by the user contains interesting attributes than during normal attribute exploration. (Measured relatively to an overall number of implications considered by the user.)
2. An algorithm using Linked Data poses fewer questions to the user.
3. An average number of mistakes (i.e. accepting an invalid implication and rejecting a valid one) made by an ML algorithm does not significantly differ from an average number of mistakes made by the user.

4   Methodology

The aim of our approach is to use machine learning (ML) to help the user during attribute exploration. A ML algorithm is to answer simple, non-interesting questions posed by the attribute exploration algorithm and leave for the user only these questions which are really interesting or non-trivial to answer.

An input of our algorithm is an ontology $\mathcal{O}$, a partial context derived from it, and two thresholds θ_a and θ_r. They are, respectively, thresholds for accepting and rejecting an implication. In an output, there is a set of probably valid implications, which corresponds to subsumptions that can extend the ontology. Details of the algorithm are described below. For sake of clarity the attribute exploration algorithm is treated as a black box (see [15] for a very good explanation), which generates the next implication to analyze.

1. Use the attribute exploration algorithm to generate an implication $L \rightarrow R$.
2. For every $r \in R$, execute the following sequence:
   (a) If $L \rightarrow \{r\}$ is already refuted by the partial context, go to the next r.
   (b) If $\mathcal{O} \models \bigsqcap L \sqsubseteq r$, mark the implication $L \rightarrow \{r\}$ as correct and go to the next r.
   (c) Compute with the ML algorithm probabilities of the implication $L \rightarrow \{r\}$ being accepted p_a or rejected p_r. By definition $p_a + p_r = 1$.
   (d) If $p_a \geq \theta_a$, mark the implication $L \rightarrow \{r\}$ as correct and go to the next r.
   (e) If $p_r \geq \theta_r$, go to the step 2i.
   (f) Ask the user if the implication $L \rightarrow \{r\}$ is correct.
   (g) Store considered implication as a new learning example. Use the user's answer as a label for it.
   (h) If the implication is correct, remember it as such and go to the next r.
   (i) Otherwise, add counterexample to the partial context. The counterexample is either autogenerated or obtained from the user.

There are two purposes for iterating over the set of conclusions R. We believe that this way the user can more easily decide if the implication is valid or not, because she does not have to consider complex relation between two conjunctions of attributes. Moreover, it makes feasible to generate a counterexample for an implication $L \rightarrow R$, by stating that it has attributes from L and has not the attribute from R.

4.1   Integration with Machine Learning

The ML task in our problem can be stated as an active learning task with a binary classification. To every implication one of two labels *valid* or *invalid* should be assigned and the user should be asked if the algorithm is unsure.

It is preferred to mark a valid implication as an invalid than vice versa, because it does not break validity of the ontology. To ensure it, we weight learning examples with relative costs of mistakes [13].

To classify an implication with a typical classifier, a way to transform it to a feature vector is required. We combine following three approaches to address this problem.

First of all, there are features made of values of measures typical for an association rules mining. Their computation is based on classes and properties of individuals in the ontology and they are computed in two flavors: with open- and closed-world assumption. The first one is typical for the Semantic Web and assumes that if an individual can not be proven to belong to a class, it does not mean the opposite. The second one, common for databases, assumes the opposite. We believe that in some cases second approach may render useful (c.f. with the local closed world assumption in [7]). Following naming convention from [12], we use the *coverage, prevalence, support, recall* and *lift*.

Secondly, every attribute is manually mapped to a SPARQL graph pattern [9] with a single variable in a head, corresponding to object identifier. Following names from [12], the *coverage, prevalence, support, recall* and *confidence* are used. They are cheap to compute with a SPARQL endpoint, as they can be expressed using only `COUNT DISTINCT` expressions and basic graph patterns (BGPs). The *lift* is not used, as it requires negation.

Finally, purely syntactic measures describing a shape of the implication are considered. Because there is always a single attribute in the right-hand side of the implication, we use only one feature: the number of attributes in the left-hand side divided by the number of all attributes.

For example, consider an implication $\{Noldor\} \rightarrow \{Elf\}$. A possible SPARQL query to the *DBpedia*, corresponding to the premises is `SELECT (COUNT(DISTINCT ?x) as ?p) WHERE {?x dbp-prop:characterCulture dbpedia:Noldor}` (the answer is $p = 17$). One can notice here that attributes are mapped to an arbitrary SPARQL BGP, not only to concept names in the remote endpoint. In the same manner, a query to cover both the premises and conclusions would be `SELECT (COUNT(DISTINCT ?x) as ?pc) WHERE {?x dbp-prop:characterCulturedbp edia:Noldor. ?x dbp-prop:characterRace dbpedia:Elf_%28Middle-earth %29}` (the answer is $pc = 17$). The third query covers only the conclusions and consists only of the second triple pattern of the previous query, the answer for it is $c = 33$. After posing these three queries, it is possible to compute all of the

SPARQL-based attributes defined above, e.g. coverage is $p = 17$ and recall is $\frac{pc}{c} = 0.52$.

5   Evaluation Protocol

As the proposed method is oriented to the end users, we are going to evaluate its practical usability. The proposed approach is implemented (see Section 6 for details). As this is not domain-specific tool and we would like to ask our students to perform usability tests, we plan to apply our method to few domain-specific ontologies concerning some knowledge of general type such as literature, music and movies. *DBTune*[2] and *LinkedMDB*[3] should serve us well as Linked Data sources. We decided on such a setup, because otherwise finding users able to answer the questions and later validating their answers would probably render impossible.

To verify hypotheses 1 and 2, we plan to ask students during a course on the Semantic Web to use our tool in one of two premade setups: with and without machine learning algorithms, similar to the setup known as *A/B testing*. We plan to collect full log of students' decisions and then compute appropriate statistics: how many questions were asked in given setups, how many of them contained attributes from the the set of attributes mentioned in Section 4 etc. Further, obtained axioms will be posted to the crowdsourcing service (e.g. *CrowdFlower*[4]). We plan to ask the crowd to verify obtained axioms. As we know which axioms were answered by the users and which by the algorithm, we will be able to perform a statistical test to verify hypothesis 3.

6   Results

So far a stand-alone *Java* application for extending OWL ontologies by the approach described in Section 4 has been developed and preliminary experiments have been conducted. Source code can be downloaded with *Git*[5] from http:// semantic.cs.put.poznan.pl/git/FCA-ML.git. The application provides flexible configuration of learning parameters and Linked Data mappings. Exporting discovered axioms to a file and comparing user's and classifier's decisions are also possible.

We did a preliminary experimental evaluation on a small ontology about characters in J.R.R. Tolkien's Middle-Earth. The vocabulary has been derived from *Lord of the Rings Project*[6] and some subsumption axioms have been added. Finally, we mapped some of the defined concepts to *DBpedia 3.9*.

---

[2] http://dbtune.org/
[3] http://linkedmdb.org/
[4] http://www.crowdflower.com/
[5] http://git-scm.com/
[6] http://lotrproject.com/

After the application of our method, statements such as $Sindar \sqsubseteq Elf$ have been added to our ontology. This statement is conformant with Tolkien's legendarium, where Sindars are tribe of elves [17]. We also noted that after a learning phase, most of the implications were answered correctly by the ML algorithm.

7   Conclusions and Future Work

We are positive that the presented approach will help the ontology engineers during ontology refinement. The preliminary experiment described in Section 6 seems to support this claim. Additionally, we combine three technologies very suitable to apply in such a setup. First of all, the main purpose of the attribute exploration algorithm is to discover hidden relations in the set of attributes. Moreover, Linked Data contain descriptions of particular aspects of the world. These descriptions are usually inaccurate or incomplete, but they should suffice as a supportive material during the ontology refinement. Finally, machine learning is a technology to make computer systems adapt themselves, so it is the appropriate tool to replace the user during repeatable, uniform tasks.

Acknowledgments. Author would like to thank Prof. Sebastian Rudolph from Technical University of Dresden and supervisor Dr. Agnieszka Ławrynowicz from Poznan University of Technology for their valuable comments and support. Author would also like to thank Dr. Mathieu d?Aquin from the Open University for a great job as a PhD symposium mentor. Author acknowledges support from the PARENT-BRIDGE program of Foundation for Polish Science, cofinanced from European Union, Regional Development Fund (Grant No POMOST/2013-7/8 *LeoLOD – Learning and Evolving Ontologies from Linked Open Data*).

References

1. Baader, F., Ganter, B., et al.: Completing description logic knowledge bases using formal concept analysis. In: Proc. of IJCAI 2007, pp. 230–235. AAAI Press (2007)
2. Bizer, C., Heath, T., Berners-Lee, T.: Linked data - the story so far. Int. J. Semantic Web Inf. Syst. **5**(3), 122 (2009)
3. Bühmann, L., Lehmann, J.: Universal OWL axiom enrichment for large knowledge bases. In: ten Teije, A., Völker, J., Handschuh, S., Stuckenschmidt, H., d'Acquin, M., Nikolov, A., Aussenac-Gilles, N., Hernandez, N. (eds.) EKAW 2012. LNCS, vol. 7603, pp. 57–71. Springer, Heidelberg (2012)
4. Cohn, D.: Active learning. In: Sammut, C., Webb, G.I. (eds.) Encyclopedia of Machine Learning, pp. 10–14. Springer, New York (2010)
5. Corcho, Ó., Roussey, C.: OnlynessIsLoneliness (OIL). In: Blomqvist, E., Sandkuhl, K., et al. (eds.) WOP. CEUR Workshop Proc., vol. 516. CEUR-WS.org (2009)
6. Dastgheib, S., Mesbah, A., Kochut, K.: mOntage: building domain ontologies from linked open data. In: IEEE Seventh International Conference on Semantic Computing (ICSC), pp. 70–77. IEEE (2013)
7. Dong, X., Gabrilovich, E., et al.: Knowledge vault: a web-scale approach to probabilistic knowledge fusion. In: Proc. of the 20th ACM SIGKDD Int. Conf. on Knowledge Discovery and Data Mining, pp. 601–610. ACM, New York, USA (2014)

8. Friedman, J., Hastie, T., Tibshirani, R.: Additive Logistic Regression: A Statistical View of Boosting: Rejoinder. The Annals of Statistics **28**(2), 400–407 (2000)
9. Harris, S., Seaborne, A.: SPARQL 1.1 query language. W3C recommendation, W3C, March 2013. http://www.w3.org/TR/2013/REC-sparql11-query-20130321/
10. Kidd, A.: Knowledge acquisition. In: Kidd, A. (ed.) Knowledge Acquisition for Expert Systems, pp. 1–16. Springer, New York (1987)
11. Ławrynowicz, A., Tresp, V.: Introducing machine learning. In: Lehmann, J., Völker, J. (eds.) Perspectives On Ontology Learning. AKA Heidelberg (2014)
12. Le Bras, Y., Lenca, P., Lallich, S.: Optimonotone measures for optimal rule discovery. Computational Intelligence **28**(4), 475–504 (2012)
13. Ling, C.X., Sheng, V.S.: Cost-sensitive learning. In: Sammut, C., Webb, G.I. (eds.) Encyclopedia of Machine Learning. LNCS, vol. 6820, pp. 231–235. Springer, Heidelberg (2010)
14. Rector, A., Drummond, N., et al.: OWL pizzas: practical experience of teaching OWL-DL: common errors & common patterns. In: Motta, E., Shadbolt, N., et al. (eds.) Engineering Knowledge in the Age of the Semantic Web. Lecture Notes in Computer Science, vol. 3257, pp. 63–81. Springer, Heidelberg (2004)
15. Rudolph, S.: Acquiring generalized domain-range restrictions. In: Medina, R., Obiedkov, S. (eds.) ICFCA 2008. LNCS (LNAI), vol. 4933, pp. 32–45. Springer, Heidelberg (2008)
16. Suárez-Figueroa, M.C., Gómez-Pérez, A., et al.: The NeOn methodology for ontology engineering. In: Suárez-Figueroa, M.C., Gómez-Pérez, A., et al. (eds.) Ontology Engineering in a Networked World, pp. 9–34. Springer, Heidelberg (2011)
17. Tolkien, J.R.R.: The Silmarillion. George Allen & Unwin (1977)
18. Völker, J., Niepert, M.: Statistical schema induction. In: Antoniou, G., Grobelnik, M., Simperl, E., Parsia, B., Plexousakis, D., De Leenheer, P., Pan, J. (eds.) ESWC 2011, Part I. LNCS, vol. 6643, pp. 124–138. Springer, Heidelberg (2011)
19. Zablith, F., Antoniou, G., et al.: Ontology evolution: a process-centric survey. The Knowledge Engineering Review FirstView, 1–31 (10 2014)
20. Zablith, F., d'Aquin, M., Sabou, M., Motta, E.: Using ontological contexts to assess the relevance of statements in ontology evolution. In: Cimiano, P., Pinto, H.S. (eds.) EKAW 2010. LNCS, vol. 6317, pp. 226–240. Springer, Heidelberg (2010)

Author Index

Printed in the United States
By Bookmasters